The
JOHNS

ALSO BY VICTOR MALAREK

The Natashas: Inside the New Global Sex Trade

The JOHNS

SEX FOR SALE AND THE MEN WHO BUY IT

Victor MALAREK

Arcade Publishing • New York

Arcade Publishing books may be purchased in bulk at special discounts for sales promotion, corporate gifts, fund-raising, or educational purposes. Special editions can also be created to specifications. For details, contact the Special Sales Department, Arcade Publishing, 307 West 36th Street, 11th Floor, New York, NY 10018 or info@skyhorsepublishing.com.

Arcade Publishing® is a registered trademark of Skyhorse Publishing, Inc.®, a Delaware corporation.

Visit our website at www.arcadepub.com.

10 9 8 7 6 5 4 3 2 1

Library of Congress Cataloging-in-Publication Data is available on file.

ISBN: 978-1-61145-012-5

Printed in the United States of America

This book is dedicated to Norma Hotaling, 1951–2008.

Norma was a beacon of hope and courage . . . an extraordinary woman who transformed her tragic experiences in prostitution into a mission of social justice for those who had been trafficked and victimized in prostitution.

CONTENTS

PROLOGUE

*Unfortunately, power is something that women abjure
once they perceive the great difference between the
lives possible to men and women, and the violence
necessary to men to maintain their positions
of authority.*
— Carolyn Heilbrun,
Writing a Woman's Life

Stefa THOUGHT SHE WAS GOING to clean hotel rooms in Paris. Instead the sixteen-year-old Moldovan, who had just graduated from high school, was sold to a trafficker by her best friend's boyfriend. Under the cover of darkness, she was smuggled into Serbia and taken to an apartment building outside Belgrade to be broken. Weeks later, she was stripped naked, paraded on a stage in front of a dozen men, and auctioned off like an animal. She was purchased by an Albanian pimp and a few days later smuggled into Italy. She walked the streets of Mestra, a town outside Venice, wearing cheap makeup, a short skirt, a low-cut halter, and stiletto heels. Throughout the night, men and women drove by in their cars, rolled down the windows, and shouted, "Whore!" But no one ever stopped to ask if she needed help, she recounted when we spoke at a safe house. Nor did any of the johns who put money down for her bother to look into her pleading eyes. To them, she was just a prostitute, their property for an hour.

One night, after yet another beating for not making enough money, she summoned up the courage to bolt from her captor.

THE PHOTO IN THE ROMANIAN PASSPORT was of a timid, happy nineteen-year-old. A warm smile radiated from a round, innocent face, and her eyes sparkled with the excitement of youth. Two years later, Svetlana was unrecognizable. Sitting on a wooden bench in a police station in the town of Ferrazaj, Kosovo, near the Macedonian border, she was almost catatonic, staring blankly at a small, brown teddy bear clutched in her trembling hand. An hour earlier, she had been rescued from a brothel.

Svetlana had been trafficked to the war-torn region for the express use of UN peacekeepers and support personnel. As a police officer tried in vain to get her to respond to his questions, I noticed numerous reddish-blue welts along the backs of her arms and legs. They were cigarette burns — one for each time she balked at taking on another john. Clearly, she had been tortured. A gauze bandage covered her left wrist. She had attempted suicide.

IRINI PENKINA WAS BROKEN after one week. She was beaten and raped repeatedly by her pimp, "seasoning" her for the scores of johns who would line up to use her body for their sexual pleasures and perversions. For the next several months, the twenty-three-year-old Belorussian woman serviced truckers and bankers, cops and sex tourists. After each encounter, she stood weeping in the shower, trying obsessively to scrub away the filth with a bar of soap. Some nights she refused to work. For her insubordination, she was beaten, thrown to the floor, and degraded anally by her pimp and his cohorts, to remind her who was boss.

When Irini had answered an ad for a job in a foreign land, she thought she was signing on to work as a waitress. Instead she was imprisoned in a dank apartment with three other trafficked women — a Moldovan, a Bulgarian, and a Ukrainian. Any fool entering her bedroom could tell instantly she didn't want to be there. Her face said it all. But the seemingly endless stream of johns scurrying in at all hours of the day and night saw her as nothing more than a Slavic whore. No one ever offered her any help. No one ever responded to her screams. Then one evening she locked herself in the washroom and hung herself with a pair of black pantyhose.

This tragic event took place in an apartment in Thessalonica, Greece, directly across the street from a police station. Irini Penkina died alone in the cradle of democracy.

BEFORE I SET OUT to research and write my previous book, *The Natashas*, on the trafficking of young women and girls into the international sex trade, I had never really thought much about prostitution. Like so many men, I had been programmed from a young age to accept all the lame excuses I'd heard about the flesh trade: that these women were making money the easy way, on their backs; that it was all about sex and no one was being hurt; that the women chose to be in this so-called profession. Throughout my adult life, I had listened to men and women parrot the adage that prostitution is the world's oldest profession. However, after hearing many such chilling personal accounts as those of Stefa, Svetlana, and Irini, detailing the horrors that women and girls — as well as young boys — are forced to endure night after night all around the world, I have concluded that prostitution is the world's oldest *oppression*. No group in society is so victimized, so brutally terrorized and abused, as the women and children who are trapped in the vicious cycle of prostitution. And what is so baffling is this exploitation continues to be one of the most overlooked human rights abuses on the planet today.

In my research for *The Natashas*, I spoke to dozens of prostituted women. Their heart-wrenching stories — of rape, gang rape, torture, maiming, murder, and coercion to perform acts they were ashamed of — ripped into my conscience. I could see in their eyes the terror of the nightmares they'd survived. I could feel the deep sadness of their souls, and I could hear the shame and humiliation in their voices. And I wondered why none of the men who had used these women could see, feel, or hear these things too. I guess it was because they simply came for sex. They paid for it, got it, and left relieved. For them the woman was nothing more than an orifice and a pair of breasts, provided for their gratification.

Over the past two decades, there has been a global explosion in the numbers of johns venturing out for paid sex with young women and children. According to the U.S. State Department's

2008 *Trafficking in Persons Report*, more than eight hundred thousand hapless human beings are trafficked worldwide every year as slaves, and most are young women earmarked for the international flesh trade. They join an estimated 10 million women and children ensnared in sex markets around the globe. Most prostituted women report servicing an average of five clients a day; some see upwards of twenty. Extrapolate from this the number of men purchasing sex on a daily or nightly basis worldwide, and the total is staggering.

The State Department report also notes that the trafficking of human beings is the third highest money-making operation for organized crime behind the sale of illegal drugs and weapons. The crime of trafficking in humans nets criminal syndicates worldwide more than 12 billion dollars a year.

What we are witnessing today is nothing less than international sexual terrorism against women and children at the hands of men, and little is being done to stop the carnage.

Numerous studies have tried to identify the reasons women get involved in the flesh trade. Poverty, chronic unemployment, domestic violence, and drug addiction top the list of root causes. Academics also cite the complex inner workings of globalization and the repressive economic policies instituted by international banks, which require impoverished nations to make drastic structural adjustments in their budgets, changes that force them to cut back on crucial social programs and safety nets. Dire or poor economic conditions, together with a weakened or non-existent social safety net, drive more and more women out of their homelands to seek jobs abroad. The harsh immigration policies of Western nations are another key factor, for they help position human traffickers as major players on the global migration scene. The increasing subjugation, objectification, and commodification of women and girls in today's societies also contribute to this scourge. The millions of young women and children who are driven from their homes only to be entrapped in the traffickers' web of prostitution betray the dark side of globalization, these academics point out.

Having seen firsthand the degradation and humiliation suffered by so many trafficked women, and having read the studies, surveys, and findings about the flesh trade, I have come to this unwavering realization: prostitution — all prostitution — is not about choice. If anything, for the overwhelming majority of women ensnared in the trade, it is the ultimate act of desperation. It is survival sex.

But when society sees these women, it chooses to view them as social pariahs, the perpetrators of seedy, immoral acts, unworthy of compassion or understanding. These women are accused of taking the easy way out, eschewing hard work and luring otherwise upstanding family men, businessmen, community leaders, and others into debauchery and deceit. I've come to realize that society's attitude toward the world of prostitution is laden with hypocrisy and double standards. While the women are stigmatized with terms laced with opprobrium and distaste — prostitutes, hookers, whores, harlots, and sluts — the users of prostituted women are benignly tagged clients, patrons, customers, and johns.

Yet it is these very men who are at the root of the problem. Men are the users and abusers of prostituted women and children. It is their demand for paid sex that is creating huge profits for crime networks worldwide and incentives for traffickers, pimps, brothel owners, and porn producers to entrap more and more victims.

In economic parlance, women are the commodity; they are on the supply side of the equation. Embedded on the supply side are the push factors — extreme poverty, lack of education, and the eternal yearning of desperate human beings to improve their lot in life. On the demand side of the equation are the men. And in demand are three key letters: m-a-n. Without men, there would be no demand. There would be no supply, either: it would not be profitable for pimps and criminals to stay in this business if platoons of men weren't prowling side streets in search of purchased sex — male buyers who are willing to close their eyes and shell out fifty or a hundred dollars for a few minutes of physical bliss while deepening the misery of countless women and children.

The stark reality is that little will be done to stop this insanity until men start taking responsibility for their actions, until men realize that *they* are the problem and that global sex slavery exists because of their insatiable demand and duplicitous behavior. Yet in most discussions, reports, and research on this calamity, they — the ultimate consumers of prostituted women — are largely ignored. They are the missing link. *The Johns* will explore this crucial, little known link in the chain of prostitution and human sex trafficking.

The JOHNS

WELCOME TO
JOHNS WORLD

The Lord told me it's flat none of your business.
—THE REVEREND JIMMY SWAGGART TO HIS CONGREGATION
AFTER HIS ARREST FOR SOLICITATION

ON DECEMBER 6, 2007, Dan Jacober arrived at the Hilton Hotel in Portland, Oregon, to meet a girl named Haley. Haley had posted an ad on Craigslist, describing herself as a twenty-something, blond sorority girl in town for a night and "not afraid to try anything." Jacober called, looking for "an hour's worth of fun." He asked her to wear black panties. They agreed on $150.

In late February 2008, David Phillips showed up at a hotel to consummate a date that he too had set up online.

Glendale James didn't bother with technology. He simply approached a woman working the street and offered her $10 for oral sex.

1

Frank Milio was a bit more generous. He sought oral pleasures as well but had twice the budget.

And on May 12, 2008, Philip Haltom got the shock of his life when his Internet liaison turned out to be a cop.

Each of these men was hoping to get lucky. But this time, for each of them, luck was nowhere in the picture. All five were arrested for solicitation as part of an undercover sting operation, and all had to face the humiliation of being outed as horny, cash-paying johns.

Their friends and family were likely shocked. Their coworkers were probably just as stunned. And they themselves no doubt cursed the moment when they gave in to their yearnings and offered to "pay for play."

But just who are these men? What kinds of lives do they lead? What made them do it? Were they first-timers or veterans? The details are sparse — as they usually are for johns — but what we do know is that they had nothing in common apart from their recourse to paid sex.

Dan Jacober is actually Sergeant Dan Jacober, a sixteen-year veteran of the Sherwood City Police Department.

David Phillips, an architect by profession, is a member of the New Brighton City Council.

Glendale James is a Chicago sanitation employee who got caught just ten minutes after he punched in at the start of his 6:00 a.m. shift.

Philip Haltom is the Reverend Philip Haltom, a fifty-two-year-old father of four who is the pastor at the Hinsdale Trinity Presbyterian Church just outside Chicago.

And Frank Milio, from Tampa Bay, Florida . . . well, he is a case study unto himself. He is probably one of the oldest on record. Milio is a ninety-three-year-old retiree.

EVERY DAY, MILLIONS OF JOHNS around the world step into their cars and set out in search of paid sex. They cruise the side streets looking for cheap thrills. They slink into massage parlors for a little "rub and tug." They swagger into strip clubs for a lap dance and a beer and then adjourn to the "champagne room" for something à la carte.

Most of their sojourns remain clandestine. Most johns keep a tight lid on what they call a hobby. Those who boast do so with caution. For the majority of johns it's a private matter, not something they talk about or easily admit. Few are proud of what they do, though many argue that it's perfectly natural. And . . . they get away with it. They remain on the sidelines while the women provide the public face of prostitution. Once in a while, though, the curtain goes up, and the public catches a glimpse of who these johns really are.

Increasingly across North America and elsewhere, law enforcement is cracking down through undercover stings. In the course of a few hours, scores of men are rounded up for unwittingly propositioning an undercover cop. But the stings aren't limited to the bars and streets. Now, more than ever, they're following the demand. The marketplace of choice in many corners of the world is the nebulous, not-quite-anonymous web of sex online. Men on the hunt for purchased sex stalk Web sites and discussion boards that offer photographs, ads, and tips. The men come across ads — like twenty-something Haley's — offering all manner of fun for the right wad of cash. Who may be at the other end, though, is anyone's guess. If the john is lucky, she's legit. If not, he's caught.

The result is a daily stream of arrest sheets and mug shots, often posted online for the world to see. Their disheveled, hapless faces express humiliation and shame, or show a lack of emotion altogether. Many look angry, others annoyed, likely perturbed that they let themselves get nabbed. But that's to be expected. What is more of a surprise is that there is really no such thing as a typical john.

Few of them look like what most people imagine men who purchase sex to be: awkward, creepy loners fixated on porn before heading out for something more real. To the contrary, many of these men look like very ordinary guys. Some are average-looking. Others are handsome. Some are young — as young as fourteen — others are in their twenties and thirties, sixties and seventies, even, as we saw, nineties. They are stockbrokers, plumbers, doctors, professors. They're also lawyers, judges, Boy Scout leaders, and accountants. Sometimes, they're men in uniform — soldiers, sailors, international peacekeepers, cops — and other times they're men of the cloth. Sometimes they're sorry, and many times they're not.

And though busted johns get named and shamed, the stories of their arrests barely make a ripple. It is only when a marquee headliner is nailed that the public sits up and takes notice.

IN OCTOBER 1987 a man who called himself Billy emerged from the Travel Inn Motel on Airline Highway, west of New Orleans. On his arm was a "working girl" from Louisiana who went by the name Debra Murphee. Billy had picked up Debra on one of the local hooker strolls, paid her no more than twenty dollars for oral sex, and then snapped pictures of her posing on the mattress.

Four months later, Billy came clean, live from a pulpit — in front of millions of people. Billy was Jimmy Swaggart, king of the TV bible-thumping hill, who raked in more than $150 million a year from his telecasts, which drew 8 million viewers weekly. On February 21, 1988, Swaggart stood before his parishioners and contritely begged for forgiveness: "I have sinned against you, my Lord, and I would ask that your precious blood would wash and cleanse every stain until it is in the seas of God's forgetfulness, never to be remembered against me anymore." The tears flowed. His flock sat in stunned silence. He was promptly suspended for a year by the Assemblies of God.

To those who had followed his teachings — and his public sermons — this dalliance was a lapse in judgment of monumental proportions, for Swaggart had single-handedly orchestrated the downfall of two other Assemblies of God ministers for sexual indiscretions. In 1986 Swaggart pounded the pulpit, exposing minister Marvin Gorman's adulterous affair with a parishioner. A year later he took delight in accusing televangelist Jim Bakker of having doped and raped his twenty-one-year-old secretary. He didn't mince words. Even after Bakker resigned, Swaggart denounced him as a "cancer in the body of Christ."

Just months after his public apology, and in defiance of his suspension, Swaggart sauntered back into his church and told his parishioners that he was acting on orders from a higher authority. Swaggart claimed that God had come to him in a dream and told him, "If [you] do not return to the pulpit this weekend, millions of people will go to hell." Convinced that the preacher man

Others are fed up with failed relationships or have simply decided that relationships aren't worth it. Paying for sex is their way of getting it without the costs or hassles of marriage or dating. The beauty of paid sex, as they see it, is that it is on their terms, when convenient, and whenever the urge strikes.

There are also the thrill-seekers who want the variety of something new and exciting in each encounter. Many are looking for a "different kind of sex" — the kind that they dare not ask of their girlfriends or wives. Others, turned on by racist stereotypes, want sex with "another kind of woman." They chase "exotic" women based on skin color to feed fantasies — of hot Latinos and submissive Asians, wild Africans and sex-starved Slavs.

Some of the men see paid sex as a treat — a bonding ritual, for instance, during a night out with the boys. Often, it's wrapped up with machismo and ego — part and parcel, they believe, of being a man.

But there is another kind of john — the kind that gets excited by the image of the "dirty whore." For him, the whore is a turn-on. She represents a femininity that is vile and evil. These men hate women. In their deluded minds, all women — no matter their age, profession, or station in society — are whores. Whatever psychological hang-ups this kind of john harbors toward women, he takes it out on those he rents. For him the woman is not there for the sex. She's there to be used, demeaned, and abused. This john — the most dangerous kind — carries around deep-seated rage, and the woman is his outlet.

One thing prostituted women know about johns that these men would rather keep under wraps is that most need to summon up their manhood before they set out on the hunt. They stir their libidos with porn and then fortify their nerve with booze — the women will tell you that most men arrive smelling of liquor. And the women say they are getting more middle-aged and senior johns who imbue their flaccid penises with renewed rigor by popping a little blue pill called Viagra.

The Internet

Many johns confide in the women they're with; many more come clean to one another on the Net. The Internet has become a one-stop shop for johns — a Yellow Pages directory, support group, and travel advisory rolled into one. It has allowed men who otherwise might not have spoken a word about their so-called hobby to break through the silence. They realize they're not alone. They can reach out and touch one another — from all corners of the globe — and take comfort in the knowledge that there are millions like them.

In the relative comfort of their homes and under the guise of a screen name, the johns share their reasons for wanting or needing paid sex, their fantasies, their escapades, their best and their worst. But they also rally around one another, offering comfort, validating each others' feelings and fears, and valiantly defending their lifestyle against attack by outsiders or creeping feelings of guilt. In the process, this community of johns has created a brotherhood like no other. To join is free and it is available around the clock, accessible worldwide, and always willing to assist. The only requirement is having the mindset of a john. Anyone suspected of being a Christian troublemaker or feminist — as I learned during the research for this book — need not apply.

What this brotherhood reveals is that, when it comes to sexuality and prostitution, johns' attitudes are remarkably consistent throughout the world. On these forums — whether in the U.S., Canada, Australia, or Europe — it quickly becomes apparent that the search for paid sex is all about entitlement, power, and control. What the john is looking for is a brief encounter where he can let go and freely express his most selfish desires. It doesn't matter whether he's with a high-priced call girl, a streetwalker, or a stripper in a bar. His wants, needs, and desires reign supreme. He doesn't have to worry about anybody else's.

Michael Bader, a San Francisco psychotherapist who has studied the dynamics of sexual arousal for almost fifteen years and has treated dozens of men who find prostituted women irresistible, addresses the problem in an article entitled "Why Men Do Stupid Things: The Psychological Appeal of Prostitutes." Bader writes that for the overwhelming majority of johns, "[T]he appeal lies in the fact that, after payment is made, the woman is experienced as completely devoted to the man — to his pleasure, his satisfaction, his care, his happiness. The man doesn't have to please a prostitute, doesn't have to make her happy, doesn't have to worry about her emotional needs or demands. He can give or take without the burden of reciprocity.

"Now, of course, these interactions are scripted," Bader adds. "The prostitute is acting. But it doesn't matter. For men who like to go to prostitutes, the illusion of authenticity is enough."

It's as if the john is producing a private porn flick: he writes the screenplay, directs, and stars. He can be mean, aggressive, demeaning, or vulgar . . . or he can be pleasant and caring, perhaps playing the part of the tender boyfriend. But his role is not to please her or worry about *her* feelings. It's all about making *him* feel good.

Perhaps the best part for the john in this erotic encounter is that he is also the casting agent. He gets to audition countless hopefuls and choose his own supporting actress. She can play a nurse, a French maid, a high-school student, or a mean, foul-mouthed, and controlling bitch.

For the duration of the liaison, the roles are clear. The john's role is most often that of master stud. The woman's is to make him feel special with whatever visual or sound effects she can muster. So if his script calls for moaning, she moans. If it calls for romance and TLC, she plays the girlfriend. For the entire encounter she has to make him feel as though he is the center of her universe; after all, he is paying.

Yet all that transpires is just that — acting. The man is buying an illusion, if only for a moment. Sadly, a lot of johns buy into the illusion and begin to believe it's real.

That, however, is but one of the perils. The pleasures may be plenty, but so are the risks. Some johns fall in love with the women they're paying; others fall for the lifestyle and believe they can never look back. Some sacrifice real relationships and families, while others never give themselves the chance to seek meaningful relationships. They may face embarrassment, of course, if they're exposed, but they also risk fines or jail time and all manner of disease. The more conscientious among them may even wake up to the cycle of exploitation they are fueling and have a hard time looking at themselves in the mirror.

But these perils are, for the most part, easily pushed into the furthest recesses of the john's mind. When it comes to right and wrong, most johns are color-blind: there's little room in red-light districts for shades of gray.

How Many Johns Are There?

Just how many johns might be prowling the streets on any given night is hard to calculate, but one thing is certain — they vastly outnumber the estimated ten million prostituted women and children worldwide, who, on average, service four to six men a day. There are numerous studies on how many men have purchased sex, but statistics differ significantly from country to country and culture to culture.

The highest rates are in Southeast Asia, with Thailand, Cambodia, and Japan leading the pack at more than 70 percent. Thailand receives an estimated 5.1 million sex tourists a year, and 450,000 locals buy sex every day.

In Europe, Spain has the highest numbers of men who have paid for sex, at 39 percent. In Germany, 18 percent of men pay for sex regularly. A German study found that 1 million prostitute users in that country buy women daily for sexual services. In Italy, 17 percent purchase sex regularly; in Switzerland, 19 percent; and in Britain, Finland, Russia, and Norway, it is anywhere from 10 to 14 percent. The 14 percent figure from a Dutch study is unexpectedly low, considering the extensive sex trade in the country and its officially liberal approach to prostitution. However, what was not considered is the high number of sex tourists that visit the country each year. In the United States, an estimated 16 percent of men have paid for sex on at least one occasion, and in the legal brothels of Victoria, Australia, prostituted women service approximately 3.1 million buyers per year from an adult male population of 1.3 million.

The difficulty with such statistics is that no one knows for certain what the actual numbers are, because most men will never admit to paying for sex.

What Men Do

Johns have remained the unexplored side of prostitution for a number of reasons. Most people have simply surmised there was nothing particularly unique about them or interesting enough to warrant in-depth research or analysis. Underlying this conjecture is a basic assumption: men who buy sex are just doing what men do. It has been widely accepted that there will always be a group of women available to satisfy men's biological needs. They are seen as a necessary evil, a sort of safety valve for when a man's sexual urge reaches critical mass. Set against the image of the prostitute — that vile temptress heaped with contempt and disgust — the man has been for the most part invisible and dismissible: a one-dimensional, usually anonymous, somewhat comical character ruled by the direction of his erection . . . in lighter contexts, a sort of mindless buffoon who thinks with his other head when his loins begin to stir. Yet this narrow, almost apologetic, and seemingly innocuous acceptance of johns has facilitated the largely uncontested, worldwide surge in men seeking paid sex.

In researching *The Johns*, I gleaned more than fifty Web sites in the United States, Canada, Britain, Ireland, Australia, and Europe in which men discuss their paid romps with prostituted women. I read more than five thousand posts on a wide range of issues written by these men. I also interviewed sixteen men who talked openly — but on condition of anonymity — about the reasons they seek paid sex. Collectively, the comments, rationales, and mindsets of johns paint a very disturbing picture and call out for an urgent and open debate on their behavior and its consequences.

It is time to stop looking at johns as a faceless footnote in what is now increasingly recognized as a very serious social problem. Men are the drivers behind prostitution. Their urges are at the core of the explosion of the global sex trade and the reason hundreds of thousands of women and girls are trafficked into sexual slavery every year. Johns may not be the most savory characters, the most likeable, or the most interesting, but it is impossible to tackle the myriad issues surrounding prostitution without taking a hard look at these men, at their character, actions, and motivations. This look must involve, above all, a rethinking of men's role in prostitution.

2

BOYS WILL
BE BOYS

Hard core is when you walk in . . . and the girls say your
mongering name like "NORM!" on Cheers.
—SEXTON, A JOHN

FROM THE MOMENT OF MAN'S FIRST ERECTION, the male sex drive takes
on an aura of almost mythical proportions, infused by centuries
of lore and widely accepted views about men's entitlement to sex.
Men need sex, the belief goes, to feel like real men, to amuse
themselves, to let off steam, or as a diversion from the cares of life.
The list of mindless excuses goes on and on, driven in part by
legend masquerading as science. Even more disturbing is the belief that prostitution is an acceptable outlet for men's urges. In
some cultures, prostitution is accepted as a means of sexual education, to help young men learn the mechanics of sex. For college

boys in the West, it's an initiation into the world of macho men. For grooms-to-be, it's a last hoorah, as it is for geezers trying to recapture their youth. For average guys, it's a way to "get the hot babe," and for celebrities and others it's a bit of sport on the side.

No wonder so many people see the buying of sex as harmless and even fun. This tacit tolerance is reflected in such mindless clichés as "boys will be boys" and "they're just sowing their wild oats." It's as if men have been given some special dispensation — some sort of social, cultural, and biological right — and the number of supposedly intelligent people who have bought into this notion is astonishing. Even more astounding is the number of intelligent men who set off on the road to masculinity with a fistful of dollars.

Boys to Men

The passage of boys to men is marked in many different ways in societies throughout the world. In some, that passage begins when adolescent boys discover a little piece of physical gadgetry in their pants, and it may conclude with the boys' initiation into the club of johns. Stories abound of brash young men venturing into brothels to rid themselves of the millstone called virginity. Rumor has it that John F. Kennedy — notorious for his sexual flings while president of the United States — lost *his* in a Harlem brothel "to a three-dollar hooker." Authors Thomas Wolfe and Leo Tolstoy also did away with their virginity in brothels. Tolstoy was dragged into the room by his older brothers, and he wept at the side of the woman's bed after the deed was done. On the other hand, Wolfe was so taken with the experience that he remained a customer of brothels throughout his life.

In 1861, before he was proclaimed king of England, Edward VII lost his virginity to a prostituted woman in a tent while he was in Ireland training with the Grenadier Guards. The experience must have delighted him, because he never lost his appetite for women of the night. When visiting Paris, he frequented a notorious brothel called Le Chabanais, which had a room with his coat of arms emblazoned over the bed. The room also contained a large copper tub that he liked to fill with champagne to bathe in with his rented women. As the corpulent monarch aged and packed on the pounds, he had a special love seat installed where he could receive oral pleasures.

In an interview with the *London Mirror* in October 2004, British rock star Chris de Burgh, then fifty-six, admitted losing his virginity to a French woman when he was sixteen, but he acknowledged that he wasn't quite sure what was happening until they got to the bedroom. "This girl said, 'Tu veux monter?' I said, 'OK,' and we went upstairs. Then I suddenly realized I was in a brothel, and I was too scared to back out. I can't remember how much it cost, but I do know that I wasn't exactly the world's greatest stud," he recounted years later. No doubt this tidbit from his early years might offer insight into his hit ballad "Lady in Red."

To this day, frat boys delight in escorting their less-experienced brethren to brothels so they can "lose their cherries." Trouble is, the first time for all these guys is invariably very, very short. Just ask Jerry Springer. In his autobiography, *Ringmaster!*, the king of American schlock television admitted he was still a virgin at seventeen when he entered Tulane University in New Orleans as a freshman. "I really knew very little about anything to do with sex. There was this place called Norma's. In the parlance of the era, it was a 'House of Ill Repute.'"

Springer's fraternity brothers were determined to show their newest members a rockin' good time. "So here we are, ten pledges, and we've been seduced into this mansion, where inside we were just stunned to find an indoor pool with all these naked women sitting around. They figured we couldn't miss here. For ten dollars, which the fraternity paid, these women would take you upstairs. The guys just said: 'Pick one and she's yours!' Now no one wanted to admit that none of us had any idea what to do. So here we are, a bunch of young guys standing around and trying to act like we're in the know. So, with a deep breath, off I went. . . . About seven seconds later it was over," Springer noted, about the same time it takes his live TV audience to chant: "Jerry! Jerry! Jerry! Jerry!"

But, of course, it's not just the future famous who throw off the shackles of virginity with a few crumpled bills. "I was in university and I was still a virgin at 21," writes one ordinary guy who calls himself Donald online. "That was really bothering me. All the guys I knew were bragging about all the chicks they were doing, and I'm sitting in my room jerking off to porn. So I decided to use the hundred dollars my parents sent me to get myself a birthday present. I checked out the listings at the back of the newspaper, and before I knew it, I was no longer a virgin. I bragged to my buddies about this chick I scored, but I never told them she was a prostitute."

Robert says he was twenty and doesn't regret the experience

one bit. "All this crap about virginity being a 'gift' that I should give to someone I love, sorry I don't buy it. I'm 22 and have been to prostitutes only a few times. I'm not addicted, and what happens between me and her stays between me and her. And if I meet a girl and she wonders about my sexual past, I'll do whatever everyone else does: lie!"

Luke describes himself as an extremely shy Roman Catholic who believed in no sex before marriage. But when he hit his mid-forties, he was still single and still a virgin. He connected with a guy in an Internet chat room who talked him into doing something about it. "He explained that he too had been a virgin unable to find the right person to both accept and love him; so, eventually, he had gone and done it with a prostitute instead. This guy was a lot younger than me by around 10 years. He then started to criticize me . . . how can I be so old and still have not have lost my virginity yet? I think that's what got me tempted to go try in the first place. I don't wish to go into too much detail; but she was beautiful, half my age, and I was extremely shy and afraid. I was so afraid that even though I had an erection, I did not come no matter how hard she tried. I simply quit in sheer bitter disgust and frustration at myself; very politely I left. Looking back, all I can say is it was a VERY BIG MISTAKE!"

To Son . . . with Love!

If there is one tradition that rates as truly archaic, it has to be the age-old bonding ritual of a father initiating his son into manhood via the brothel. In a 2004 interview with *Playboy* magazine, three-time Oscar-winning movie director Oliver Stone revealed that, when he was in his midteens, his dad sent him to a prosti-tute to lose his virginity. Until that fateful day, Stone's life had been spent in an all-boys boarding school and boys-only summer camps, where he had almost no social contact with girls. So his father, a Wall Street financier, stepped in. "My father was a gen-erous man and I love him to this day for it."

Stone has fond memories of his first time. "For me it was great," he told *Playboy.* And apparently he wasn't the first man in the Stone family to have taken this path to first-time intimacy with a woman. "There's a great tradition of that, I believe," Stone said.

Leo is an alumnus of a British all-boys boarding school. When he graduated, his father dispatched him to a brothel. "I think he was worried I might be gay. I wasn't. I just didn't have the time or opportunity to meet girls. It was a strange experience and I might add, a very quick one. I learned where to put it and within a few moves, it was over and done with. I was too nerv-ous to enjoy it. That was my first and last time going to a prosti-tute. I prefer intimacy, and that was simply mechanical. When I got home, my dad was beaming. Said he was proud of me. I didn't feel proud. I felt stupid."

Picture it: a father looks up from his morning paper and asks his sixteen-year-old, "Son, have you had sex yet?"

The boy hesitates. "Not with anyone else . . ."

"I mean with a woman."

The boy chokes on his juice and looks around fervently, fear-ful his mother might walk in.

"Well, son, it's time you became a man. Let's go for a drive. I'm taking you to a brothel." The father's message is twofold: passage into manhood in this forum is seen as an accomplishment and, more alarmingly, if you have money, you have the power to buy a woman.

Hangin' with the Boys

Stag parties the world over are notorious for paid hanky-panky. Whether revved up by big-screen porn fests or visions from yesteryear of a stripper jumping out of a cake, best men are routinely arrested by vice cops across North America while cruising hooker strolls in search of the evening's entertainment. For some men, there is nothing more best-manly than dispatching the groom into a washroom for a blow job.

"Me, my best man and three ushers all headed to the Dominican Republic for a wild weekend of debauchery," boasts one man online. "We got these amazing-looking prostitutes and banged away. It was like a wild Roman orgy. We drank and we banged. We switched partners. It was great. I'll never forget it. Of course, I'll never tell my wife."

For groomsmen, weddings are sometimes all about the stag party, one last go at their buddy's premarital freedom. Today the bachelor party has taken off like a red-hot rocket. "Stag tourism" is sweeping North America, the United Kingdom, Australia, and Europe as best men hook up with party-planning travel agencies offering unforgettable stag weekends. The lure of cheap booze and "exotic Eastern European strippers" has British, German, Italian, and Scandinavian stags swarming to Europe's sin capitals — Amsterdam, Berlin, Warsaw, Budapest, Riga, and Prague — for a weekend of prenuptial debauchery. In North America, stag-party planners offer their expertise in virtually every major city, with Las Vegas and Atlantic City cornering a hefty cut of the herd.

Colin boasted that the stag he hosted as best man took half a dozen buddies to Las Vegas. "It cost a total of $14,000 and it was worth every penny. We got the VIP treatment and front-of-the-line service at every club we went to. The most incredible thing was the girls. Every one was a ten, a real knockout. They could have been *Playboy* centerfolds. We were treated like gods. When we left for home, we remembered an important word of advice: what happens in Vegas, stays in Vegas!"

Norman was going to prove to the groom and all six of his buddies why he was the best man. He contacted a notorious tour agency in Riga, the capital of Latvia, to make all the arrangements and handle special requests.

"It wasn't cheap, but this was my mate's last weekend of freedom and the lads wanted him to go out in style. We were met at the airport by a white stretch SUV limo, and inside were two strippers who weren't the least bit shy. That evening we had a steak dinner with the wildest girl-on-girl sex show. Then it was off to a strip bar for some totally nude lap dancing. The groom groped enough breasts to get him through the next ten years of his marriage! It was a magnificent weekend of debauchery."

But not all stag parties result in happy endings.

A British groom-to-be lamented that nine of his lads took him to Prague for a weekend stag. "It was like being in a porn feature. There were gorgeous prostitutes stripping for us and doing things to each other. We all got sloshed, and I ended up having sex with two of them. When I woke up, there was a woman sprawled naked in bed beside me. I couldn't believe what I had done. I got really upset and ashamed. I'd never done anything like this before in my life, and I thought if my fiancée ever found out that would be the end of us. My mates swore she would never hear of it, but she did. One of the guys told his girlfriend, who was to be a bridesmaid, and she just couldn't keep her mouth shut about it. My fiancée had a regular fit and called off the wedding."

For Jeffrey, getting married meant making a commitment to be faithful to his bride-to-be. "I was deeply and truly in love with my fiancée. Then the lads took me out for my last night of freedom and it all changed. I don't remember much, I got so hammered, but a few days later I went to a doctor who told me I had an STI [sexually transmitted infection]. I was so ashamed of myself that I called off the wedding. I couldn't go through with it, knowing that I had been with a prostitute a week before taking my vows."

Another time-honored bonding experience is the guys' night out, and the venue of choice is a nudie bar. Men howl and hoot while swilling beer and stuffing dollar bills into the G-strings of strippers wrapped around brass poles. As the evening progresses and the mind-numbing effects of alcohol take hold, the lap dances kick in. A totally naked woman grinds on a man's lap until he either runs out of money or ejaculates in his pants. However, if the price is right, he will be invited to the "champagne room," where the champagne may not be real but the sex certainly is. The men are asked to pay three hundred dollars a bottle, but what they're really paying for is the entertainment.

"I enjoy going to strip bars if only to admire gorgeous female bodies," says a stockbroker from New York. "Watching beautiful women strip helps me release the stress of the day and occasionally, when the mood strikes, I go to one of the back booths for another kind of release."

Throughout North America and Australia, the strip bar has also become a regular haunt for the business lunch. As men in suits eat their burgers and watch completely naked women grind, gyrate, and bend over onstage in front of them, a waitress walks up and politely asks, "May I get you anything else?"

"Here in Australia, we think nothing of going to a strip bar for a business luncheon," Mick explained in an online post. "It's just a normal thing you do with your mates. After all, it's legal. We eat, talk a little shop, and if you're in the mood for a little lap dance for dessert or want to head off to the VIP room for a quickie, no one really gives a damn.

"But it does make some of the women in the office go a bit mad. After all, they can't come with us. I mean, it would make things a tad awkward, if you get my drift," he added.

R & R

Soldiers on R & R—a rest and relaxation break—and sailors on shore leave are notorious for paying for sex. For them, it is also a rite of passage, usually the last course after a wild night of chugging copious jugs of beer. This is the classic example of "boys being boys," as high-ranking officers wink and nudge at the antics and chaplains sit conspicuously silent. This tacit approval by military brass worldwide has created a sense of entitlement among young men in uniform. The bodies of girls and young women are just a few dollars away wherever they are stationed.

On scores of sex Web sites, retired military men and veterans offer boasts about their sexual conquests while serving their country—whether on R & R from combat, on shore leave after months at sea, or on UN peacekeeping missions in war-ravaged nations like Kosovo and Bosnia and Herzegovina. These men never speak about their conquests in personal terms. For most, their sexual escapades while on leave are the stuff of bravado, and the women they rented simply pieces of faded flesh.

"I was in the U.S. Navy for years, and when my ship wasn't bombing Al Qaeda we were in ports fucking, drinking, partying, and getting fucking hammered like there's no tomorrow," a retired American sailor bragged on an online john site.

One nation that was once high on the list for the sexual escapades of military men is Thailand. In the mid-1960s, the Land of Smiles became a major playground for American servicemen on R & R from combat in nearby Vietnam. They jokingly referred to it as I & I (intercourse and intoxication), and for sex-starved GIs and marines, it was anything goes in the Bangkok go-go bars.

"Here we were fresh from the killing grounds of Vietnam and there are all these hot, young Thai babes just waiting to romance us," a former marine called Gunner reminisced. "I remember walking into a massage parlor with a few of the guys, and there were easy one hundred gals in pink kimonos sitting on bleachers behind a glass wall waiting for their numbers to be called. We could have our pick—one, two, or three. They catered to our every wish. We had the time of our lives."

Nowadays, a popular pit stop for American sailors—in fact, for sailors the world over—is the Philippines: "Manila and

Angeles City are a paradise for getting laid and it's real cheap. We would dock and within minutes we were in the bars having our pick of hundreds of young beauties, all panting to get us in the sack for just a few dollars," a john called Sailor Rob crooned. "I love the navy when we pull into port in places like the Philippines. It makes all those months at sea worth every minute."

When Lorne was in the U.S. Army, he was stationed for a time along the demilitarized zone in Korea. "Next to the base was this tiny village with bars filled with Filipino and Russian women and a few Korean chicks. They were our stress relief. We'd head in for a little I and I while an MP [military police] stood outside to make sure there was no trouble. We got free rein of the place. We got hand jobs, blow jobs, and for the entire package we went to a back room. This was not something you wrote home about!"

Servicemen sometimes do establish longer-term relationships with women they pay for sex. One American soldier on leave from his tour in Germany who hooked up with "the perfect woman" in Amsterdam — "Czech, smallish but perky breasts and not a day over twenty-two" — spent every other weekend for six months buying blocks of time with his new "girlfriend."

"Of course we spent a lot of time fucking, but we also spooned for hours, talking about life in America and life in Prague. I'd bring American cigarettes from the base commissary and cosmetics from the BX [base exchange]," he recalled.

For the most part, though, these men in uniform are not interested in the women they use but only in the sex. They remain willfully blind to everything else, no matter how glaringly desperate the woman's situation might be.

Olenka, a nineteen-year-old Ukrainian, sits across from me in a coffee shop in Sarajevo chain-smoking cigarettes. She is tall and thin, her skin is pale, and her dyed-blond hair is cropped short. She stares nervously down at her ruby-red fingernails as she recounts her six-month descent into hell as a sex slave in a bar in the northern Bosnian town of Tuzla. Olenka was just seventeen at the time, but the nightmare still haunts her. She takes a long drag from a cigarette and begins her story.

"I went with between eight and fifteen men a night. I did not want to have sex with any of them. If I did not do as I was told, my owner said I would be beaten to death. This man was cruel and vicious. You did not cross him."

In the months she was held captive, Olenka figures she was raped more than 1,800 times. The men each paid the owner fifty dollars. She never saw a penny. On one particularly harrowing evening she was passed around to a dozen soldiers. The men were rambunctious, celebrating a birthday in the bar. One of their buddies had turned twenty-one. She was the birthday present for the entire platoon. Whatever the UN peacekeepers wanted, she was forced to give.

"The entire time, I must smile and make them believe I am enjoying this humiliation," Olenka said in a barely audible whisper. "These men were animals. They cared nothing that I was there as a prisoner. They simply wanted sex."

She doesn't know the names of any of the men who used her, but she remembers the uniforms and the insignias emblazoned on their shoulders — American, Canadian, British, Russian, German, French. Many were soldiers. Some were police officers with the UN. Others were among the thousands of workers — with the myriad international aid agencies or with the UN — that flooded the region after the war with Serbia. Many times she pleaded for help. Some of her international "patrons" had cell phones dangling from their belts. She asked them to let her make just one call.

"They all refused. All they cared about was they had bought me for the hour and I was there for their pleasure. One of them told the owner I asked to use his cell phone. For that, I was beaten and left in a cellar without food for three days."

When Olenka was finally rescued in a raid on the bar, she recognized eight of her "clients" among the UN and local police who carried out the bust.

Lights, Camera, Action!

For decades, the idea of guys just being guys has been fueled by Hollywood and the off-screen antics of movie stars. Throughout its history, some of Tinsel Town's most beloved leading men have frequented women of the night. John Barrymore once rented an entire brothel for a week in Madras, India, to try out a variety of positions from the *Kama Sutra*. Handsome silver-screen stars Richard Burton, Marlon Brando, and Errol Flynn all had flings with women working as prostitutes. Clark Gable admitted that he often hired high-priced escorts because he could "pay them to go away." The problem with regular women, he once quipped, was they "stay around wanting romance and movie lovemaking."

Hollywood movie mogul Louis B. Mayer knew he couldn't keep his leading men from misbehaving, and the last thing he needed was a weeping one-night stand turning up pregnant on a film lot or a gossip columnist getting wind that a major star was seen slinking away from a house of ill repute in the wee morning hours. So Mayer provided his celluloid royalty an outlet — he set up a clandestine bordello just off the MGM lot and filled it with starlets who didn't pass the screen test. Mayer also intensely disliked gay men. He wanted his matinee idols to be known as he-men and used his private brothel as a way of screening out actors who were closet homosexuals so he could cancel their contracts.

One Hollywood prince put to the test was James Stewart, whose homespun charm, morality, and decency at the age of twenty-five were cause for concern and whispers on the MGM lot. In his biography *Jimmy Stewart*, author Marc Eliot claims that the star of *It's a Wonderful Life*, who was raised in a strict Presbyterian household, had no desire to have sex with prostituted women, but his manager left him with no choice. MGM scout Bill Grady is quoted in the book as saying, "I had to lay down the law to him. I had to tell him, 'Jim, if you don't go and give a manly account of yourself at least a few times, Mayer and the others will think you're gay. So get your ass over there and get those rocks off with at least two of those broads.'" According to Eliot, Stewart reluctantly complied.

In 1995, *Two and a Half Men* star Charlie Sheen, once notorious as "Charlie the Machine," was forced to testify at the trial of infamous Hollywood madam Heidi Fleiss, where he admitted under oath to spending at least $53,000 on twenty-seven of her call girls in 1992.

In October 1996, Oscar-winner Jack Nicholson allegedly hired Christine Sheehan and another woman for a threesome, promising them each a thousand dollars. When it came time to pay, the ego-swelled actor apparently growled that he didn't have to pay for sex. According to Sheehan, he then got violent, grabbed her by the hair, pounded her head into the floor, and threw her out of his home. She sued, and the following year Nicholson shelled out $32,500 after she promised to drop the charges and keep quiet.

In a profile in *The New Yorker* in 2000, comedic actor Jerry Lewis revealed that as a young man he had been a glutton for women in prostitution, but he also admitted that he didn't know better. "I was like a kid in a candy store. I mean, it was nothing for me to knock off four broads in an afternoon. We'd go by the numbers. 'Twenty-three A for Mr. Lewis, please! No, Twenty-four A is the blonde; twenty-three A is the brunette.' It was just wonderful! The thing that was not wonderful about it was that there was no morality. I had no morality. I had no guilt. I thought: This is what men do."

The alumni of famous johns also comprise celebrated composers, authors, poets, and athletes. American composer George Gershwin had no trouble attracting willing women, yet he often frequented brothels. Besides Thomas Wolfe, authors Victor Hugo, Ernest Hemingway, and H. G. Wells all admitted to dalliances with rented women. Even children's-fable writer Hans Christian Andersen crossed the line, and F. Scott Fitzgerald sought out the companionship of a prostituted woman after his wife had been locked up in an insane asylum. While living in Venice in 1818, English romantic poet Lord George Gordon Byron rented a palace and filled it with prostituted women for his enjoyment.

Sports figures are notorious for their sexual exploits off the field, but probably none more than baseball legend George

Herman "Babe" Ruth. Ruth is said to have known the locations of every brothel and every red-light district in every city where his team played. The famous home-run hitter favored professionals, known in the parlance of the time as "sporting girls."

Nothing stirs the tabloids more than when an A-list movie star gets caught in flagrante delicto with a woman of the night. For Hugh Grant, whose middle name happens to be John, the night of June 27, 1995, will presumably be forever etched in his mind. This is a man who had everything going for him — good looks, charm, lots of money, and international fame. Women swooned at the sight of him. He could have had his pick of gorgeous groupies. Yet sometimes having everything doesn't seem to cut it.

In the wee morning hours on that fateful day, Grant cruised along Hollywood's Sunset Strip in a white convertible BMW and zeroed in on a streetwalker known on the stroll both as Little Red Riding Hood and as Divine Brown. Anyone who saw her could understand why. She had a shock of red hair, wore pink lipstick, and was strutting her stuff on scarlet-red stiletto heels. The actor eased over to the curb. The two had a brief chat, agreed on a price — sixty dollars — and the woman climbed into the car.

Grant drove to a nearby side street, parked, and Red went to work under the dash. The actor got so excited that his foot kept hitting the brakes, causing the brake lights to flash on and off — a signal that caught the attention of two LA cops on patrol. An officer rapped on the windshield and ordered the two startled occupants out of the car. A mortified Grant and an unflappable

Stella Marie Thompson were arrested and charged with lewd conduct in a public place.

When the overnight police arrest sheet was made public, the tabloids in the United States and Britain erupted with headlines over Grant's disheveled mugshot: HUGH-MILIATED, LEWD GRANT, HUGH'S SORRY NOW, and BLUE HUGH. From any vantage point, it looked like the actor's career was up in smoke. His public-relations handlers were in a panic. So Grant went into scramble mode, and he came up with a very simple plan of attack.

He decided he wasn't going to rummage about in the excuse box. Instead, he bit the bullet and publicly apologized. He hopped a spin cycle, making the rounds of the TV talk-show circuit, and pled his case on *The Today Show, Live with Regis and Kathie Lee, The Tonight Show with Jay Leno*, and CNN's *Larry King Live.*

Leno opened the interview by asking Grant: "What the hell were you thinking?" To which the actor replied with a mumble, "I'm not one to go around blowing my own trumpet." The audience broke into laughter. Then, on a serious note, he added, "I think you know in life what's a good thing to do and what's a bad thing, and I did a bad thing . . . and there you have it." Grant told Larry King, "I could accept some of the things that people have explained: stress, pressure, loneliness — that that was the reason. But that would be false. In the end, you have to come clean and say, I did something dishonorable, shabby, and goatish."

In a press release, the actor confessed he had done "something completely insane" and that he had "hurt people I love" —

his girlfriend at the time was supermodel and actress Elizabeth Hurley — "and embarrassed people I work with." After entering a plea of no contest, Grant was fined $1,180, ordered to attend an AIDS awareness program, and put on probation for two years. On the steps of the courthouse, a lone female fan held up a placard that read, "I would have paid you Hugh!"

Governor John

On March 12, 2008, the world got the latest installment of the ever-popular serial of famous johns caught with their pants down. Though fully in the tradition of the usual saga played out in tabloids and newscasts — otherwise respected celebrities, politicians, and preachers make spectacular fools of themselves on account of the urge, sending their careers into a tailspin and their PR ratings into freefall — this latest chapter offered one of the more shocking and unexpected reversals of political fortune in recent times.

The subject in question was known in high-end prostitution circles merely as Client Number Nine. In public life, he was the tough-talking, squeaky-clean, ride-the-moral-high-ground governor of New York State, Eliot Spitzer. With jaw squared, eyes cast downward, and his wife Silda stoically by his side, Spitzer stood before a battery of TV cameras and resigned from office, citing "private failings." Those failings involved his penchant for high-priced call girls, on whom he'd spent a purported $80,000 over several years. The specific liaison that brought him to his knees was a $4,300 hour-long tryst at a Washington, D.C., hotel.

"I've acted in a way that violates my obligation to my family and that violates my or any sense of right and wrong," Spitzer told reporters.

The forty-nine-year-old father of three teenage daughters had a weakness for browsing the Internet in search of relief. He found it in the offerings of the Emperors Club, an exclusive prostitution ring offering a stable of fifty escorts — rated on a "seven diamond" scale and costing one to five thousand dollars an hour — available for appointments in New York, Miami, Washington, London, and Paris. Crowning itself "the most preferred international social introduction service for those accustomed to excellence" and trumpeting its expertise in "introducing the most impressive models to leading gentlemen of the world," the Emperor's Club proved too hard to resist. The governor joined as a platinum member.

What Spitzer showed on that bleak March day of his public humiliation was that he was no ordinary john. He was the ultimate hypocrite, who betrayed not only his wife and family but also the dedicated people in the hard-fought movement to put an end to the trafficking of women worldwide. He had violated the spirit of the very antitrafficking legislation he'd championed as attorney general of the state and signed as governor, which went into effect on November 1, 2007. That law is among the toughest antitrafficking measures in the United States, giving law enforcement the tools necessary to go after sex traffickers and johns. On passage of the legislation, Spitzer stated, "Those who exploit innocent people and children . . . are subject to strict punishment under state law."

Yet he had been just another john. For Spitzer to have been

part of the demand that fuels global sex trafficking was an enormous slap in the face to thousands of voters and supporters, to those working in the human-rights and women's movements, and to the women victimized by the trade.

Norma Ramos, co-executive director of the Coalition Against Trafficking in Women, based in New York, said: "The contradiction and hypocrisy of Governor Spitzer being a supporter of the recently passed New York State antitrafficking legislation, while he himself is part of the demand that fuels sex trafficking, constitutes an enormous betrayal of the human rights and women's rights movement that works to end human trafficking."

However, while the owners, management, and so-called escorts involved with the Emperors Club have been charged with various offenses, Client Number Nine has managed to escape the long arm of the law. He could have been charged under the Mann Act of 1910, which prohibits "interstate transportation of women for immoral purposes." Federal prosecutors looking into the prostitution and money-laundering operations of the Emperors Club caught Spitzer on a wire-tap arranging for Ashley Dupre, aka Kristen, to travel from New York to Washington for a rendezvous at the Mayflower Hotel on the eve of Saint Valentine's Day. Under the Mann Act, that's a no-no.

On November 6, 2008, the U.S. attorney for the Southern District of New York, Michael J. Garcia, announced that his office had no plans to prosecute Spitzer for "any offense" connected to patronizing prostituted women, meaning the only punishment for the former governor's trysts will be an utterly wrecked career and reputation. "After a thorough investigation, this office has uncovered no evidence of misuse of public or campaign funds,"

Garcia said in a statement. "We have concluded that the public interest would not be further advanced by filing criminal charges in this matter."

Garcia added that although there was evidence that Spitzer violated the Mann Act, none of the other factors that traditionally weigh in favor of bringing charges was present, such as the use of minors involved in prostitution, or the commercial or other exploitation of them.

Norma Ramos argued that by allowing Spitzer to walk, the Department of Justice "has sent an unmistakable message that it is acceptable to buy and sell women, this in the face of growing evidence of the true nature of prostitution and its relationship to human trafficking."

Court Jester

Ronald H. Tills had a reputation as one of the toughest sentencing judges in western New York during his ten years on the bench. But it turns out that while dishing out hard time, the New York State Supreme Court justice was also committing crimes.

The distinguished-looking, bespectacled, silver-haired seventy-three-year-old was the entertainment coordinator for the Royal Order of Jesters in Buffalo, New York, from 2001 to 2007. The Jesters, a fraternal organization with 23,500 members across the United States, is dedicated to "mirth and merriment." To become a member, a man must also be a Shriner or a member of the Masons.

Tills took mirth and merriment to untold levels — below the belt. From 2001 to 2007, he personally recruited call girls and ferried them across state lines to service Jesters at club meetings in New York, Pennsylvania, Kentucky, and Florida, and at Niagara Falls, Ontario. In October 2007, he arranged for prostituted women from three different states to service a Jesters meeting in Brantford, Ontario. These actions are all felonies under the Mann Act and carry a maximum penalty of ten years and a $250,000 fine.

In a plea agreement the embarrassed former justice acknowledged arranging in September 2001 — while he was still a judge — for prostituted women to attend a meeting of the Buffalo chapter in nearby Dunkirk in order to have sex with members of the club. He also admitted that he committed a crime, that his conduct was wrong, and that his judgment was terrible. He will be sentenced in January 2009 and is expected to get twenty-one months for his cooperation in the case. A former police captain and a former law clerk to Tills pleaded guilty earlier in connection with the investigation.

Federal investigators believe that Buffalo was not the only Jesters chapter involved in transporting prostituted women across state lines, according to court papers filed by Assistant U.S. Attorney Robert C. Moscati. "This organization maintained chapters throughout the United States, including in western New York, and it was the custom of these chapters to host periodic meetings, usually on weekends, for their members," Moscati stated. "At most of these meetings, some members of the organization would be tasked to arrange the presence of women at the meeting, for the specific purpose of utilizing the women to engage in sexual intercourse and other sexual activity with the organization's members in exchange for money."

Prosecutors said they learned about the Jesters' involvement while investigating prostitution and human trafficking crimes associated with massage parlors in Niagara and Erie Counties.

Getting the Hot Girl

Many ordinary guys — the kind without the glamour or privilege of celebrity — are not satisfied with ordinary girls. What they want they perceive as beyond their reach: not the average girls but the babes.

Hot Stuff, who is thirty-five, says that when he was twenty, he could never get the hot girl. "You know what I mean, bros," he explains. "So, mongering is a way for me to get that choice girl. I just want to experience the beautiful side of life before I die. If it means going to TJ [Tijuana] for a nice time or the PI [Philippines], then that is good."

Another, who calls himself Sleazy, interjects that he is not going to pay for sex with "an average girl. I'd rather wank off to a porno," he says. "If I'm gonna be spending my hard earned cash I want to spend it on things that I can't get otherwise, which is stunningly beautiful women."

Rod is thirty-eight, on the pudgy side, balding, and, in his own words, "not much to look at." Once a year, in February, this systems analyst treats himself to a two-week sex vacation in the Philippines. He's been doing this since he was twenty-six. "It's what I look forward to all year. I get to bed the hottest babes who think I'm really cool. I know I could never, ever get one of these girls to go out with me back home. There's no way. But on vacation, they gush all over me. I get my pick and have to push so many of them away. It's my paradise."

One reason these and other average guys vie for the attention of paid hot girls is their skewed view of average women. "So-called normal girls are boring," said one john, "but I'll sport fuck them if only for the count."

On another site, a john signed in as Anon reported that while on the dating circuit recently he "chatted up a few normal girls to see the difference in the way that sexuality is handled." He continued, "When I'm with a working girl, the conversation goes straight to sex . . . and sex is automatic. But when I start talking to these normal girls, they don't seem to be all that interested in sex. It is super boring. Not that I have dated much during my lifetime, but this seems pretty dull. It makes you wonder how sex would ever happen at all with most of these girls. Now I can see why the demand for hookers is so high. Getting these girls in bed is like trying to draw water from a rock."

Recapturing Youth

In the macho world of johns, nothing is more cliché than aging men who nourish their swollen or battered egos by renting the bodies of very young women as a means of recapturing their youth. The boasts of men in their forties, fifties, and sixties who've "bagged" eighteen- and nineteen-year-olds choke the discussion forums on Internet sex sites. Men also banter about the magic elixir that has renewed their sexual prowess and replenished their stamina: Viagra.

"There is no substitute to screwing a different 18 year old girl each time, any female will eventually get older and become boring sexually," Devilman offered.

"She was barely eighteen," another john crowed. "She was easily a nine in looks and a body to die for. I got her for the entire night and all it cost me was $100!"

A fifty-one-year-old john acknowledged that "There is no way a twenty-year-old would ever go on a date with me, never mind sleeping with me. But when I go to a twenty-year-old prostitute and show her the money, she doesn't say 'no,' and I get what I want: a date with a hot chick."

Another, who calls himself Lance, expounded on the joys of Viagra: "I'm fifty-six and my sex life was almost flat-lined. I couldn't get it up, and when I did, I couldn't keep it up. And then the pharmaceutical industry finally got something right. That little blue pill has given me the go-power of a twenty-year-old. I feel like the Energizer Rabbit. I just keep going, and going and going."

His boast was backed by another fifty-something john. "When a hot, young babe says to me that she's never experienced such longevity, I, of course, don't tell her it's all because of Viagra. I want her to believe that us old guys are better than the young ones. What we lose in recovery power, we make up in staying power."

3

LOVE AND MARRIAGE

My wife is not adventurous. She hates giving oral. She hates taking it from behind. She hates being on top. She likes the traditional way: me on top. So when I go out to see a hooker, it's non-traditional all the way.

—A MARRIED JOHN ON WHY HE PAYS FOR SEX

WHY DO MEN CHEAT? There are so many reasons. Why do men cheat by buying sex? Most will likely tell you they're not fulfilled. Because each situation is unique, it's impossible to make generalizations. The Internet, however, is rife with locker-room talk as to why men in relationships pay for sex on the side. In one respect, these cybervignettes reinforce many of the stereotypes of cheating johns: wife not interested . . . wife too conservative . . . husband has needs that can be met only by a pro. But some stories surprise. At one extreme are men who vilify marriage and

41

relationships through and through. At the other are those who continue to profess love for their wives or insist that what they do is actually good for their marriage. Some don't see their behavior as cheating. Others don't care, because they blame their wives for their sorry lot in life.

Though there is precious little connection between their loins and their heads, there certainly appears to be a direct line to these johns' stomachs—they're curiously fond of pithy one- or two-liners, particularly if they employ food metaphors.

"In marriage you get occasional sexual relief, not a Broadway play. It's usually a baloney sandwich, not a banquet," writes one.

"At home I'm always getting hamburger," writes another. "Occasionally, I want filet mignon with all the trimmings."

"After a year, everything became humdrum. The sex dropped off to once a month. . . . All the sizzle was gone from the bacon."

"Marrying a normal girl is like cooking your own meal at home or using a dial-up connection. It's way more difficult and slower than paying for sex with working girls."

And my favorite: "Buying sex is simply like going to lunch without your wife," says a john who likes to eat out a lot. "You're hungry, you eat. Sometimes you eat together." And apparently sometimes you don't.

Why Do They Do It?

It's surprising how many johns claim to love their girlfriends or spouses. The problem is, that claim is almost always followed by a big, fat BUT. Reggie, a British john who shares his story online, insists that he loves his wife and would never leave her. "I really do love her. She's great with the children, she's got a warm way about her, and she's a fantastic cook.

"But she's gotten real fat. She tips the scales at 280 and looks like a bleeping hippo," he complains. "I have absolutely no interest in having sex with her. To be honest, the thought of seeing her naked turns my stomach."

His solution is to seek out sex with what he coolly refers to as "working girls." "I'm a man with certain needs and it gets a little tiresome masturbating to porn on the Internet," he explains. "So one night, I took the plunge and headed off to a massage parlor where I got what I needed." He hasn't looked back.

Was it worth it for him? Hard to say. The massage may have met his physical needs, but emotionally it came up short: "The entire experience is detached," he says. "No kissing, no cuddling, no passion . . . It's just cold sex. There is no emotional involvement whatsoever."

Yet, if the lack of intimacy in the encounter bothers him, there also seem to be no repercussions with respect to his feelings for his wife. He professes suffering no pangs of guilt for cheating on her, probably because he believes she's partly responsible.

"I'd like to make love to my wife," Reggie claims, "but she's got to stop being a human disposal unit and shed the blubber. There's no way I can ever get it up with someone who looks that gross."

"I love my wife," says another married john, but he quickly adds, "I love women." His Achilles' heel: "You know the old saying: variety is the spice of life." For him, variety in his sex life is a must. Obtaining it in the safest, easiest way is his prime concern. "I learned a very important lesson early on in my marriage.

I once got involved in an affair, and it nearly cost me an expensive divorce. It took a lot of apologizing, begging, and promising to be a good boy before my wife took me back.

"What I learned from all that is the easy way to get variety is to pay for play," he confides. "The pro knows why I'm seeing her and it's over in an hour. It's like I've gone out for a long walk and my wife is none the wiser." For him, paid sex — or "pay for play" — is less risky than an affair. With the pros, he says, "there are no hiccups along the way."

Another attached john, who calls himself Super Stud, is in his mid-thirties and has been married less than a year. In that short time, he admits, he has had sex with "maybe 40 women." He goes on "sexcursions all the time out of the country. I am a monger and unfortunately for my wife I can't shake it," he says. "Since getting married I have just gotten better about hiding it." He says he agrees with his therapist that he is emotionally immature.

Theo, another john, has a different kind of problem: he suffers from a Madonna-whore complex. "You marry for love," Bill asserts, "but if you want to fuck like a dog, you go to a whore." Bill and other johns have strict views about what type of sex is acceptable with a partner or wife. Normal sex, the bread and butter variety, is fine. Kinky sex is too dirty: practicing it with his wife would make her a whore.

Men who subscribe to this view tend to see women in one of two lights — either tainted or pure. According to psychologists, these men often marry women who remind them of their mothers. The wife becomes the Madonna figure — a "good" woman to be loved, cherished, and protected. Because they see their wives as virtuous and pure, these men dare not engage them in anything "dirty" or degrading. Yet by the same token they are excited by and don't want to forgo the dirty side themselves. For that, they sneak out with a fistful of cash. Their encounter with the "bad" woman can never be about love, because to them she is only a whore. It can only be about sex.

"I enjoy kinky sex," explains Bill. "That's what turns me on — anal, giving facials, talking dirty. I can't do these things with my wife. I love her and she's the mother of my children. I hire a whore to do those things. That's what she's there for."

"I didn't marry a whore," says another john called Elliot. "I don't want a whore to be the mother of my children. But let's face it, sometimes you just want a whore who you can screw with wild abandon. That's why I go to prostitutes."

Larry has been married for six years but says he pays for sex twice a year: on his birthday and just before Lent. He treats himself because he lusts after a certain kind of sex that he would never imagine seeking from his wife, but with him it's less clear that he wouldn't *want* to. He seems more concerned with marital peace. "Sex with a whore is always better and that's a fact. You just get to do things that you wouldn't ever imagine doing with your wife," Liam says. "God, if I asked my wife for some of the stuff I've done with whores, she'd bloody well go round the bend!"

And then there's Paul. He says getting married and having a daughter is "the best thing" that has ever happened to him. He describes himself as hardworking, says he has a nice home. Trouble is, the sex that is available from his wife is "boring as hell," he explains. This he attributes to her simply being a wife. "A good wife is many things but almost never a good whore." Put differently, "mongers who are accustomed to having it their way will never be satisfied with the way a wife does it," he says. Or another: "Most wives give you a place to put it, but damn few are good whores."

What he's looking for is someone who will do whatever, wherever, and whenever he asks. "I want sex my way from start to finish, and a good whore follows my lead or directions," Elliot says. "She bends and twists and spreads and kneels, and maybe can even be creative."

Pangs of Guilt

That married men cheat by buying sex on the street, paying for extras in a strip club, or seeking an "out call" on the Net we know from numerous sources — police sting operations, delighted reports in the media, and the men's own boasts and shared confidences online. But are they ashamed about what they do? Do they see it as a betrayal of their partners? Do they see it as different from adultery?

Oddly enough, in the eyes of some attached johns, paying for sex is not actually cheating. Cheating, they believe, would involve something more sinful or compromising — some sort of feelings for the women with whom they're having sex, a greater investment of emotions. They also don't think there's any loss in sex at home; it's not as if their pay for play means there's less play with the wife.

"C'mon, I don't think it's hard for most guys to give a wife all the sex she wants. You're not cheating her out of sex," Liam says. "Now I do think having a girl friend is cheating. That's asking for trouble."

Paying for sex, he insists, is relatively harmless. "We don't know their name. We don't care who they are, and . . . who really cares if we ever see each other again?" Seeing prostituted women, he seems to think, is somehow more virtuous than having a typical affair. "I bet most men whose wife leaves them due to infidelity has to do with an ongoing affair, rather than a one-time purchase."

Some wandering husbands, like Frank, feel guilt-free because they claim straying in this way hasn't affected their marriage. "Going to a prostitute is how I get sex," Wayne explains. "I don't feel like I'm cheating and I certainly haven't noticed a change for the worst in my marriage. My wife doesn't want it and I do. If she would have sex with me, I wouldn't go to a prostitute."

Other married johns, like Keith and Wayne, take it one step further and actually convince themselves that they're doing their wives a favor. Keith has been married for twenty-two years and has been paying for sex on and off for the past sixteen. "That's when the last of our four kids was born and that's when our sex life came to a screeching halt," he recalls. "Don't get me wrong. My wife and I have a fantastic relationship. We get along well. We don't fight. That is we don't fight anymore. We did whenever I was in the mood and she had the proverbial headache. I hated having to beg like a dog for a bone, and having sex just to procreate wasn't how I envisioned marriage.

"Anyhow, my frustration eventually led me to a prostitute and I got my needs met," he explains. "Since then, everything has been okay at home. I'm pretty sure my wife suspects I see a pro but she's never asks and I don't tell.

"I think she's content that I don't bother her for sex and I'm happy 'cause I get sex when I need it and how I want it. I don't get into kinky stuff, but it is hot and heavy," Keith admits.

Wayne is more blunt. "I really believe going to a prostitute has helped my marriage. Most of the time my wife doesn't want to have sex, and it has been the cause of many an argument. So I book an appointment with a sex provider, and now my wife and I don't have arguments," he says.

One john who calls himself Stickman strikes a more sour note, blaming "inconsiderate" wives for their husbands' straying. "Men pay call girls for sex when they are not getting what they as men want from their wives," he claims. "Happy, sexually fulfilled husbands tend not to wander. When a wife stops meeting her husband's needs in favor of her children's, what is a healthy man to do? Masturbate or find a new cow to replace the one he married. This is the question every sexually frustrated husband faces."

Marriage, Monotony, and Money

For some married johns as for some unmarried ones, paying for sex is a frugal, well-calculated choice: "I've been through a divorce once before," says Colin. "I should have learned my lesson the first time but I was ruled by my dick.

"Before long I got dragged into another marriage. After a year, everything became humdrum. The sex dropped off to once a week and it was missionary or nothing. All the sizzle was gone from the bacon. I'd leave if I could afford it but I can't. I'd be out on the street begging for nickels and dimes just to get by."

However, Colin has found his release. "Whenever I get tired of missionary sex, I go see a prostitute. Then it's show time! I can howl like wolf and she can purr like a contented kitten, and when I leave I'm one happy customer."

"My wife and I put on a good act," writes another attached john, who uses the screen name Stewing in Purgatory. "In front of the family, we are always smiling and joking. But I know she can't stand living with me and I feel the same towards her.

"We do it for the kids, the in-laws, and our close circle of friends. I know if we divorced, it would be a disaster socially and I don't think either of us could handle the fallout. So we stay together and every so often when the urge hits, I see a working girl to get my rocks off. Otherwise, I think I'd go completely insane."

SINGLE
BY CHOICE

Mongering has perhaps warped what I want in life. Because now all I want to do is stay single and fuck whores forever!
—A JOHN WHO HAS CHOSEN TO PAY
FOR SEX RATHER THAN DATE

W HEN TIMES ARE TIGHT, people look for ways to save money. "These days, it's cheaper to rent than to buy," says one man. He's not talking about videos, cars, or a place to live. He's talking about sex. Bargain sex.

For some men, cheap sex means sex that is bought. The other kind is harder on the wallet, or so claim the thousands of single johns for whom dating and relationships are a hefty and risky investment. The costs of courtship are high. The payoff — sex — uncertain, leaving many pining for more cost-effective erections. Their answer is to remain single by choice and to pay for play rather than pay for a date.

51

the women they are using. For these johns, it all comes down to prostituted women as a disposable commodity. "Maybe I'm just more impatient," says one younger john. "I grew up in the age of fast food and hi-speed internet. I want sex NOW. Not in weeks, months? Years?!"

At the other end of the spectrum, there's the aging cruiser not wanting to lower his standards: "As I grew older — and not wanting to go down too much in my standards of female companions — I found out that just paying for it certainly takes a lot less effort, time and even money."

And in the middle are busy professionals too wrapped up in their careers to care about — or succeed at — dating.

Allan, a thirty-one-year-old business consultant from London, says he used to spend a lot of time trying to meet women in clubs and bars. Not anymore. "Some of my friends are fully aware that I visit prostitutes," he says. "Many of them do themselves." Why the switch? It's a "mixture of the convenience and . . . time," he says. "I work very, very long hours."

Mark, a thirty-seven-year-old stockbroker on Wall Street, is another up-and-comer married to his career. "I work in a very stressful job and put in a 72 hour week. I'm always on my Black-Berry or my laptop. I don't have time to do the dating thing.

"Every time I've started dating a chick, she's dropped me because she whines that I love my job more than her. Hey, I make a huge salary, drive a Porsche, and own a penthouse condo. You don't get all that by sitting on your ass.

"I just got fed up with all the hassles of dating," he admits. So he now goes to "the classiest escorts. It fits my busy schedule."

The Hassles of Dating

Pay for play — which some johns shorten to P4P — may be easier, cheaper, and more of a sure thing. But even more important for many single johns, as the previous examples show, is that it is also hassle-free. There are no attachments, no pesky emotions, no hurt feelings on either side. A "working girl" gives them what they want, when they want, without any of the "issues" they may encounter in a relationship.

"I've been trying for ages to get together with girls who I thought were the one, only to get passed up for somebody else," says one. "I gave up and decided that I'm going to start buying. . . . It's a better alternative for me. It's hassle free and guaranteed."

The desire to dispense with "emotional baggage" is a common theme among these single johns. Others speak of eliminating the "drama" of relationships. Both have become mantras on the chat boards and discussion forums of the john community.

"Sometimes paying for it is better. You avoid ALOT of girl-friend issues!!! Some of my exes, here in the UK, have been too much drama. At least with a hooker, they leave afterwards," says one john.

"As a monger, I put up with far less bullshit over [sex] because I know I can get my needs met without the drama if I want or need to," says another.

Yet another john, called Piccadilly Circus, agrees: "It's a lot cheaper, easier to get, and involves less emotional baggage than a date."

A cruder explanation comes from Malcolm, a computer

technician in Toronto. "Every time I go on a date . . . and I mean every single time . . . the woman brings a ton of emotional baggage to the dinner table. I don't have the time or the inclination to listen to her problems. A prostitute knows exactly what I want — her open mouth on my hard cock."

But the simplest comes from Shaft, who sums up the lifestyle in seven words: "Paid mongering is better. No emotional tie-ups."

Jaded

For another group of johns who reject the hassles of dating, the motivation is a failed relationship or marriage. Marvin, a car salesman, explains his choice by equating his marriage with prison. "I just got out of a three-year prison sentence," he wrote. "It was a costly divorce but it was worth getting away from all her complaining. Every time I got home from work, it was bitch, bitch, bitch. All she did all day is sit on her fat butt, watch soap operas and then micro-wave me a Stouffers dinner. My wife was a freaking drama queen with the perennial headache.

"I no longer will go out with any woman on a date because I don't want and don't need the drama," he continued. "Now when the urge hits, I call up a sex provider and she gives me exactly what I want — searing hot sex with no complaints, and better yet, no insults."

Another john, who calls himself Roadwarrior, says he too won't ever marry or even date. His reasons are twofold: two marriages, two divorces, and "two fortunes lost."

"Chasing women is a pain in the ass," he wrote. "Far too much aggravation for me. No, I'd rather pay for it right up front.

Paying for sex stops all the 'I wanna get married' stuff from the gf [girlfriend]. Doesn't set you up to get raped in divorce court after you have worked your ass off for years to get ahead and you can relax and enjoy yourself without all the drama that comes with living with a female."

Overall, he concludes, the women he paid treated him better than the ones he didn't. "If I had to compare the ones that treated me right [with] the ones that didn't, I'd have to pick the ones I paid over the gf/wife."

Steven, another disenchanted john in the same camp, counts his blessings that he *didn't* get married. "All I ever got were complaints from my girlfriends. Thank God I never married any of them or I'd have blown my head off by now," he says. "I enjoy my providers. They ask me how my week went and they tell me I'm the greatest lover they've ever had. I know they're a bunch of lying whores but at least they make me feel like Tony the Tiger — GREAT!"

Maximum Pleasure, Minimum Fuss

For many johns the biggest benefit of all is that there's no wondering how the date will end — and they do consider these dates. "At the end of the date with the prostitute you know you are usually going to get that release," says one john. "But the drama queen girlfriends I have dated, they get so wound up that after six months of dating they still don't feel comfortable to take you back to their house and screw all that frustration out of you."

"I am a single guy," says another. "No girlfriend and wouldn't want one. I like pretty women and sex."

And then there's Finlay: "I find it empowering that I can fulfill my manly needs whenever I want with minimum fuss.

"The best bit is that I can leave afterwards," he adds.

His story is not unusual. "I've now been single for a while and I can tell my friends find it strange that I'm not interested in trying to get non p4p when we are out, but I'm not really interested for many reasons.

"In my present state of mind my chances of entering into a relationship with a [Western woman] are nil. And I've actually never been happier, which I think people find strange (they think I'm not getting any, but little do they know), because its human nature for some people to always have to be with someone.

"So for me personally, mongering has perhaps altered/warped what I want in life. Because now all I want to do is stay single and fuck whores forever!"

5

I'M JUST
A LONELY GUY

*I pay or I be lonely guy. Loneliness is a killer. I don't like the
lonely life. And not easy to find woman in my life.*
—Online posting on the World Wide Sex Guide

THREE MEN, THREE CONTINENTS, one thing in common: they're lonely,
they can't get women, and they've become resigned. The first, an
American who calls himself Lonely Guy: "I've always been a shy
guy. All my life I've been fat, and on the looks meter I'm about a
three. No matter where I am, I see women look at me and roll
their eyes. I constantly suffer from feelings of rejection, and as a
result, I've never had the courage to ask a woman out.

"I didn't go to my high school prom or my college gradua-
tion. At work, I sit in my cubicle and keep to myself.

"I am thirty years old and I've never had a relationship with a normal woman. So I guess you can say I am an ideal candidate to go to prostitutes."

The second, a twenty-four-year-old Brit who goes by the name Sleazy: "Women are like a Rubik cube or jigsaw puzzle. It's hard to figure them out. They live on a different planet. Even sometimes talking to or watching female relatives, I'm thinking wtf [what the fuck]? I don't understand them. They are on a higher level.

"Any time I did make a slight effort to talk to a girl or go for meal, which was not often, I would want to get the hell out of there or get drunk as fast as possible.

"It's a sad fact to think I never ever had and will never have a girlfriend . . . I'll just have to stick to hos and put other women out of my mind completely."

And the third, a kindred spirit from across the globe: "I am Ram Man from India. I understand your problem, sir. Like you I not had sex for many years, especially in teens and 20s. Not easy to find the women for good relations and sex. Go to club waste of the money and the time. Girls not friendly these days. So I pay for the good sex with hot-totty. It is very sad but I have no choice.

"I pay or I be lonely guy. Loneliness is a killer. I don't like the lonely life. And not easy to find woman in my life."

Lonely Guy admits that, since he is painfully shy, he has been watching porn for years, starting as a teen:

It was my only source of release. I watch the soft core stuff. Still do. I don't like hardcore. It's just vile.

Every time I log onto one porn site or another, there are

all these ads for prostitutes. Then I found a number of sex sites where all these men brag about all the pros (prostitutes) they've had sex with. All the things they did with them. How easy it was and that none of the women reject guys no matter how unattractive they are because it's all about money.

One night, I was reading the ads on Craig's List and this one woman's picture caught my attention. She was so beautiful and sexy and Asian. Her name was Lily and the ad said she was twenty-three. She was asking for two hundred kisses. I figured that meant two hundred dollars.

In my wildest fantasies I knew I could never, ever get a woman like her but I was feeling really desperate and really horny so I called.

The woman only did "outcalls," so she came to his apartment.

I could tell the second she laid eyes on me that she was disgusted. I thought for sure she'd walk out but she didn't. She got right down to business.

I handed her the money and she asked me to take off my pants which I thought was kind of strange and quick. It wasn't about sex. She was checking me out for signs of STDs. I felt really uncomfortable being naked and inspected like that.

Once that was over, she got all undressed, put a condom on me and got on top of me. She started moaning and going wild and in less than a couple of minutes it was all over. She got off, took off the condom, dressed and just left. That was it.

I have never felt so stupid in my entire life. It was totally embarrassing. I had convinced myself that this was something that would make me feel good about myself, maybe give me some confidence. Instead, it had just the opposite effect. Right from the moment she arrived at my apartment, I knew she didn't want to be there. I could see she was disgusted by the look of me.

But she was there to do a job and I paid her to do something I knew she didn't want to. It was all cold and mechanical. All the moaning was an act, probably to make me cum fast. I've never gone back to a prostitute since.

"I'm twenty-two, never been on a date, never been in a relationship, never kissed a girl, never had sex, nothing, and it will probably stay that way forever," laments a would-be john, Ceylon. "The nervousness is so intense I will never, ever be able to talk to any girl I'm attracted to. I guess I have to live with the fact that I will be alone forever, that I will never know what it's like to be in love with a girl who loves me back.

"I figured out how to lose all the excess weight and keep it off for five years now," he continues. "I figured out how to make a shit fucking load of money, yet I can't seem to figure out this love shit. Maybe I should go to Pattaya and fuck prostitutes and accept the fact that that's all I can and will get — meaningless sex with no love."

And then the anger: "Fuck this friendship bullshit. It's so stupid, and girls are all idiots," he exclaims. "I bet they'd be blown the fuck away if they only took the time to try and get to know me. I'm deeper, smarter, funnier and nicer than most of the assholes that they'd end up with. Ah fuck 'em. I really should book a ticket to Thailand and forget about this love shit."

*   *   *

THE LONELY GUYS' STORIES prompt an outpouring of advice — some sympathetic, some crude — on the World Wide Sex Guide. One experienced john offers, "Never say never for Christ sake. You are 24-years-old. You got your whole life ahead of you. I understand your problems with not talking to girls all your life and it's okay. Many young men have been through this stage in life. You are just breaking out of your shell.

"You must also accept the fact that going into the dating world you must accept rejection. Everybody has been rejected. It is part of the process."

In the end, his advice is simple: "Just go overseas and get laid."

Another seasoned john echoes that thought: "What you need is for an age appropriate girl to fuck your brains out and spend some time with you listening to you pontificate about your boring life and ideas about life, the universe and everything and generally stroking your ego (I'm sure this will be a tremendous treat for her!!!). Save your money. Take a trip to a GFE destination like the Philippines, Colombia, possibly Argentina."

A john called Rake offers these sage words: "Go to a monger destination and give it a try. As you probably know, you will be risking addiction to cheap rental pussy. Keep a close hold on your wallet. Since you have not had success with women at home, you might lose your mind when an attractive young woman pays attention to you and gives you pussy. You might be a prime candidate for exploitation by a rental girl. All is not lost. Enjoy."

"Going to Bangkok is not giving up on anything . . . love is where you find it," says another. "You're young and all young people go through what you're going through, some earlier than others but trust me you are normal." Besides, he adds, "I know one-eyed, fat, old men who can get laid. . . . Be brave. Trying and failing is much better than a life of quiet desperation."

He offers a final postscript: "If you go to Thailand, enjoy the country and the culture. Getting laid is extra."

MARTIN IS THE LIFE OF A PARTY. Everyone at work and in his social circle loves him. He is jovial, charming, and friendly. But just beneath the skin beats the pulse of a very bitter middle-aged man.

"Look at me. I'm short, I'm bald, and I'm not all that much to look at," he said, sitting in a downtown Montreal bar. "All the women in the office adore me. When I go to parties, all the women joke and kibitz with me. They'll rock and roll with me, but none of them will slow dance with me. I ask women out and at the end of the date, I get a kiss on each cheek and a thank-you for a wonderful evening. That's been my life since high school."

Looking around the bar, I ask, "What kind of woman interests you?"

Martin points to two Quebecoise brunettes sitting at a nearby table. They are stunning.

I take a sip of my beer and tactfully suggest that maybe he's aiming too high.

"Why shouldn't I aim high? I don't consider myself chopped liver. Why should I settle for something I don't want? I'm a really nice guy. I own a condo. I own my car. I have a great job. I have money in the bank. The only thing I don't have in my life is a woman to love."

"Have you ever tried a dating service like E-harmony or LavaLife?" I ask.

"I've tried them all. I get instant replies when I write about myself . . . my likes, my dislikes, my dreams, wants, and desires. The connections pour in. They all love my responses. And then they *nudge* me to post my picture, and when I do the connections go dead. I get zapped into cyberspace."

Martin stares at the two brunettes, who have since been joined by a couple of guys in swank Armani business suits, who are obviously on the make. "Look at them. Two freakin' losers, and those women think they've just hit the jackpot. I'm the freakin' jackpot. I can't understand why women like that fall for jerks like them."

"They're just looking for what you're looking for," I offer.

"Well, I'm no longer looking. I've given up on the dating scene and spending tons of money on dinners, plays, and movies. My dates for the past few years have been call girls. I see women that are incredible. I spend an hour with them, and they give me all the loving attention I want and need."

"I doubt that it's loving," I suggest.

"I know it's not love. I'm not an idiot. But at least it's something."

"Ever fall for one of these women?"

"Yeah, I did. It was a big mistake. I started seeing her regularly and tried to convince her to leave sex work. I told her I would take care of her."

"Somewhat like the guy in *Pretty Woman*," I said.

"Yeah, but she didn't see it that way. She told me she had a man in her life and she wasn't interested. Then I made a big mistake. I asked her what kind of man would allow her to be a prostitute other than a pimp. She told me to leave and never come back. Since then, the girls I see are just about business. I mean we have fun for the hour. They're all really nice to me, and I enjoy my time with them."

"And when you leave?"

"I go back to my solitary existence. I go back to being lonely," Martin said.

"You've given up?"

"How many times can a guy pick himself up after being rejected over and over again?"

"I'm sure there is a woman out there who would love to be with you."

"Sure, but she's not what I'm looking for."

"In other words, she's the flip side of you and you don't want that," I said. "I wonder what she must feel, but then, you'd know."

Martin looked down at his drink. He didn't respond.

PAUL HAS TRIED TO FIND a girlfriend. For the longest time, his dream was to get married and have children. But no one would have him, so reluctantly he turned his attention to prostituted women.

"I'm intelligent. I have a good job. I'm considered good looking but I have a disability," he wrote. "It seems when women see it, they can't get past it."

Paul is a paraplegic, bound to a wheelchair. "I broke my back eight years ago in a skiing accident. It took me a long time to overcome the shock . . . to stop feeling sorry for myself. Not long after the accident, my fiancée faded from the scene. She couldn't handle it. As for me, I managed to get it together with counseling and a lot of support from my parents and brothers."

After a few years of therapy, Paul was zipping about on a basketball court, meeting new friends and dealing fairly well with his situation. But there was one important thing missing from his life—female companionship.

"Life can get very lonely when you're bound to a wheelchair. I may have lost the use of my legs, but the plumbing was in perfect working order. The thing is, I couldn't even get to first base with any women. They were friendly and all, but not one would go out with me. It was like I had some deadly disease."

Paul and his wheelchair-basketball teammates often commiserated about their lack of female company. "More to the point, we were a bunch of sexually frustrated guys, because we weren't getting laid."

One evening, a friend of Paul's confided that he regularly sought out the companionship of prostitutes.

When he told me that, I rolled my eyes. I couldn't believe that he had been reduced to paying for sex with some whore. He got really pissed at my reaction . . . called me a moralistic, insensitive bastard, and left.

Over the next few months, I thought about his situation and realized that maybe he was right. I really, really wanted to have female companionship. I wanted to touch a woman's body, but going with a prostitute was anathema to me. Not that I'm religious or anything like that. It's just the thought of paying for sex and having sex with a whore who's been with God knows how many guys in a week just turned my stomach.

Then one evening I found myself browsing exotic sex ads on the Internet, and before long I was on the phone. I told each one about my disability. I was pissed off that so many of them said no way. I couldn't believe these whores had standards. They'd go with some married jerk that no doubt treats his wife and children like dirt, but they wouldn't go with me 'cause I'm disabled.

But Paul persevered and got lucky on his fourteenth call. "She did outcalls, and didn't even charge me a premium. But I have to admit that I felt really disgusted with myself . . . with what I have been reduced to. It was just sex, very mechanical and nothing all that memorable. Still, it was good to touch a woman."

Since that first time, Paul says he's become a regular john. "I have a stable of women I can call when I want companionship . . . found them all on the Internet. Still, when they leave, I feel this twinge of guilt and anger inside. I hate doing this. I hate that I've been reduced to this, but it's all I've got. It's either this, or spend my time alone in my room masturbating to porn."

6

THE GIRLFRIEND
EXPERIENCE

Many of us like to buy into the fantasy that the girl we are with is happy to be there and is enjoying herself.
—A VETERAN JOHN

THE BELIEF THAT JOHNS are only out for sex is widespread. For many, that's true, but some crave the illusion of romance as well. They want to feel, if momentarily, a connection with a woman, even if it's merely because she is paid. While these men may pay for sex, what they're really shopping for is a make-believe girlfriend, and there are plenty to be found. Women who play their roles well can make these johns believe the fantasy that the intimacy is real and the liaison is more than just sex. The john is having a girlfriend experience, or GFE .

"The girls in Thailand (like the Philippines and to a lesser extent those in Cambodia) are willing to play, and convincingly, the role of a girlfriend, and to not only stay the entire night with a monger but to have sex several times," says one such john. What's more, he adds, "and of considerable importance to many mongers," is that they're willing to "cuddle up and give the pretense of showing warmth and love of the kind that men experience in the best of relationships and marriages."

"GFE is just what it says," explains a john who calls himself Heatseeker. "You interact with your companion like you would with a normal girlfriend. I mostly think it's the non sex part of your time together that makes it a GFE, like going to a movie, bowling, going out to eat just like you're out on a normal date with a normal girl only you're with a hooker."

"A GFE is typically a non-rushed session where the provider caters to your every need without balking," explains another.

Dave from Phoenix says for him the GFE is "like renting a girl friend for the hour instead of the more cold, detached hooker type pro. Most importantly, GFE is natural, not mechanical or forced. No matter what kind of play is desired, it should feel like the real thing. For Dave, the real thing, involves "having an emotional and intellectual connection with a provider like you would with a real girlfriend, not just a body for physical sex."

Dave also offers a somewhat New-Age definition of the GFE when he describes what he most relates to in the experience: "universal love, which many people don't agree with our culture's definition of love. GFE and love can be for the moment. It doesn't have to result in falling in love that many are so afraid of. It is more like standing in love of a unique spirit of a person and seeking to express this universal love by sensual pleasure giving touch, sensuality and sexuality."

For another john, GFE is "most of all about being a sincere mutually desired human reaction. It is the opposite of the women being treated like a sex toy and the man an ATM machine."

What becomes clear from reading many such postings is that the GFE is considered a premium service by many johns the world over. It is valued not only for what it offers but for what it allows these men to forget.

"In the context of this hobby, it means that for the duration of the encounter the provider does not make you feel like you are participating in a business transaction," says one.

Sexton speculates that "the majority of clients . . . don't need or want affection from our provider," but "there are some of us who get off on an even deeper level getting that affection." For johns like this, the GFE provides a more fulfilling or meaningful experience. "[W]hen I'm with a provider who gives me a GFE," he says, "it satisfies me on a deeper level."

GFE enthusiasts readily admit that they're paying for a fantasy — not just sex — and that they do so because believing the woman is happy to be with them makes them feel good.

"We all know what we are signing up for when we hire a professional," says a john who calls himself Voyageur. "In fact many of us go this route for the specific purpose of avoiding emotional commitment and having a clean and pleasant break when the deed is done. Even so, many of us like to buy into the fantasy that the girl we are with is happy to be there and is enjoying herself."

Some johns set slightly lower standards. "GFE is when she lets you lick her toes and . . . pretends she doesn't really think that you're the most disgusting creature on the planet!" confides another.

A john who calls himself Beach Comber explains that the GFE involves "more fondling and touching rather than just, 'Oh, stick it in, baby.'

"If I'm really attracted to the provider," he says, "a little kissing and groping is a nice build-up to the main event. It's a lot less mechanical and more like you're actually being intimate with your lover after a romantic night on the town. . . . It differs immensely from the mechanical provider who asks you up front how much you're going to tip her and won't allow any touching. For some, this type of service is okay. For me, I like the idea of being able to pretend that I'm really with someone who digs me for an hour and then be able to leave and pull the same gig a week later with a different girl.

"GFE or not, it all boils down to no commitments."

The Boyfriend Experience

While many johns pine for the girlfriend experience, some want to feel like they're returning the favor. The fantasy for them takes on an added dimension as they offer the women a boyfriend experience (BFE). A john called Zeus explains, "When you can come along and they feel that 'BFE' from you . . . from your attentiveness and willingness to listen and treat them like a regular woman, they pour into you more and that to me is when you will have your best experiences because she is comfortable and there is a level of trust. It's a good feeling when they feel that they can unwind and open up. . . . [S]he sees something in the guy that reassures her of something — that there are decent guys out there after all."

For these johns, the warm-and-fuzzies that come from casting themselves as the boyfriend adds to the magic of the encounter. Some actually convince themselves that the women want their attention and bask in their client's affection and trust. "Their profession is a very lonely one," Sexton ruminates. "Most of the time their clients don't give that affection they need."

Offering this affection, these johns believe, elevates them to the ranks of Most Eligible Client. "You'll find the majority of these women do this trade to provide for their families and to make a way until they can truly get out of it," Zeus insists. "You won't find many that do it because they 'love it.' When they meet someone whose company they enjoy or feel a sense of comfort and calming from, they tend to latch on to that because they are truly desiring that brief attention and personal time in their lives. You'll be surprised at what they really share and express during the quiet and comfortable moments."

All this "bonding" can't help but loosen the johns' grip on reality. Some grow to like the women they rent, or form strong emotional connections. They mimic the rituals of dating, bringing flowers and chocolate, walking with the women down the street, holding hands, laughing like lovebirds. For many, the women become surrogate girlfriends — lovers, yes, but also confidantes and friends. Sometimes, though, the johns buy too much into the *Pretty Woman* fantasy, and the blurring of their two worlds starts to wreak havoc.

Johnathan was thirty-nine when he jetted to Thailand on his first sex excursion. "Read about all the cheap and wild sex on the beaches in Pattaya and figured I needed some of that. I went completely crazy. I fell in love and almost didn't go home but after I told the girl about my plans [to quit his job and move to Thailand], I saw this expression in her face. I was nothing more than an ATM machine to her and if I couldn't supply the cash, she was going to move on to someone else. Love had nothing to do with it."

Ryan, on the other hand, always wanted to be a monger. "But on my first attempt I fell in love with an eighteen-year-old escort," he admits. "She wants to get married in Manila. I'm from the U.S. Her family is all excited. I'm like the fucking hero to them saving their daughter." But the fantasy seems to be wearing thin. "I tell you, if I had to marry I'd rather marry a slutty escort than a good girl, but fuck, now this bitch goes away for hours under suspicious excuses and I don't know what to think. She comes back and says how much she loves me. My heart says to trust her, but my head says fuck you, dump her ass and head to the nearest brothel. What do you think about this?"

Nothing sets off alarm bells for veteran mongers like proclamations or even mere hints of love. Try as they might, they can't see beyond the labels. To these johns, the women will always be "hookers," "sluts," and "whores," and it pains them to see their novice brothers so vulnerable, so sappy, so inexperienced, so deceived. So they resort to a tough-love intervention of sorts, hoping to slap the budding Romeos into accepting their version of the truth.

"Never fall in love with a prostitute," warns one jaded john. "Just think about all the dicks she's sucked and that should bring you back to reality."

"There's no such thing as, 'falling in love with a hooker,'" says another. "Bang her, pay her, move on to the next one, problem solved. End of story."

"You can't turn a ho into a housewife," argues a third. "[W]hat would you expect of her besides keeping your nuts drained? Is she educated? What type of employment is she capable of holding down?"

"Remember, you pay a hooker once," he adds. "You pay a wife for the rest of your life. How will you feel when she doesn't want to fuck (you) any more? How much of a 'relationship' would you have left?"

But when the pithy one-liners don't seem to work, they pull out the heavy artillery. Upon reading Ryan's post, a veteran monger implored the brotherhood to write in and set their smitten brother back on the path of sexual enlightenment.

"We've all been there," the veteran noted. "Tell him he's making a huge mistake."

In no time, the boards were inundated with stories about the time his brethren were "hooked by a hooker," and "mercifully" saw the light. Ryan read and was saved.

A john called Bullrider admonishes: "One important thing for less experienced mongers who may read these posts to keep in mind is that the same pro who delivers the GFE is still a hooker. Once a woman is a hooker that is a very hard mentality to shake. A hooker is also a hustler, a street operator, and often associated with criminals — often pimps and drug dealers. Yes, this even applies to so-called high end girls. She is high end because she charges more. Do not ever believe the sweet act from a pro."

These seasoned johns are hardened. They don't feel guilt, they don't let themselves feel sympathy for the women, and they certainly don't do anything so ghastly as mistaking the tingling in their toes for love.

"We're all vulnerable to their advances," admits a john who calls himself The Saint. "They are good at it, making us feel as though we're taking the moral high ground by getting them out of the bar scene and supporting their families. But ask yourself the question: Why should you? The fact the family is poor is not down to you, her joining the bar scene wasn't your fault so why cough up hard earned cash to correct a situation that wasn't of your making?"

The GFE View

Monica arrives at the coffee shop dressed in jeans, a loose red sweater, and a khaki blazer. She looks like the girl next door, except in her day-to-day life she's a call girl. On Craigslist she describes herself as "26, charming, classy and easy going." Her premier service is the GFE, which she offers for "200 roses an hour."

"I get a lot of clients wanting different things. Most men want straight sex as in wham, bam, get their rocks off and leave. Some want stuff they've seen on porn videos. And I have a number of regulars who want the girlfriend experience.

"I know what each one wants and needs. First I greet them with a big hug. We chat for maybe ten minutes in my living room before we head off to the bedroom. We make love, usually for about 20 minutes. I know how to make men come very quickly. Lots of moans and groans and wild writhing! It's funny. These guys actually think they're superstuds and believe they're making me go crazy. All part of the GFE! Make them feel great about themselves."

"You sound bitter," I suggest.

"Watching the parade of johns come through my door has made me somewhat bitter," she replies.

"What bugs you most about them?"

"The guys want me to act like their girlfriend. What they want is someone to whine to, someone to listen to their stupid rants about their wives or their girlfriends. Like I could even begin to care about their pathetic lives. But I fake interest, 'cause that's my job. It's what I do best. Fake!"

"What do they rant about?" I ask.

"Oh, 'My wife doesn't want to give me oral. My girlfriend doesn't want to do anal.' A couple of guys told me their significant other had the nerve to call them pigs for even suggesting it. So they come to me. I'm their pig. Imagine, they're looking for a girlfriend experience, and to them it's all about giving it to me up the ass or giving them oral. When we're lying in bed later, they tell me they wish their wife or girlfriend was more like me. Then their relationship would be perfect."

"What else do they expect from you?"

"Like I said, it's mostly someone to listen to the bullshit that is their life. 'My wife doesn't understand me. I wish she was more like you. All my girlfriend talks about is getting married. I wish she was more like you.' Sure, you want a whore to be your wife! I don't think so. I'm a diversion, a fantasy, an escape from the humdrum and boredom," Monica says.

"What else do they talk about?"

"Their kids. Oh, they're so proud of their kids. I've had guys come here, do me, and then head out to pick up their kids to take them to Little League or ballet class. They show me pictures of their children. That's when I feel most like a whore. I think about their perfect little lives . . . the white picket fence, the three-bedroom bungalow in the suburbs, the naive wife cooking supper and giving him a kiss as he comes home after spending an hour with me. Sometimes I cry because I know that to these men I'm a prostitute and nothing more."

"Any men ever get stuck on you?" I ask.

Monica laughs. "Oh, yeah. I always keep an eye out for nut jobs. I get guys who couldn't get a date if their lives depended on it. They are just too . . . well, let's just say they're not good looking—bald, fat, and a personality as boring as dust. My radar goes up when they start bringing me red roses and chocolates. I *know* I've got trouble when they bring me jewelry—watches, gold bracelets, and necklaces with hearts on them. When I hear them mumble the word *love*, I tell them either cool down or I cut it off."

"Do they cool down?"

"Most don't. They get into this savior complex. They want to rescue me from this life of sin. Here they are coming in and sinning, and suddenly I become their Pretty Woman and they want to take me away from 'this life,' as they call it."

"What do you tell them?"

"I tell them it's over and not to call me again. I screen all my calls. I never answer a blocked call, so if I see their number pop up, I don't answer. And I tell them if they ever come to my door unannounced or I catch them stalking me, I'll call the cops.

"I had one regular who was married. He wanted to leave his wife and kids. I showed him the door. I will not let myself fall for a john, because I know one day, when life isn't so rosy, he'll bring up my past in the heat of an argument and call me a whore. I don't need that shit. I know what I am, but most of all, I know what he is."

"Which is?"

"A lying bastard who cheats on his significant other, or a loser who either can't find a real girlfriend or doesn't want to put work into a real relationship," she says caustically.

"What do you tell these guys when they are leaving after an hour of the GFE?"

"Oh, I play the girlfriend role to the hilt. I pout a bit. I tell them that I'll miss them and I can't wait to see them again soon, and once they're out the door I go and take a long, cold shower."

7

I WANT IT
MY WAY

I see a lot of masochists. I get a lot of corporal session requests.
I get a lot of requests from people to have me pee on them.
I don't know why.
—A New York City dominatrix

For the vast majority of johns, a tryst with a prostituted woman is a sexual turn-on in and of itself, and venturing out into the night in search of the forbidden fruit is part of the thrill. It's like taking a walk on the dark side. Some men may see the woman as a whore, others as a seductive temptress or enchanting vixen. But there are men who look at these women through entirely different eyes. They see her as an object to be controlled, because it's *their* experience and *they* have the cash. In the world of johns, they call the tune, and the rented woman has to play it. Some johns play nice, others risqué, while others get downright violent or mean.

"I don't hire prostitutes for the conversation," Bryan writes. "That's not what I'm paying for. I get enough conversation at home. The wife never shuts up. I pay a prostitute for a good time and that means using her mouth for my pleasure. I pay her to give me what I want and in my book when you pay the money, you're the boss. I give the orders and she follows them. So if I want anal or something a little bit out of the ordinary, I get it. Otherwise, I'll find someone else. There are plenty of whores in the sewer willing to do what I tell them for cash."

Another john called Daryl points out that "If after agreeing to go to my hotel room to share with me love's magic moments the girl then suddenly becomes less charming and friendly, I drop her. I don't expect them to sing and dance and yodel, but I do expect the acting to be a part of the game from start to finish. Can't pretend that you like me? Then you get nothing. I'm acting too honey. . . . When I tell you that I love you and that you are the most beautiful woman I have ever seen, I am acting. Get with the program."

A third says he likes his sex rough. "I want her to know she's being fucked by a real man. I want everything — oral, vaginal, anal — and I end it by giving her a facial. . . . [I]f I am going to pay them, they better do as they're told."

Joseph Parker, clinical director at the Lola Greene Baldwin Foundation for Recovery in Portland, Oregon, says that most of the johns he has seen in Portland do not respect women and don't want to. They want control. "Real sexual relationships are not hard to find. There are plenty of adults . . . who are willing to have sex if someone treats them well and asks. But there lies the problem. Some people do not want an equal, sharing relationship. They do not want to be nice. They do not want to ask. They like the power involved in buying a human being who can be made to do almost anything.

"Some people do not want real relationships, or feel entitled to something beyond the real relationships they have," Parker continues. "They want to play superstud and sex slave. . . . If they need to support their fantasies with pictures, videotapes, or real people to abuse, the sex trade is ready to supply them. For a price, they can be a legend in their own minds."

Parker adds that johns would deny any intent to harm anyone, and might even claim empathy for the women, but this doesn't mean that they'd ever stop or help anyone escape the industry. "He does not care whether the person he is using is unwilling or unusually vulnerable. He simply feels entitled to whatever he wants, whenever he wants it. If someone is hurt, that is not his problem. He feels that the fee he pays covers any damages." This is why johns do not want to have an extramarital affair. "[T]hat would require them to be nice to the woman. They want to have sex on demand in which they do not have to be nice."

What Do They Want?

So what are these men looking for? It varies from man to man. The "nice" john only wants to feel like a stud. He wants the woman to moan and groan and make him believe that he's rocking her world. Many other johns engage in activities normally considered taboo or risqué. Top on the list for many is raunchy sex: positions, penetrations, and performances they've seen on porn but know they can't get from their girlfriends or wives. They demand rough and verbally abusive encounters. They want "around the world" sex, so-called golden showers, which involve urination, and threesomes. Cliché fantasies — women dressed as nurses, French maids, or schoolgirls — are popular items on the menu. For the truly bizarre, some seek out paid sex with pregnant women, while others are turned on by women who are lactating.

There are also a lot of very nasty men who treat the women they rent with absolute disregard and disrespect. These misogynists make no apology for their vile actions. They routinely refer to the women as "whores, skanks, and sluts" and a long list of other derogatory names. For these men, the women are wicked and invisible. Their advice to other johns is to use them, abuse them, but never, ever trust them.

On a wall near a hooker stroll in Amsterdam, scrawled graffiti illustrates what some men think of prostituted women in the land of liberated and legalized paid sex. "Fucking whores, you must be fucked until you drop on the ground," reads one.

A john on a sex site comments that whether the woman is a streetwalker or a high-end call girl, "They are all prostitutes. They are whores. They are not ladies." He instructs fellow johns that a whore cannot tell the buyer "what they can and can't do. Last I checked they had no say. They take what they are given, get paid for it and shut the fuck up. If they don't like it, they can get a real job and stop fucking wasting our time with their fucking dumb whorish ways."

His advice to prostituted women: "Shut up, get fucked, get paid and fuck off, that's your job, not being all demanding. If you're so well educated get a real job. Fucking whores who don't know their place piss me off."

Every day, sadistic johns seek out prostituted women to degrade in the most dehumanizing ways. A lot of these johns want to dominate the women physically, and some go further. Their perversion has as much to do with their rage against women as it does with sex. Their objective is to harm and humiliate. What they do to the women is, in a word, sick. These men take out their rage on the most vulnerable members of society. Because these women are generally viewed as tainted and expendable, the men know they are less likely to be held to account for their actions against them.

Some of these johns discuss their predilection for domination on the popular International Sex Guide site. One, called Drill Sergeant, solicits advice on where he can "buy girls for harder SM [sadomasochism] use such as whippings, fisting, 'rape,' bondage, and various pain games."

Another, called Romeo, asks for contacts for "girls" he could use for "water sports," or golden showers. "I want to piss in a girl's face. I would like to piss in a girl's mouth, open or closed. . . . So if you have a toilet, mature or young, contact me," he writes. His request is answered by Arranger, who says he has women "who will do masochism," including golden showers.

A third john boasts that he had a twenty-two-year-old "maid" in Kyiv, Ukraine, whose role was to be raped by the "house lord." And a fourth simply states, "I am a sadist. I enjoy inflicting pain. I enjoy punishing my subs [submissive women] and the extra added bonus is when the sub makes a mistake that deserves more punishment."

Other men rave about their own sadistic pleasures, including fisting anally and vaginally, ejaculating in a woman's face, slapping, hair pulling, and crude verbal abuse.

Then there are the johns who want to be dominated. They pay women to insult them, mock them, beat them, tie them up, urinate on them, and abuse them. This may look like the man relinquishing control, but in reality the john has surrendered nothing. Domination is his fantasy. After all, he's still paying. What he wants done to him is simply an act. It is all part of a game that he has constructed. Any thought that the woman has power is only an illusion.

"It's been a fantasy of mine to be dominated and humiliated by a woman. My wife is not interested in doing it. Any suggestions?" asks a john in London.

On a New York sex site, a man eager to be forced to lick the bottom of a dominatrix was directed to an article featuring an interview by such a woman. In the article, entitled, "Everything You Always Wanted to Know about S&M Dungeons . . . But Were Afraid to Ask," Mistress Alina was asked about her most frequent request.

"I see a lot of masochists. I get a lot of corporal session requests. I get a lot of requests from people to have me pee on them. I don't know why."

And who are her clients?

"Fucking middle-aged white guys and a lot of them are divorced — well, a lot of the guys in their 40s are divorced, a lot of the older guys are married and their wives have no idea," she said.

Interestingly, the idea of going to a dominatrix doesn't seem too popular with many johns. When someone seeks advice on where to go to be dominated by a woman, only rarely does he get a recommendation.

The Nasty Bastards

On most sex-site discussion forums, johns vehemently deny abusing the women they rent, but the undeniable fact remains that women in prostitution are subjected to violence and abuse at the hands of men who pay them. It is a daily occupational hazard. In fact, there is no other job on the planet fraught with so much danger as prostitution, and in no other so-called profession are so many women murdered each year.

A study released in April 2008 that delved into the minds of 110 Scottish johns found that 10 percent of the men believed that rape of prostituted women is not possible. Twelve percent believed that the concept of rape in the context of prostitution simply doesn't apply. Twenty-two percent said that, once they pay for sex, customers are entitled to whatever they want. More disturbingly, 10 percent admitted they would rape a woman — any woman — if they thought they wouldn't get caught.

This response may indeed represent a mere subset of johns — the kind that even regular johns decry as "nasty bastards" — but this type of john is responsible for an alarming rate of violence toward prostituted women.

In a 1998 international study of 475 people in prostitution in South Africa, Thailand, Turkey, Zambia, and the United States, 55 to 82 percent reported being physically assaulted, 50 to 78 percent reported being raped, and up to 75 percent reported being raped by a customer.

The London School of Health and Tropical Hygiene released a study titled *Stolen Smiles* in June 2006. Researchers interviewed 207 trafficked women from fourteen countries; the women, who had been rescued, were sold into sexual slavery in twenty-four countries, more than half in the European Union. Researchers found that nearly eight out of ten had been physically assaulted by traffickers, pimps, brothel and club owners, and johns. Ninety percent had been physically forced or intimidated into performing sexual acts. They were kicked while pregnant, choked with wire, burned with cigarettes, hit with bats and other objects, dragged across the room by their hair, punched in the face, or had their heads slammed into walls and floors. A full 61 percent said they had been threatened with a gun to the face or knife to the neck.

Another study in Minnesota in 1994, which looked at sixty-eight women in prostitution in that state, found that half had been physically assaulted by a john and that nearly a quarter of these had been beaten so severely that they suffered a broken bone. "The apparent randomness of violence by johns is frightening," Ruth Parriott noted in her study. "Two of the women told horrendous stories of assaults so vicious that they spent time in a coma. In both cases, there was no prior argument with the john to warn the women of danger. One woman displayed a picture of herself on a ventilator in the hospital as she noted wonderingly that the john had already paid her twenty dollars, and 'he never even took it back.' He did, however, drag her behind his car before leaving her for dead."

Similarly, a 2001 study of forty American and foreign women in the sex industry in the United States revealed that 64 percent had been victims of physical violence, with some of the injuries so severe that the women were permanently disabled. One-third said they were subjected to sadistic sex acts. Forty-four percent had a weapon used against them.

These aren't isolated incidents. Study after study reveals shocking levels of abuse. The "Oral History Project" by WHIS-PER (Women Hurt in Systems of Prostitution Engaged in Revolt) in Minneapolis, Minnesota, found that 74 percent of the women interviewed had been assaulted; of those, 79 percent were beaten by a john. Half had been raped, and 71 percent were victims of multiple assaults.

The studies show that the women are not only beaten, they're beaten repeatedly. In the early 1990s, the Council for Prostitution Alternatives in Portland, Oregon, collected data on violence against women from fifty-five survivors of prostitution. It found that 81 percent had been victims of aggravated assault — defined as "horribly beaten" — an average of forty-five times a year. Seventy-eight percent had been raped by their johns an average of thirty-three times a year. Forty-three percent had been physically abused or tortured by men an average of five times a year, and 47 percent had been abducted by men an average of five times a year.

Research has shown, time and time again, that for women in prostitution there is no such thing as a safe place. Studies show that johns victimize women on and off the streets. Half of the women in escort services have been raped. In strip clubs exotic dancers are sometimes threatened with a weapon or with rape. Their clothes are ripped, they are slapped, grabbed, and they have objects thrown at them. Women working out of private homes are also victims of frequent violence: 21 percent report being raped ten or more times.

But the riskiest and most brutal venue for women in prostitution is the streets. Johns typically cruise side streets where they can pick up women for cheap, fast sex. Most of the women who work the stroll are desperate, damaged, or destitute. They may be hooked on heroin or crack cocaine; most are controlled by a violent pimp. These women are the most likely to encounter violent johns who take pleasure in inflicting pain and suffering, who deliberately set out to physically harm, humiliate, and rape prostituted women. For such men, these street women are fair game to be hunted down and beaten.

Over the past two decades, the world has witnessed horrific reports of serial killers stalking women working the streets. In the United States, there is Gary Ridgway, the Green River Killer, who pleaded guilty in November 2003 to murdering forty-eight prostituted women in the Seattle and Tacoma, Washington, area. He boasts that the real number is seventy-one. In 2006 in Vancouver, Canada, Robert Pickton, a pig farmer, was charged with the murders of twenty-six prostituted women. He went to trial on six slayings, and on December 9, 2007, was found guilty of second-degree murder on all charges. And in February 2008, forklift truck driver Steve Wright in Ipswich, England, was found guilty of murdering five drug-addicted prostituted women in 2006. Every one of his victims was tortured, then killed.

These slain streetwalkers — like the scores standing on curbs in Los Angeles, Dallas, New York, Chicago, Miami, Toronto, Vancouver, and Montreal; or in London, Paris, Athens, Vienna, Moscow, Berlin, Rome, and Kyiv — were drug-addicted. Many had been forcibly addicted by their pimps or men who duped them into thinking they were loving boyfriends. Others got addicted long before their entry into prostitution in an effort to dull the pain of a childhood filled with physical abuse or incest.

Pickton's victims sold their bodies for five, ten, and twenty dollars to get their next rock of crack cocaine, which they purchased from their pimps. In return, they allowed themselves to be degraded and humiliated, to be treated worse than animals, to be urinated and defecated on, to be beaten and tortured. These were marginalized women. Most were outcasts from a child welfare system that had long abandoned them, and all were victims of a society that looked at them as worthless whores.

Welcome to Rape Camp

For men who fantasize about violent abuse but fear the consequences of doing it in person, the Internet has once again stepped in and provided an outlet for their rage.

In late 1999, Dan Sandler, a thirty-five-year-old miscreant from Ashland, Oregon, was going through an acrimonious divorce. He developed a venomous hatred for American women and decided to get even. Sandler flew to Cambodia, where he corralled a number of Vietnamese women who had been trafficked into the sex trade in Phnom Penh. His objective: provide an outlet for jilted men to take out their pent-up rage at Western women on Third World women.

Sandler launched a cybersex Web site that began: "Welcome to the Rape Camp! . . . It's not just a live video chat, it's an international experience." The site featured nude Vietnamese women in sexual bondage. They were blindfolded, bound, and gagged, and some had clothespins clipped to their nipples. He invited visiting cyberjohns, paying from fifteen dollars for ten minutes to seventy-five dollars for an hour, to "humiliate these Asian sex slaves to your hearts content." The men would relay their demands over their keyboards, and within minutes they would be enacted.

Sandler also advertised Cambodia's flourishing sex-tourism trade on his Web site, targeting johns who are "sick of demanding American bitches who don't know their place." The site offered to assist tourists in finding cheap flights, hotels, and brothels. It also dispensed advice for naive first-timers. "Don't pay in advance," it counseled, "and don't be bashful about sending her back if she doesn't do as advertised or if there is some major attitude shift."

In various newspaper interviews, Sandler rationalized his rape camp by contending, "They're selling these women anyway in prostitute houses, where they have to have sex with 10 men a day and get AIDS." Sandler was unrepentant about his maniacal objective. He hoped the site would "promote violence against women in the United States . . . I hate those bitches. They're out of line and that's one of the reasons I want to do this . . . I hate American women."

Rape Camp triggered outrage among a group of local officials, and Sandler was arrested. Facing five years in prison for violating the law on human trafficking and sexual exploitation, he appealed to the U.S. government, which eventually intervened with the Cambodian Interior Ministry, arranging for him to be deported rather than prosecuted. In early November 1999, Sandler was kicked out of Cambodia and banned from ever returning. He has never been prosecuted in the United States.

HOW DO
THEY FEEL?

*I feel no guilt whatsoever. I am getting what I need
and I am helping them get what they need. No one
is being hurt. . . . I do not believe that God would
send me to hell for acting on my natural instincts.*
—A JOHN WHO CALLS HIMSELF LOADED

EVER WONDER HOW JOHNS FEEL about their hobby? Do they feel
guilty, embarrassed, conflicted, ashamed? What do they think of
women who rent their bodies? Do they look beyond the surface
and wonder why they're there? Are they concerned that they're
taking advantage? Do they have sympathy? Do they wish they
could stop?

There's no single answer. When it comes to feelings, johns
are all over the map, running the gamut from those who, once the
deed is done, immediately feel guilty and slink off into the night

to those who are proud to be "feeding her family" or whose sole preoccupation is "How soon can I do this again?"

But one thing is clear. The average john seems to have trouble looking in the mirror, because if he looks critically at what he does and allows his conscience to wander, he may not like where it goes. The dedicated john has developed many skills for self-protection, rationalization heading the list. It's his way of preserving the desperate illusion that prostitution is inherently OK.

Johns are attuned to the power of words and are well aware of the stigma of paying for sex, so most don't call themselves "johns" or "prostitute users," nor do they like the term "prostitution." "Prostitute" is too value-laden, too controversial a word. They prefer more neutral terms, like *provider* and, for themselves, *client*. Those who want to cloak what they do with the perceived respectability of commerce speak of a "business transaction" and call sex a "service." To them, the women are "sex workers," "service providers," and "working girls," or "WGs." Others who prefer a more mystifying approach borrow from the terminology of book clubs and gamers. Buying sex, they maintain, is simply their "hobby." They become "mongers" or "punters" or "hobbyists." The creative euphemisms flow freely, as do the excuses, and there's no limit to the linguistic gymnastics.

So why go to all this trouble? Because they can't handle the truth. Their rationalizations are a matter of self-preservation.

Charity with a Twist

Sometimes, the johns' thinking is just so outrageous that it truly challenges the imagination. "They should erect a statue at the

Bangkok airport in my honor for all the poor families I've helped with my hard-earned money," jokes one sex tourist.

The irony is astounding, yet johns who travel to poverty-plagued lands often see themselves as doing something commendable. The money they proffer is so desperately needed that even demanding sex in exchange takes on an aura of valor. They see themselves as lending a hand and speak proudly of supporting the women's families. In the twisted corridors of their minds, they become benefactors, some even believing that they're modern-day heroes, as the john quoted above demonstrates. For them, charity begins below the belt line.

One such john joining an online discussion on whether women in prostitution are trafficked or exploited conceded that "Maybe it is true. Maybe these women have horrible, depressing lives. If they do and to the extent that they do, I'm a few hours of easy money. I'm a free meal." He was reacting to reports by the U.S. State Department and others concluding that women in prostitution are often trafficked and beaten, with many experiencing posttraumatic stress disorder.

His defense: "It's not a cake walk hanging out with me, but I don't leave any posttraumatic stress disorder in my wake. . . . The only thing I torture is the local language, something I've found most of these girls find funny." He too is convinced that he has done many a good deed, boasting of how some of his regulars seem grateful: "[A]t least a couple of these girls would tell you, I'm one of the best things that ever happened to them. . . . One of these girls seems to be convinced I saved her mother's life. I believe her more than I buy those State Department numbers."

Equating mongering with charity is one of the more

stunning self-deceptions in the psychology of johns. But some take the charity card to the next level, actively seeking out disaster and despair. One john who identifies himself as William gripes about poor women who are "too proud" to accept handouts in exchange for sex: "They want to help themselves, even when they can't. . . . However, an earthquake or tsunami may change their behavior for a few weeks." His advice: "Sometimes you need to travel in places that have been hard hit by some natural disaster. Let's suppose you provide shelter and a comfortable bed to the prettiest peasant girl in the village hard hit by an earthquake. Then she will be truly grateful to you." How does he feel about himself? "There is no better feeling than being able to help those who really need your help the most!" he exclaims.

Reflections . . . Deflections

William may enjoy basking in the glow of what he sees as charitable deeds, but the more common recourse among johns is to sweep emotions aside. To survive, they've developed virtually impenetrable armor and a line of defense to justify their behavior. The most popular is the stoic belief that what they're doing is perfectly natural.

"The drive for sex is in the man's genes. It's totally natural. It's biological. He must have sex," says a john called Derek. There is nothing more "natural than the biological need of men to have sex," insists another. "Wanting to have sex with beautiful women is a natural male tendency," writes a third, repeating the mantra.

At the heart of the matter is whether it is natural for men to pay to have their "natural needs" met. For an overwhelming number of johns, the answer is a resounding yes. "There is nothing more natural than two adults having consensual sex, even if one of them has to pay for it," asserts Rocky.

What some johns see as the honest and natural approach is actually less harmful than the alternative. "I think mongers like us who are open and honest about our excursions are far less harmful than those who are ridden with guilt trying to cover up their lives with countless lies," writes Beach Comber. "Don't get me wrong, I'm not peeing my pants to tell my mother that I sleep with sex workers or visit massage parlors on a somewhat consistent basis, but I'm certainly not ashamed of what I do. I go to get a normal natural need met with other consenting adults."

Shame, in fact, is in short supply, as johns are particularly adept at deflection. In one online discussion, a participant asked if any of the older men ever experienced the "walk of shame" when strolling down a Third World city street holding hands with a much younger rented woman.

"No 'walk of shame' for me just 'the stride with pride,'" responded one.

"[It] would be a walk of shame in your own backyard," said another. "But when you're on the other side of the world man, who cares?"

A third boasted that there is no greater feeling than walking "with a scantily clad hottie on each arm. The look of disbelief on the tourists is priceless," he says. "The men are thinking how they can escape the old bag for a few hours. The old bags are pulling their men into the closest seafood place."

In another context, a regular called Rounder argued that if he suffered from shame, he wouldn't be a john. Mel, another john, was blunter: "Shame only afflicts people with morals. I have no morals."

While some, like Mel, boast about having no morals, others callously suggest the unthinkable. "Go to where people are hungry," advises a twenty-one-year-old who uses the handle Diehard. "Go to a poor country. Go to poverty plagued lands and find the women there. They will love you," he insists. "They will take care of you. They will take it up in the ass for you. They will suck it raw for you. They will swallow for you. They will massage you. . . . They will do anything for you . . . for so little money. So little, just so they can have their next meal and live."

Countless other johns insist they are absolutely and wholly guilt-free. "I feel no guilt whatsoever. I am getting what I need and I am helping them get what they need," writes Loaded. "No one is being hurt. . . . If it wasn't me, it would be someone else. I do not believe that God would send me to hell for acting on my natural instincts."

"Yeah, I feel terrible pangs of guilt when I'm reaming their assholes . . ." jokes another, Addick. "But I'm Catholic so I go to confession so I can fuck them again the next week."

"It beats flipping burgers."

If they're not feeling the guilt in their guilty pleasure, it's probably because johns have convinced themselves of two things: one, there's nothing wrong with paying for sex, and two, the women they're renting really don't mind. There's nothing wrong, they maintain, because it's perfectly natural, just a business transaction like any other. And the women actually like it; it offers quick, easy cash.

"These women earn way more than working in factory or behind a desk," insists a john called Assman. "And don't tell me women don't like sex. They love it. So it's a job . . . and they get to do something all people love." To top it off, he insists, "They get paid a lot of money . . . more than the average women."

Johns of Assman's breed seem preoccupied with the money aspect, insisting that the women have actively chosen to do this job and comparing it to other low-status work, claiming that selling sex is the easier and even more respectable option.

"Money is money," says a john on an Irish site, "and if they choose it over making some chips in McDonalds fair enough." While he half admits that women may find prostitution degrading — "Some might find working in a fast food place degrading" — he has no sympathy for anyone trapped in sex work: "Everybody wants to avoid what they have to do to make money."

"I don't feel that sex is any different than any other service I pay for," says a regular called Longhorn. "I pay a doctor to put his fingers up my ass. I pay a man to dig up my septic tank cover and pump out the contents. I pay a lady to come here and clean my bathroom, and without doubt not one of them wishes to be here or do what they do. . . . But I'm sure almost every one of the women has and will allow men access to her body for sexual pleasure without being paid." In short, he feels "no guilt about paying a woman for access to her body. Perhaps they should feel guilty about taking my money."

These johns have convinced themselves that prostitution is a sweet deal, one that helps women afford luxuries like houses, cars, and jewelry. "Prostitutes are in it for the money, not because they're trapped or in terrible situations," opines a john called Ned. "It's a job that probably nets a few grand a week, for working maybe 3 days. Scenario: woman is renting house, wants to buy house. Has no education, etc. Can't walk into well paid job. But can prostitute herself three nights a week, make a few thousand a week and have enough cash in a year or so to put a substantial deposit down on a house. She is exercising a choice. It's not questionable whether she exercised choice in the issue, she did. She could have chosen to continue to rent. That indeed is what most women in her situation do."

Some get very defensive when the conversation turns to whether there really is a choice and insist that, no matter how you look at it, it's still a question of economics. One, who calls himself FarEastLover, reacted vehemently to the suggestion that prostituted women are often trafficked or forced. "I don't give a damn," he insists. "They have a choice as to whether or not to sell pussy and make some money or marry some slug and be poor all their lives. My opinion is this: If they are selling pussy, I'm buying it. Take that feminazi bullshit rhetoric some place else."

It's a common tactic: attack the messenger. The die-hards do this at the drop of the hat. To them, anyone who questions their lifestyle is either a "Christian fundamentalist," a "man hater," or a "feminazi pig." When confronted, they lash out, defending their hobby to the bitter end.

"Are you yet another Christian fundamentalist here to preach at us about morality? Are you hoping that you will make us feel bad about our hobby?" one john fumes. "I feel more guilty receiving service from an underpaid fast food worker or cleaning lady." He also vents rage at anyone who suggests that women in prostitution are exploited or coerced. "Are you assuming that prostitutes are all victims who are forced into the life? Bullshit. Everybody is unique," he says. "There is a percentage of the female population that is more open sexually and/or has few qualms about trading sex for cash," he continues. "To many, it is their best option for a quick buck. Many of them actually even enjoy their work."

He's not alone in his thinking. One of the biggest hot buttons for johns is whether the women they're renting are acting of their own free will. When they speak of economic choices — women going into prostitution because it pays or because there are no other viable options — they often do so with determined indifference: they're determined to prove their point but indifferent to her situation. When the question turns to coercion, however, and whether she is forced into prostitution through violence or threats, their indifference is replaced by anger or blissful denial. They've never seen it, they claim, and they don't care to know.

"I didn't see any chains."

Johns may not like to talk about morality or ethics, and they often go on the offensive when challenged by an outsider, but they do sometimes engage in a candid discussion if prompted by one of their own. On one site, for instance, a guilt-ridden john referred to studies showing that "few activities are as brutal and damaging to people as prostitution." He noted in particular one study cited by the U.S. State Department conducted by California psychologist Melissa Farley. It concluded that "60 to 75 percent of women in prostitution were raped, 70 to 95 percent were physically assaulted, and 68 percent met the criteria for post-traumatic stress disorder in the same range as . . . combat veterans and victims of state-organized torture."

On another major site, one troubled john confided that he had been reading about the sex trade, including the trafficking of women from the former Soviet Union and countries like Thailand, Burma, and Cambodia. "These reports indicate that a significant percentage of these women are sex slaves who are brought into the sex trade against their will, forced to work and live under horrible conditions and actual or the threat of violence, and bought and sold like cattle. I do not know if this is true or not. I have always chosen to believe that the WG [working girls] I have encountered were women who chose this life, in one way or another and for one reason or another, whether good or bad."

His misgivings were enough to spark some reflection and an interest in what others thought. "Do any of you ever feel any qualms about this hobby on a moral/ethical standpoint as contributing to the exploitation of women?" he asked. He claimed that in his two decades of mongering, he had "rarely observed any woman who appeared to be under any significant duress or pressure to work in the profession other than the pressures of poverty and materialism." As to whether he would continue if it were true: "I would not partake if I believed that I was supporting slavery."

One by one, the johns participating in the online discussion asserted that they too had never seen any exploitation. "I ask if they are forced into it and most say no and that the money is better than another job that don't pay shit," replied one.

"Ninety-nine per cent of mongers purchase as a willing buyer a service from a consensual adult willing seller," said another. "I assume twenty-one years of age to be an adult. If she is twenty-one and selling unless I see explicit evidence otherwise (which I have never seen) I believe her to be a willing seller."

Some johns do acknowledge that some women are forced, but even they take care not to implicate themselves. One, for instance, agreed that the risk of trafficking may be higher in places where there is demand for certain ethnic groups but stressed that he himself doesn't partake in "those kinds of establishments": "African girls working in Germany, Romanian strippers in Canada, and of course even within a country, they might be hauling girls in from the country to work clubs in the city. But I don't really like those kinds of establishments. I'd rather meet a girl on her home turf where she can 'be herself.' . . . So I guess it depends on how one goes about one's mongering," he concludes.

Sometimes, the johns make it clear that they just prefer to stick their heads in the sand. "I am unaware if the man owning the corner store or the man who comes to clean out my septic tank is under pressure to sell his service or his wares because of a drug habit, being coerced, blackmailed, or ordered by a judge for back alimony. . . . [T]hat happens to be a fact of life in this less than perfect fucking world. We don't always get to do what we want to do. We all make choices. Unfortunately the choices offered aren't always what we would like them to be." What it comes down to for him is this: "If I don't see a chain on a person's leg, then I know they have a choice."

The irony can be staggering. One of these john sites conducted a poll asking whether "mongering leads to the international trafficking of sex slaves." Almost 75 percent of the
respondents said yes, but none admitted to using the trafficked
women themselves. These are the same men who frequent sex
tourist pits like Thailand and rave about purchasing foreign
women. They convince themselves that a Ukrainian woman
working in a brothel in Germany, a Thai woman in an Australian
massage parlor, or a Romanian woman in a Canadian strip club
is there because she has chosen to be there. Refusing to look beyond the surface, these johns prefer to believe that a sex slave's
smile is her consent.

So, yes, denial is alive and well. So too is the age-old tactic of
shifting blame. Even when johns accept that trafficking might lead
to the exploitation of women around the world, they often take offense to any suggestion that they, as users, are part of the problem.

"Is it just possible that it isn't the guy's fault that some pimps
don't at least have some sense of humanity in them?" asks one.
"But we'll blame the men anyway because that's easier than trying to figure out how the so-called human traffickers are able to
do what they do.

"There are reasons why people are exploited in the first place
that have little to do with satisfying the wanton lusts of the evil
male. I suppose it's useless at this juncture to point out that they
wouldn't be so easy to exploit . . . if somebody gave a rat's ass
about them. No. Nobody gives a shit until somebody is fucking
them and then it's officially a full-blown tragedy."

Johns of this stripe revile feminists who claim that prostituted
women are victims of exploitation by men, but some go even fur-

ther, flipping the argument on its head and contending the true victims are, in fact, the johns:

> Not only is this complete bullshit, it's the other way around. MEN are the ones being exploited by these whores. The urge for men to have sex, and to be aroused by sexy women is a completely natural evolutionary trait that is the driving force behind reproduction and has a heavy influence over mankind's success. While men can control their actions, they cannot control the urge. This leaves men open to abuse and exploitation.
>
> Whores, strippers and porn stars all abuse this urge so they can make money. Men hand over wads of cash for these women to take their top off, to view porn and to stick their cock in their ass. None of these things have any real value yet men are driven to buy their services over something they have no control over. Sure it's entirely possible to stay away from these whores, in fact a lot, if not most men do, but the urge will always be there and there will always be men who succumb to this urge, and give into these exploiting whores.
>
> It's an addiction just like any drug and whores are like the drug dealers who exploit a drug user's addiction. The difference is it's a natural addiction that cannot be cured (unless you do something drastic, such as cutting off your balls).
>
> In the end everyone makes the choice to be involved. Women make the choice to be the exploiters, and men make the choice to be exploited.

"I used to feel guilty!"

Occasionally, when the conversation turns to scruples, some johns do admit to suffering from guilt, but this quickly prompts waves of conciliatory pats on the back and recommendations for corrective action. "Sounds like you're suffering from a severe case of 'Catholic Guilt.' You're not alone," replied one. "I dealt with some of the same feelings you described for years. I think every monger has people in their lives that they wouldn't want to find out about their hobby. I don't think anybody's mother would approve, to be quite honest." But his "me too" message had a lesson: pangs of guilt, he said, "will keep you from enjoying yourself and preoccupy your mind with irrational thoughts."

"I feel guilt about it," admits another, called Lex. "I think, though, it's mainly the thought of my mother finding out. I'm sure most of us can relate. There are other people in my life as well who I would feel as though I really disappointed if they knew I was into this kind of stuff." His post brought out of the woodwork even more johns admitting that they too sometimes felt guilty or ashamed, though most advise putting such feelings aside, letting go, and enjoying the moment.

"Catholic guilt and thoughts of my family and friends finding out made me a bit uneasy," confides a john called Down Under. He "used to feel guilty about this hobby for years." But he learned a coping strategy and found mental strength in numbers. "As time went on, I learned, through sites like this, that we are not alone. There are millions of men across the globe that share this common interest. We like women! If that's a crime, then I'm guilty."

Any Regrets?

Men who buy into the lifestyle may spend a lifetime buying sex. Veterans speak of mongering for decades. Others, still young, claim in online posts that, having partaken, they never want to stop. But the choice to continue or let go is an intensely personal one.

Some men don't question it. They've become lifers and have no intention of changing. A twenty-three-year-old Brit who calls himself Sir Dick says he wants to keep doing it forever. "It doesn't cross my mind. I want to die shagging. That's how I want to go out," he says. "A bottle of Viagra on my night table, a grin on my face and a sweet young sexy pro telling the coppers I went out with a wild moan of ecstasy emanating from my lips."

Ask these men whether they have any regrets, and you'll likely hear a resounding chorus of "Hell no!" But a john called Man Whore allowed that he has just one. "My only regret: Why did I wait so long? Why did I waste so much time and money dating normal women and not getting laid when all I had to do was hire a sex worker? Now I'm making up for all those lost years and I'm finally enjoying what man was put here for."

Another says his only regret is that he isn't rich. "If I had lots of money, I'd been spending it on whores. I'd be banging them day and night in every hot spot on the globe. Thing is I'm an ordinary Joe with a job that leaves me with just enough play money to take a two-week sex vacation once a year."

For these hardcore johns, it's clear. When it comes to buying sex, they do it, love it, and can't imagine being without it. For other men, however, it's more complicated. Ian bought sex on a half dozen occasions. "There was the thrill of doing something dirty, the first few times," he confesses. "Then that wore off and after the next few I was the one feeling dirty. I realized going to prostitutes wasn't for me."

On the other hand, Randolph, a randy British john, admits he is troubled by media reports of women in the trade being forced, beaten, and raped. "These are the effects of my 'hobby' laid bare. That's the kind of person I am, when all is stripped away. . . . That is what I have now helped to sustain, taken advantage of; it's what my money and actions have contributed to," he lamented. Yet for him too the end game doesn't change. "The thing which in some ways bothers me the most is my almost boundless capacity to just simply ignore what I have done, and fully plan to do again."

Another john shared Ian's disappointment at the emptiness of paid encounters. "I don't know how many times I've said to myself, this is the last time. I'm not doing this ever again," he wrote. "There I am in bed with a complete stranger who probably thinks I'm a disgusting man and she's letting me be intimate with her for money. Then when it's all over, I feel so empty inside that I just want to get out of there. I always make this promise to myself and a month later, I can't help myself. I go to another provider." These men are trapped. They want to stop but don't. The emptiness — or guilt — always loses out to the urge.

Others make no pretensions of quitting but become disillusioned when they realize that paying for sex is devoid of meaning. "Do people actually, seriously, feel better after it's all done with?" asks one. "[E]very time I've paid for it, there is an emptiness after that usually lasts a few days. And it's really weird, because I understand that sex should be just a physiological release, and, intellectually, I do not see anything wrong with paying for sex. But there's still that something missing. I can't help but sound like a homo, but there is really something special about having sex with a girl you love, and who loves you, that you just don't get with a whore."

"I think, subconsciously, we go to whores looking for that . . . for a moment at least, we'll feel loved," he continues. "I don't personally care what people do, one way or the other. But, in the end, I don't think people like the idea of waking up next to a whore . . . right? They want to wake up next to a person they really care about, and who cares about them."

Other johns agree. "[I]t's in the man's nature to fuck around . . . [but] it's also in the man's nature to find at least one girl whom he trusts, who cares about him, who can comfort him when the times are hard.

"Living your life without having such a person beside you isn't pleasant for most people," he observes. "Prostitutes can indeed spice up your life, yet a man can't live on spices alone."

Whether or not they stop, there may come a time in their lives when johns realize that their choice has not been without cost. Twenty-two-year-old Jon's biggest regret was losing his virginity to a woman for whom he had absolutely no feelings. "She didn't know me, didn't care for me and had probably done a dozen men that week. I was just a business transaction. I felt like such a fool when it was over. What a stupid memory to carry in my mind. I shouldn't have listened to my mates."

Vince, forty-four, calculates that in his twenty-two years as a monger he has spent a small fortune paying for sex. "I have really nothing to show for it. The memories are a drunken haze of strange women with no names or names I can't recall. I have no relationship. No wife, no kids. My brother and sister know what I'm all about and don't want me near their families. Now as I'm getting older, it's finally hit me what a total waste my life has been. I allowed myself to be ruled by my dick, not my heart and I'm paying an even bigger price for it. My life is an empty shell."

"My regret is I got caught," writes forty-year-old Gary, "and it ruined my marriage. My wife's at home taking care of the three kids and I'm spending money on whores. She got suspicious and hired a private investigator to follow me. Now she hates my guts, I'm paying a fortune in alimony and I can't even afford to see a prostitute even if I wanted to. Trouble is I loved my wife and everything I worked for is in the toilet all because I couldn't keep my fly zipped up."

A fourth man was slapped into contrition by the law:

I was named and shamed into it. I was arrested in an online sting by the cops. I met what I thought was a prostitute on Craigslist. Turned out she was a cop and when I got to the hotel room, I was busted, taken to the police precinct, photographed, fingerprinted and charged with solicitation.

That would have been okay but then the cops posted my mug shot on line and someone in my church saw it. I knew something was wrong that Sunday when I went to mass and the pastor asked to speak to me in private after the service. He didn't come on like I was an evil sinner but he told me I had to repent and tell my wife. That's when I really began to regret what I had done. I realized I had made a big, stupid mistake and I had to make amends. It took a lot of time, counseling and healing before my wife finally forgave me although I know it's always in the back of her mind.

Confessions of a John

Norman was a teenager when he first paid for sex. "I'm the classic story. I lost my virginity to a prostitute. I was eighteen, horny, and not getting beyond third base with any girls. So I paid twenty-five-dollars and hit a homerun!

"It wasn't like fireworks lighting up the nighttime sky or anything even approximating that," he admits. "It was quick. Over in probably fifteen seconds." He laughs.

"I don't remember a thing about the woman, but I'll always remember the rush in my brain about going to see a prostitute. I knew inside I was doing something dirty. If my mother ever found out, she would have hit me over the head with a ladle. I'm sure my old man would have laughed. But never in my mind did I think it would lead to a lifestyle and a serious problem."

Norman, a retired engineer who is married and has two sons and five grandchildren, continued patronizing prostituted women for almost half a century. For the first two decades, he stayed home, but at thirty-eight he started vacationing abroad. He has been to the Netherlands, Costa Rica, Brazil, Romania, Russia, Columbia, and the Dominican Republic, to name a few, and he figures that over the years he has spent $250,000 on the women alone.

I am sitting with Norman in a coffee shop. When he heard I was writing a book about johns, he approached me, wanting to tell his story.

For the past two years, he tells me, he has been clean, with the help of Sex Addicts Anonymous. I ask him what made him stop.

Norman stares at the wall for a moment and then looks down at his coffee mug. "I was diagnosed with prostate cancer. My sex life is over, and who knows if I'll be around in a year."

He takes a deep breath and continues. "About a year ago, I decided to tell my wife everything . . . everything I had been doing all these years behind her back. She was devastated. I thought she would ask for a divorce, but she didn't. She stays with me for the sake of the children and the grandchildren. She cried a lot at first. She's over the initial shock, but I don't think she will ever get over it totally.

"I needed to clean the slate. I wanted to get all this . . . out of my head. I needed her to forgive me," he says. "She says she's forgiven me, and maybe in some small way she has. At least my mind is a little calmer."

But there is a nagging regret that jabs at Norman's conscience. He admits that he had never thought much about whether the women he paid were forced. "For a lot of years, I never thought about it," he says. "I figured they were all in it for the money. When I went to foreign destinations, I didn't speak the language, so there was little if any conversation.

"But I realized something about myself a few years back. I had never really looked into the eyes of any of my dates. I'd look at their face but I never looked into their eyes."

One night in Prague, he finally noticed. "I hired this beautiful escort. She was in her midtwenties. I think she was Russian or Ukrainian. . . . She was brought to my hotel room by a guy with no neck. I noticed right away that she looked embarrassed and scared. I had no way of knowing what she was thinking. We couldn't communicate.

"Then I looked into her eyes. There was this haunting sadness and a fear in them." But Norman went ahead. "I had already paid so I had sex with her. When it was over, I went to the washroom to clean up and when I came back into the room she was crying. It was the first time I had ever felt ashamed inside for doing this."

Norman admits that it ruined his vacation. "I didn't really feel up for much after that. So I headed home. Not much later, I read a few articles on this phenomenon of trafficked women — girls being kidnapped or tricked into prostitution, being taken to another country and forced into prostitution by gangs of pimps. I got the feeling then that she was definitely trafficked. There was no way she wanted to be there. I knew that even before I had her."

I ask whether this changed his view of prostitution. "Not right away," he replies. "What did change is I started looking at the women I'd hire. I mean looking beyond their looks and their body. What I began to notice is that while most smiled and said how happy they were to see me, there was a certain look in their eyes, and slowly I began to feel more and more uncomfortable with myself and what I was doing. It wasn't like some sort of epiphany or anything like that. It was this gnawing feeling in my gut."

"Guilt?" I asked.

"I never felt guilt. I just did it because I wanted sex and I'd bought into all the clichés — all this about the oldest profession, that men need sex, and prostitutes were doing it for the money. Guilt never entered my thought process," he recalls, "that is, until that night in Prague."

"What happened?" I asked.

"I kept seeing her face. I kept seeing the fear in her eyes, and I'd see her crying. She made me think how many of the prostitutes I had sex with — and they number in the hundreds — were really doing it because they wanted to. To me, I was buying a product. They didn't exist as people. They were just whores. And all of a sudden, I start asking myself, 'What have I done?'

"I know what I've done is despicable and dishonorable. I used a lot of women because I had the cash and they were selling. I didn't think much about their situation. I only thought about my situation. It's taken me a long time to get to this point in my life and to come to terms with it. All I want to do is somehow make amends."

Asked if he had any words of advice for other men following in his footsteps, Norman was initially reluctant.

> There isn't much I can say that will make most of them ever change their ways. They don't care about the women they sleep with. Sex is the thing. And who am I to give advice? I'm a life-long monger.
>
> But if I had one bit of advice, I'd ask them to look into the woman's eyes. That will tell them if she wants to be there or whether she's been forced into it. All drug addicted hookers are forced to do it. All poor women are forced into it. When I look back at the hundreds of women I've paid for sex, I know that most didn't want to be prostitutes. If anything, they should be called destitutes and I used every single one of them because I didn't care. I would say the majority of women don't want to be whores and men should think hard about what they are doing and quit deluding themselves with excuses and lies.

MONSTER
WOMAN!

Since time, man has tried to please woman. As woman
gets more, woman wants more. Stupid man gives more.
So today we find ourselves stuck with this monster woman.
Does she appreciate what man has done? No, "give me more!"
—A JOHN WHO CALLS HIMSELF FOOTLONG

MANY MEN PAY FOR SEX because they're ruled by their loins. They
want sex, need it, so they go out and find it. But there is another
group of men who pay for sex for ideological reasons — or, at
least, they have developed an ideology to justify purchasing
sex. These men speak of class wars and hatred and "monster
women" — women taking their jobs and taking over the family,
women who are greedy, needy, self-centered, and spoiled, women
who have been brainwashed into believing that they're actually
the equals of men.

What these johns all have in common is that they are profoundly uncomfortable with empowered women. They resent
feminism (or fear it) and long for traditional roles, for a time
when men were men and women were . . . milkmaids. Some hark
back to the days of the Great Depression, when their grandfathers
were assured the "big piece of chicken," while others seem ready
to head all the way back to their ancestral caves so they can drag
their women around by the hair.

These men spread blame around to everyone and everything
that has contributed to this perceived unfair state. They accuse
television, the media, and educational institutions of propagating
the lie of equality and empowering women. They have scathing
words for employers (including their own) for letting women into
their offices and boardrooms. Feminism shoulders monumental
responsibility for all of society's ills, while anyone advocating
equality between the sexes is a "feminazi" (men or women) or a
"feminist eunuch" (men). They are particularly harsh toward other
men who in their ignorance or weakness have yielded to the feminazi creed. But the biggest culprits are women themselves.

These men insist that they aren't misogynists. That would
mean they hate *all* women, and they claim that they don't. They
reserve their disdain for Western women, particularly American
women. They complain so much about them they've developed
a shorthand: WW/AW. Third-world women, on the other hand,
are revered. Women from poor and backward countries that have
not yet been invaded by the "feminist plague" are as they should
be, these men insist: docile, submissive, still dedicated to their
men. These women make them feel manly, appreciated, and, despite the language barrier, understood. Asian women are espe-

cially prized because they are particularly passive, these men assert. The curious thing is that they draw these conclusions not based on any real relationships or substantial interaction; their views are shaped solely from experience with red-light districts, massage parlors, and strip clubs visited during sex junkets abroad.

Wounded by a perceived profound inequity and furious with the "bastardization of the Western male," these men do what any other warriors without backbone do: they grab their weapons and head for the hills. In this case, though, their ammunition is the dollar, and their refuge from the war of the sexes is prostitution. For them, prostitution is the last bastion of manhood, where the old order they all long for remains intact. It is a place where men with cash in hand can wield dominance over women. Men can be kings and women maidens, or women can play the masters if the men allow it. Everything revolves around the man. The woman is there for one purpose: to serve and please.

The problem is that the men who have created this caricature believe that all Western women are corrupted, including those soliciting in the streets. For them, to resort to prostituted women necessarily means getting on a plane and escaping to a faraway nation, preferably impoverished, where the women are still "pure." The benefits are multiple. Their dollar goes further. The women, often young and beautiful, are exotic. Driven by poverty, they cater to their customers' every whim. And the men don't have to worry about what people seeing them might think.

To make sense of it all, and to staunch any pangs of guilt, these men persuade themselves that *they* are the victims. In their topsy-turvy world, Western women have driven them to patronize prostituted women in foreign lands. On numerous Web sites, they speak of the "unfairness, inequity and unreasonableness found within Western male/female social and romantic interaction" and claim that contemporary Western women blame men for centuries of oppression. Painting a portrait of greed (Western women are materialistic), manipulation (women are now in control), impossibly high standards no man can ever meet, and a cold, unappreciative heart, they have convinced themselves that men have become second-class citizens, forced into servitude to meet women's needs. Women, however, can never be satisfied. When relationships fail, women rob men blind, leaving only a fraction of what they have spent years or even decades to build. When relationships last, men still lose, doomed to lives of mediocrity as women go on using them and their wealth. The icing on the cake for many of these men is that Western women are whiny and neurotic. If their feminazi ways have not pushed men away, women's chronic complaining surely will.

History Through Their Eyes

To appreciate how skewed their views of women are, consider the philosophizing of three johns. The first is an American who goes by the online name Footlong. "The female syndrome started just after this country was discovered. It has progressively gotten worse in time. "Here's why," he offers.

> The pioneers trekked west. Upon finding the new land, the first thing that happened is the female said, "No, I cant live in a wagon." So man built a house. Then she said "I need a house with a wood floor." So again man provided. Well as things de-

veloped, we find now that female says, "I am tried of doing dishes." So man invents the dishwasher . . .

Since time, man has tried to please woman. As woman gets more, woman wants more. Stupid man gives more. So today we find ourselves stuck with this monster woman. Does she appreciate what man has done? No, "give me more!"

Now, to continue to the next step: now female turns into hippo. Yes, no more whales in the sea. They are walking on land.

The result is overweight female, dictating to man. Tell me: are we so hard up that we need an overbearing, self centered, dictator female to rule us?

Well, after 3 marriages, losses over one million dollars total, I am seeking an ASIAN female. Why? Because they respect man, they give to man, they live for man. No I don't want a slave. I want respect and a pretty woman.

The second, Caveman, is also American. He gives American women the benefit of the doubt, or so he thinks:

It's not that American women are defective or stupid or evil (at birth, anyway). They are inundated by misinformation from early childhood by marketers who are trying to sell them shit.

My Grandmother, who raised her children during the depression, knew that Grandpa was going to get the "big piece of chicken" and no one was going to eat any food until he blessed it. I would imagine that the vast majority of our Grandmas lived by the same set of standards.

This, of course predated the "Golden Age of Television." The decomposition of the family started at the same time as "soap operas" first appeared. Marketing strategists found that they could earn millions selling shit to women who were at home while their husbands were out earning. They came up with more shit that these women "needed" and it paid off big time . . . escalating to the point where it became impossible to acquire all the shit these women were now convinced they "needed" on just the husband's salary so women started to flood the workplace.

What happened next is history. Women CIOs, CEOs and COOs are popping up everywhere in direct competition with men whom they've been convinced are not smart enough or good enough or rich enough . . . [They] are everywhere with hordes of aspiring replacement women in their wake. Welcome to Amazon Nation, brothers. Are you really expecting a blowjob from one of these hustlers? Yeah, maybe while she's setting you up to take you down but as soon as she becomes your handler . . . she will become the de facto head of family and your role will be limited to supporting her ambitions, aspirations and whims, sacrificing your own.

"It wasn't 3rd world women who shaped my opinion of American women," Caveman confides. "[H]ell experience did that. It was third world women who saved me from a world where I knew I'd never get the 'big piece of chicken' no matter how hard I worked, loved or bled," he laments.

The third john, who calls himself Slickdick, speaks fondly of a time when women stood by their men. "There was a time when women were nothing more than a daughter or wife — as if that is a really bad thing, but I think there was a time women were happy to be nothing more than a daughter and wife. Women used to be proud to bear children or by standing by her man.

"A woman of the past was taught bearing the kids and raising them with love in the family was their greatest achievement.

Now it's how many hours they can work and the size of their bank account."

The situation today? "Western women are being taught in media and entertainment that western men are not to be taken seriously and their needs are not important," he writes. "I agree, what can we men offer the women anymore like we used to? They can have their own job, own car, own money and security, all we can do is get them pregnant and ruin their figure and cost them that job cause they are expected to have the baby."

Caveman seemed more concerned with the blame he felt he was shouldering for the inequities of the past. "I agree with what you are saying about today's woman," he responds. "[T]heir mothers and grandmothers have told them about all this oppression, and the women have internalized this hate. But let's be honest. The 30 year old woman I see in the store buying steaks while I get the government cheese cause she took my job — she was never cattle, and was never oppressed, but she wants to hate me for things I never did, and for things that never happened to her. I get the hate for things that happened to her grandmother from some man that has long been dead."

"Who made them slaves?" he adds caustically — or pathetically. "I am not guilty."

So what's a guy to do?

These three gave up Western women altogether. The first escaped the "monster woman" by turning his sights to women from the East. The second, sorrowful over the size of his share of chicken, fled to where the women are poor. "It's not a case of we men falling victim to our own greed. This is the direct result of having lost a class war," he says. "Now all we can do is travel to

3rd world countries in an attempt to rediscover our proper place in the social food chain and maybe get our wounds licked by women who've found themselves even lower on the economic food chain than us." And the third, consumed with intergenerational hatred, boasts about his exploits in Brazil. "I do ok with the yanks in America, but I do much better in Rio."

Thousands of men are following suit.

And So They Run . . .

Turned off by the newly "liberalized" woman or despondent about their own role in the West, these men see zero prospects for happiness at home, so, with their libidos in hand, they head off to foreign lands.

"You're not ever going to get good lovin' from Western women. Save your hard earned money and head to Colombia, Costa Rica or the Philippines," suggests one. "The women there will treat you the way men deserve to be treated — with respect and lots of good lovin', and it won't cost near as much as dating an American behemoth."

"I have had it with WW and their feminist crap. P4P is much less hassle," says a john called Sam. "That's why I spend as much time as possible in Bangkok where the women know how to treat a man right."

"I monger in the Philippines and Thailand because the women make me feel like a real man. Western women make me feel like an ATM machine," says another.

These johns truly believe that they are treated better in

Asia — and in other parts of the developing world where they pay for play — often attributing the difference to a more neutral media or the fact that feminism has not yet left its indelible mark.

"[W]omen's attitude towards men is immeasurably better anywhere in Asia compared to the West," claims DownUnder, an Australian. "Asian women have not been encouraged to despise men by the media and education system as is the case in the west . . . Go East young man!!!!!!!!"

Scores of other johns who have also experienced the thrill of "exotic" women are only too eager to offer advice. "Guys, don't date WWs," writes one. "My advice: save your money and travel. If you add up all the money spent on dating, courting, marrying, and divorcing, it's simply way more expensive than taking vacations every few months to South America or South East Asia where you can get all the sex you want with all the beautiful women you can ever imagine, and all for so little money. And the only baggage you have when you return is your suitcase."

Johns admit that sex travel changes their attitude toward women, but they maintain that it's the lesser of two evils. "[T]he long term effects of mongering are probably not as detrimental to one's psyche as the long term effects of exposure to '1st World' women," says one. "Mongering does change a guy's attitude toward women, but at the same time I started mongering because of their attitude toward men," says another.

It's a popular theme. Ask these men what drives them away, and they'll point to Western women's ideas, attitudes, and values.

"Many domineering 'western' culture women DRIVE me to drink," rants one. "Bitches who are NEVER satisfied, no matter what. Mongering enables men to find out there are good ladies out there!!! Just have to look around."

"This attitude is a MAJOR reason why I look for romance with foreign women," reveals a john called Jerome. "Foreign women are much less likely to think they 'don't need a man,' " he explains.

Phil saves his daggers for the women in the United States. "More and more men in the US are finding it more worthwhile to kick AWs and their attitudes to the curb and seek out foreign women for sex."

"I think that MOST American women are not suitable for men," gripes another. "This is why . . . guys like us seek women from different nationalities. We want women without American attitudes, values."

Footlong has an even more cynical take. "USA sucks for females, unless you like getting a new house and furniture every four years. I say boycott the American female. Leave her in the cold. They have plenty of blubber to keep them warm."

The Effects

For johns whose answer to their problem with Western women is an airline ticket and a bulging wallet, the biggest draw abroad is their belief that they will finally be treated like princes. But for many, it's more. It's enlightenment, they say. Traveling for sex, they claim, opens their eyes.

"When an American man spends substantial periods of time with foreign chicks, it becomes a truly enlightening experience," says a john called Libertine. "Many American women have been politicized from a feminist perspective. As a result they expect to be freed from their traditional roles while showing no sympathy or appreciation for men who maintain theirs. A relation with an American woman is almost always an unbalanced one because of this.

"I think a lot of guys end up 'trapped' by the unavoidable investment they make when they start dating an American chick, and so they start yielding and yielding so they can get that pussy. Instead of yielding, they should take a trip abroad!!!"

"[N]ot all American women are bad," admits another American john, but "so many are bad it's real hard to see the good ones." Traveling, he says, is a good reference point that helps men distinguish one from the other. "I feel sorry for some of the men who have never had a chance to travel and see the light," he says. "A lot of men here deal with women who are bad and think they are doing good because she is a little better than the last chick they had."

Countless other johns see paid sex abroad as a measuring stick that helps them judge the women at home. "It gives us an edge," says another American called Per-view. "It puts everything into perspective. When a woman tries to control a guy using sex, mongering gives the guy the guts to reassure himself that he's fucked better."

A john in the United Kingdom is quick to agree. "I can relate to this quote a lot. You put British girls into their place, as you know a better product is out there!!!"

His views are seconded by a Brit who goes by the name Assman. "I don't give a damn about women in the UK. I have screwed a lot better else where," he says. Mongering reminds him how "lucky" he is and makes him "feel sorry" for his other friends. "They are stuck with some really ugly trolls unable to go out and try something new and better. They are totally under the whip because they are afraid they will lose the troll they are currently with." He, on the other hand, feels thankful for all the experiences he has had. "Out of all my many friends there is only one other who has enjoyed the same life I have with many, many wonderful beautiful girls who know how to make a man feel special. Yeah I do feel more appreciated when I am with girls from outside the UK."

Feeling appreciated is a common theme. "By creating all kinds of alternatives to having a competent man be an integral part of the household, men have been thrown out of the family by society as whole. Even literally!" says another john. But traveling is an escape. "[J]ust traveling around a fair bit, I've found that women 'appreciate me' a hell of a lot more in some places than in others," he says. "Sometimes, it's not what you are but what people think you are, and women in particular, especially in the 3rd world, will idealize men as saviors."

Some men admit that when they started traveling for sex, they gave up entirely on Western women. "The nice thing about international travel is that a man gets to see there are options, and what is considered normal behavior for women at home, is not normal in many other countries," Per-view explains. "Before I went to the Philippines and Mexico I was disappointed in American women. After visiting the Philippines and Mexico a few times enjoying hookers, I am VERY disappointed in American women.

"Do I sound bitter about American women? Well, I guess I

am," he admits. "I have not dated an American woman in 8 years." The reason? "The GFE from working girls all over the world can not be matched by AW," he explains, adding that he has considerable experience, having had "many, many, many AW experiences over the years."

Duce tells a similar story. "I first mongered in 1990 in Pattaya. I haven't had a 'proper relationship' with a western woman since. Only one night stands. I have thought about bringing an Asian lady back with me as a wife. But how long would it be before she gets infected by our sick media's feminism? Heaven would quickly turn into hell."

Colin refers to the "hassle of it all not being worth it as there is something better available."

And Jerome admits losing interest in American women — or at least being less tolerant. "I monger outside the US," he says. "I have [seen] that foreign ladies have much more marriage-friendly, male-friendly attitudes than do US women. Mongering with foreign women has made me much less willing to view AW for anything other than strictly platonic relationships, and even then . . ."

But it's not just Western women who are frozen out. These johns admit that mongering alters their views of women in general and even of the traditional family. "I have no doubt that 'mongering' can affect how one views the opposite sex, but I have little to no interest in a traditional life," says one. "That is: a wife, a house, a 9–5 job, 3.2 kids and church on Sunday. It's simply not for me. For those who view this as domestic bliss, good for them."

"My mongering career only started three years ago," says Finlay. "But I can see mongering has seriously altered my perceptions of women and attitude toward life in general. For starters I'm average looking, so in the real world, more often than not I've had to fuck average women with the odd attractive one. After fucking beautiful p4p women I just can't bear the thought of going back to average women. Firstly, obviously for reasons of aesthetics, however I also find it empowering that I can fulfill my manly needs whenever I want with minimum fuss. The best bit is that I can leave afterwards."

"I have to say there is one serious long-term effect of mongering," says a third. "You're used to sexually experienced women who can readily accommodate any sexual position you wish, almost any sexual technique." This, he says, stands in stark contrast to the women he has been with in a more traditional sense. It also affects how he relates to his partner. "The only real negative effect of long term mongering is it lowers your BULLSHIT threshold and makes you quick to sense an onset of manipulation on the part of your S.O. [significant other] and pull the plug on it immediately.

"On the positive side, mongering lowers your blood pressure, reduces your chance of experiencing heart disease, increases your optimism and self assurance and inspires self improvement (workouts, learning new languages, following currency markets and researching travel deals). It also improves prostate health and makes your dick bigger."

Doom and Gloom

Though johns are so incensed or fed up or turned off by what they see as the onslaught of feminism—and the women it breeds—that they strike back, by taking their libido elsewhere, the vast majority ensure that they have a return ticket home. Some return but don't bother with relationships, saving themselves entirely for the foreign women who treat them right. Others return to marriages or relationships; though they talk, they're not willing to walk. Third World women offer an escape that helps keep the deplorably imbalanced social order intact. They keep life tolerable, offering a temporary reprieve whenever time and finances allow.

But for some men, today's modern woman is far more toxic, and the society they live in intolerable as a result. These men have such an aversion to what they call feminist values that they contemplate fleeing, never to return. The challenge, however, is in finding the utopia that has not yet been infected, as they say, by the feminist plague.

One such john is Rock, a thirty-year-old from the States. "I am planning on leaving the USA because I feel it is over for a man here that wants to find sweet women," he says. "For all you NON USA members, I want to WARN you—that if we let the AMERICAN LIBERAL WOMAN spread her ideas and emotions to YOUR country, you and every other man will be DOOMED."

Rock says he has used prostitutes in the past, but at this stage in his life, he is seeking something more permanent, so he turns to his fellow johns for help.

"Where are good places to go for USA English speaker who wants to escape the culture where women live in fairytales and other brainwashed USA westerners are not going to come there anytime soon and spread the evil thoughts?"

As the discussion unfolds, he reveals more about what is pushing him to run away:

> I have a 4 year degree, make good money, but at 30 years old find all my friends are lonely or divorced. Most often the woman has put impossible expectations and strains on the relationship — they have become shopping machines and it's so much easier to take the credit card and go shop their problems away than to stay at home and deal with REAL issues.
>
> American women are the most power hungry people I have ever encountered. I don't blame them, they are taught to be that way from little girls. I just don't want to be around them anymore.
>
> I hope America changes for the better, and I wish all the men willing to stay in AMERICA good LUCK finding a sweet girl, but I have had it with them and am getting older and can't waste anymore time.

At its core, the issue for Rock seems to come down to money and control. "I don't have many good years left for intimacy," he says, "and if I am going to get that met, I have to get as far away from this mindset as possible or start using my money to control women and in turn create new power mongers."

Johns' Dilemma

It's all about power, dominance, and not losing control. These men see the world changing around them — it is no longer a world that revolves around the male — and they feel profoundly uncomfortable with this new brand of equality. It's something they don't understand and cannot accept. Many speak wistfully about man's traditional role — one emphasizing dominance over women — while belittling modern women who have refused to remain under heel. They see women's attempts at securing their own happiness as attempts to do away with men. Everything has become a zero-sum game: every win for a woman is seen as a loss for a man.

Gone are the days, for instance, when men could take pride in being the undisputed head of household. Gone too is the pride that comes from knowing that they are the de facto providers. Today's women are breadwinners alongside men. Rather than see this as advancement, these men see it as competition and loss of stature. Today's women are partners in marriages and families, but these men see them as taking control. Women today may share their partners' dreams, but they will likely also have dreams of their own. Rather than celebrating their partner's goals, these men see women as unsupportive and selfish. They blame modern women for turning their comfortable, ordered world on its head and creating something odd and foreign, contrary to the "natural" order of things.

Many of these men have also lost confidence in what they represent as men. They express doubt, even anxiety, over what they can contribute and what they can give a woman who already has it all, and they gripe about being devalued — or undervalued — by women, who, in their eyes, now wield the power.

So they marshal their defenses. They cast themselves as victims, insisting that women are taking advantage of them. They feign indifference, claiming not to care whether they end up in a relationship with one of these women at all. And many get nasty — really nasty.

Yet the more they're pulled (kicking and screaming) into the world of so-called liberalized women, the more they reject it. But they can't do without women because they can't do without sex. They want it when they want it, on their terms alone. There's the physical urge, of course, and the physiological release — what they'll describe as a natural need — but there's also a deep desire to maintain some sort of control, and sex has always offered a way to exert dominance over women.

They convince themselves that they won't get what they want from the reviled liberated women, so they construct fantasies of far-flung sexual nirvanas where the women, usually dirt-poor, are all too eager to please. In these places, where the balance of power is comfortably weighted in favor of men (for now), particularly men with money, they try to recoup at least some of their manhood, reclaim their confidence, and nurse their wounds.

10

TRAVELING
JOHNS

*Most of us began as children. . . . Our parents are poor and they
sell us. We obey our parents. We have no choice.*

—Mei, a twenty-year-old veteran
of the Thai sex market

As DUSK FALLS, hundreds of young women make their way into a
sunset of glowing neon lights on Patpong Road — Bangkok's infamous red-light district. For most, there is no bounce in their
step, no smile on their faces in this so-called Land of Smiles. They
are going to work, but what they have to do to earn a wage is far
from ordinary. They are bar girls, and their job is to hook a john
for a night of paid sex.

By 11 p.m., the sound of outdated rock and disco music pulsates, and the narrow road is jam-packed with swaggering, grin-
ning *farangs* (foreigners) in search of a body to rent. They come

133

from all over the world — the United States, Australia, Britain, Canada, Europe, and Japan — and within seconds of entering the road they are greeted by scantily clad Thai women who work in tandem trying to catch their attention with a wink and the ubiquitous smile.

Up and down Patpong, persistent doormen vie for business like carnival barkers under a rainbow of neon, promoting clubs like Lipstick, Fire Cat, KISS, and Gold Fingers.

"You want sex?"

"Come watch fuck show!"

"Many ladies want you."

"Cheap beer. Lots of ladies. Please, you come!"

A sweaty doorman beckons as he pulls back a curtain for a glimpse inside. The bar is packed with young women in skimpy yellow bikinis.

Freelance touts push glossy brochures into the hands of foreigners offering massages, hand jobs, and blow jobs. The photos show dozens of young women wearing numbers attached to dusty pink, flaming red, and azure blue kimonos, all of them smiling. They are perched on bleachers, waiting to be selected for the evening.

While the street action is mind-rattling to the uninitiated, a whole different world unfolds just a floor above. I take a deep breath and follow a rowdy group of Australian backpackers up the staircase to a club called Queen's Castle. Inside, it is very dark, with two rows of tables around a stage set up like a boxing ring. I head for the bar, and as soon as I sit down I think this is a bad idea. I look over to the door and map out a rapid retreat as a young woman in a yellow bikini throws herself into my lap.

"Hello, handsome man! You like me? I come to your hotel."

I politely push her off. "Just came for the show."

"You like? I stay with you tonight?"

"Not interested. Just came for the show," I insist, more firmly now.

She leaves with a pout and heads over to another table with a lone, balding farang in his forties. She plants herself on his lap, and he grins wide. His hand slides onto her thigh and they both laugh.

On the stage a dozen women in bras and bikini bottoms gyrate mechanically to the Eagles' "Hotel California." They look totally bored. Some stare blankly at the ceiling, others at the walls. They rarely look down at the audience.

Then the vagina shows begin. The first act features a naked woman pulling yards and yards of a colorful silk scarf from her vagina as she dances around the stage. She is followed by another woman who shoves one banana after the other into hers and shoots them into the howling crowd of foreign men jamming the stage. A tattooed, thirty-something American picks one up, peels it, and jams the entire banana into his mouth to a chorus of hoots. A third woman lies on her back and fires darts from her vagina at balloons hanging on the ceiling. She is an expert shot, hitting wherever she aims. Other vagina acts involve dropping ping-pong balls into a small cup, puffing a cigarette, and slowly pulling out a string with a dozen razor blades attached to it.

"That was so cool!" one of the Aussie backpackers shouts to his mates.

As they hit the street, a tout collars them. "You want animal show? Dog with woman? . . . You see python snake. She put in pussy."

"What do you say?" one of them asks his friends. They laugh and follow the man to another sex venue.

All up and down the sex *sois* (side streets) of Bangkok, a parade of prostitution tourists ogles the seemingly endless procession of pretty young women. Approaches are made, prices are whispered, and the haggling begins. Once an agreement is reached, the couples disappear into the crowd holding hands like romantic lovers.

Inside Goldfingers, a middle-aged German pays the barman a "bar fine" for the woman he's just ordered. He's five-eight and well over 250 pounds. She is tiny, all of 90 pounds, and looks like she's just sixteen. As she approaches the bar, her expression says it all. She is repulsed but quickly offers up the requisite smile. In Thai culture, a smile (*yim*) can mean many things. It can mean happiness, but it is also used to mask embarrassment, tension, anger, resignation, fear, and remorse. In this case, I figure, it is *feun yim*, which means "I am being forced to smile even though I don't want to."

Thailand is *the* sex destination for prostitution tourists. Airlines from all over the world land daily at Bangkok International Airport and disgorge herds of johns in search of paid sex. Not one of these men seems the least bit concerned that he is actually breaking the law. Despite the openness of the practice, the fact remains that prostitution is illegal in Thailand. But the foreign money from sex tourism is in the billions, enough to make corrupt and (not-so-corrupt) politicians and police turn the other way.

The first real sex tourists were American GIs, when Bangkok became a major center for R&R during the Vietnam War. In no time, their forays into the bars and brothels of Bangkok pumped millions of U.S. dollars into the Thai economy, and when the war ended government and business leaders wanted to keep the foreign exchange coming. To this end, they promoted the sex-tourism industry. Their efforts have surely paid off. Today sex tourism accounts for half of all visitors to Thailand, with the annual income from prostitution making up between 10 to 14 percent of the country's gross domestic product — and it is still growing.

I head toward another well-trodden Bangkok sex destination, the Soi Cowboy. In less than a minute I am approached by a twenty-year-old veteran of the Thai sex market. She is slender, with long, black hair and very white teeth, and she speaks English fairly well, so I offer to pay for a little conversation and a drink. She smiles and agrees. We sit down at an outside bar.

She tells me that her name is Mei and that she comes from the north of Thailand. She recounts being sold into a brothel at the age of six. She was trained to give *yum-yum* (oral sex), and for the next half dozen years she serviced hundreds of sex tourists and locals. Then, when she was twelve, her owner sold her virginity for one thousand dollars, paid by a Japanese businessman who abused her for an entire week. For the next two years, she was considered a hot property in the underground child sex trade before she was sold into the massage-parlor industry. When she turned sixteen, she hit Patpong. She now knows the Bangkok sex scene and how to play it. She knows who to target and who to avoid. She is a sweet talker and has an inviting smile, but her eyes are cold, hard pits.

when you are not looking at her, you would realize her true feelings. It's like being at Disneyland and seeing the smiling cartoon characters which is all behind a mask. The more I go to Thailand the more I see this mask. It's subtle but I see it more and more.

At daybreak, another curious spectacle begins to unfold with the rising sun — droves of bar girls emerging from the hotels and guesthouses, many on the arms of last night's farangs. They look tired, used, and — even after so many years in the sex trade — a little ashamed. Many disappear into the morning mist, heading home to their own beds. Others have signed on for another day. They walk holding hands with their johns like boyfriend and girl-friend. The men, wearing Hawaiian shirts and the grin of conquest, usher their rental girls through the streets in search of a place to treat them to breakfast. The young women wear their *yim soo* smile, which means, "my situation is so bad, I may as well smile."

WHILE THAILAND IS THE NUMBER-ONE sex destination on the planet, traveling johns are popping up wherever there are poor and destitute women. In Southeast Asia (especially the Philippines and Indonesia), Central and South America (Costa Rica, Colombia, and Brazil), Africa (Ghana, Kenya, and South Africa), and the former Soviet Union (Russia and Ukraine), sex-tour operators are setting up shop and advertising "romance tours," and the johns come flocking. But one place in particular has emerged as a new sex destination extraordinaire.

The travel brochures sell fun in the sun — pristine beaches dotted with swaying palm trees, spectacular volcanoes, and a lush tropical rain forest rich in exotic plants and wildlife. Costa Rica is bursting with natural beauty and justly markets itself as a mecca for ecotourism. Each year, almost two million people visit the country to soak up its breathtaking scenery and bask in the sun. The government's tourism bureau promotes life in this Central American paradise as *pura vida*—the pure life!

But there is a sinister side to Costa Rica that the government doesn't boast about, and it springs to life with the setting sun. Under the cloak of darkness, a different breed of tourist swaggers out of hotels and motels seeking all forms of carnal pleasure. They are the sex tourists, and thousands of them fly into the country every month from the United States, Canada, and as far away as Europe. They flock there because prostitution is legal, the women are plentiful, and the sex is cheap. It's cheap because the locals are desperately poor; these so-called tourists know their dollar can go a lot further than at home. They also know that, given the distance and the anonymity of the place, they can do things with virtual impunity, things they would never try in their own countries. And because corruption is rampant, it is easy for a john to bribe himself out of a sticky situation, should the need arise.

Over the past decade, this tiny tropical nation has become *the* hot spot for sex tourism in the West. In fact, thanks to a raging torrent of testosterone-laden johns flying in from North America, Costa Rica is now known as the Bangkok of the West. Costa Rica is fewer than three hours from Miami, and little over five hours from New York or Toronto.

I had heard of Costa Rica's steamy side while researching my last book, *The Natashas,* but I didn't see it for myself until 2004, when I visited the country to do an investigative documentary on sex tourism. First I hit the Internet to learn what sex tourists had to say about the country; I was astonished at the sheer volume of postings.

"This is Disneyland for the single man!" Sneaker wrote on one Web site. "The girls are hands down the best."

"If you are 35- to 75-years-old, hock everything you own and go to the Del Rey Hotel and the world famous Blue Marlin bar," another john recommended.

"If you are looking to nail hot chicks day and night, go to Costa Rica," Fisherman suggested.

"Costa Rica is the best place in the world to get laid," Jay declared on another Web site. "The place to go is the Blue Marlin bar. There are hundreds of beautiful young women. This place is gringo paradise."

The Del Rey, a must-see on the sex tourist junket and lauded on Internet sex sites for its hundred-dollar "happy endings," is centrally located in San José's Zona Blue, which teems with strip clubs, massage parlors, and sex clubs masquerading as discos. The hotel looks impressive from the outside, painted a historic pink with elegant white trim framing the windows and doors. The street is alive with the buzz of taxis and cars. Crowds of tourists pack the sidewalks — both men trolling for a catch and curious gawkers checking out the scene.

On a steamy October evening, I ventured into the hotel's notorious Blue Marlin bar to look around. The scene was surreal. The stuffed head of a magnificent trophy marlin towered over the packed room. Tacked to the wall below were dozens of insignia patches left behind by satisfied cops and firefighters from places like New York, Detroit, Chicago, and San Francisco. Three flat-screen satellite TVs were tuned to an NFL football game between the New York Giants and the Dallas Cowboys. This is purported to be a sports bar, after all, though no one seemed the least bit interested in beefy guys tackling each other.

Dozens of soft-around-the-waist, middle-aged white men perched expectantly on bar stools and chairs scattered across the dim room, while scores of young and stunningly beautiful women worked the room, trying to make eye contact and score a date. There was a smorgasbord of girls, most in their late teens, just waiting to be bought for an hour or the night. Men who frequent the Blue Marlin are jokingly referred to as fishermen trolling for *ticas* (Costa Rican women). What they use for bait is the American greenback.

I sat down beside a balding, craggy-faced man with a sizable beer gut bursting the buttons of his cheesy Hawaiian shirt.

"My first time down here," I began.

"Been here eight times in the past three years. Ever see so much nice ass in all your life?" he asked with a laugh.

"Just one long parade."

"Your mind just starts to break down after a while," he said, reaching over and grabbing a young woman's butt. "If you really want to whore it up, you can stay here, take her upstairs to a room. In a way, it's like living in a whorehouse."

He was right. The Del Rey is nothing more than a brothel posing as a hotel. It's a sordid meat market for North American sex tourists, who have their choice of nubile teenagers and young women, often at a bargain-basement price.

Throughout this nation of four million, the sex trade is booming. It is estimated that of the 1.9 million tourists who flocked to Costa Rica in 2007, more than half came from the United States and Canada, and a quarter of them were single men. In fact, sex tourism is starting to challenge ecotourism as the number-one foreign draw. The trade has spread like a virus to most of the seaside towns on the Pacific and Caribbean coast. One such town is Jaco on the Pacific side. It looks like a typical beach resort, overflowing with souvenir shops, bars, and restaurants catering to tourists. But look a little closer and you'll notice something out of the ordinary — a lot of pale older men walking hand in hand with darker women young enough to be their daughters, or even granddaughters. These unlikely pairings are everywhere — in restaurants, on the beach, poolside at hotels — and when the sun sets, the traffic moves to the hot spots for some "gringo groping."

A favorite haunt is the Beatle Bar. When I walked in, Bruce Springsteen's "Hungry Heart" was cranked to the max. Johns jammed the bar and tables, surrounded by gaggles of preening young women in skin-tight clothing. In an alcove at the back, above a pool table, a Canadian flag was draped on the wall. I sat down at the bar, ordered a cold Imperial, the national beer, and struck up a conversation with a hefty man in Bermuda shorts, argyle socks stuffed into black leather sandals, and an XXXL T-shirt emblazoned with Mick Jagger's flaming tongue.

"Name's Victor," I said. "I'm from Toronto."

"Robert. Chicago," he replied.

"Nice looking chicks."

"You can have any one you want. Do what you want, and come back tomorrow and pick another one. What a place! It's a regular paradise."

"What's the cost?" I asked.

"If they say a hundred, I'd say fifty."

I grabbed my beer and scouted the situation. A man in his late thirties was sprawled out in a chair at a table laden with empty beer bottles. He was plowed and exuded the demeanor of a pompous ass sitting on a throne. Three women were vying for his attention.

"Got your pick tonight," I shouted as I passed by.

"Every one of these girls will fucking go home with you for fucking nothing, dude!" he replied, beaming. "Any one of these girls. Some cheaper than others. Some are real cheap."

"How cheap?"

"Cheap. I mean like, you know, twenty bucks."

"Yeah?"

"Seriously man, Work 'em down! Work 'em down!"

And so it goes throughout the night and into the wee hours of the morning in dozens of bars up and down the coast — platoons of over-the-hill foreign men cruising for sex with local women.

A young woman approached me at the bar and asked if I was interested.

"Only in conversation and a drink," I replied with a smile.

She sat down on the bar stool and ordered a glass of ersatz champagne, no doubt cheap apple cider. I winced as the barman handed me a twenty-dollar tab.

"Hoping to meet someone tonight?" I offered.

"That's why I am here. And you?"

"Just interested in conversation," I said, looking around the bar at all the aging, big-bellied men.

She said her name was Juanita. She was wearing a clingy orange dress. She was very attractive; I put her age at about nineteen.

"What do you think of these guys?"

"They are all pigs, but what am I to do?"

I shrugged, not about to tell her to go look for a real job when the prospects were limited.

"Any guys ever get rough with you?"

"A few. They think because they pay, they can do what they want."

"What do you fear most?"

"AIDS. Many of my friends have AIDS, and they still work. Many men want sex without a condom. They tell me that and I say no, go find someone else."

"Smart move."

She ordered another drink. I smiled. "I hope you're getting a cut from this."

"I do."

"Ever get asked to be filmed?"

"A few times. I always say no. This girl I knew was video-taped and then she found out it was on the Internet. She went to a café for Internet and found herself. She ran screaming from the place. She begged people if there was anything to remove this from the Internet and was told it was there forever. The next day, she was found dead. She cut her wrists."

"You want to be here?"

"None of us want to be here. Look at these men. They are grotesque. Most are old enough to be my grandfather. They come here and take Viagra and think they are great lovers. They are fools with money, and they know we are desperate. That is the only reason we come here. We are poor. I do this because my family needs to eat. I do this to survive. These men do this for pleasure because they have money."

"Does your family know what you do?"

"They don't ask. I don't tell them. That way, there is no shame except for what I carry inside me every time I do this."

With that, Juanita finished her drink and left the bar with her sights set on a thin, balding, fifty-something john.

A moment later, another tourist parked himself on the bar stool beside me. He was in top shape and, I figured, in his forties, and he looked like one mean bastard. On his lower right arm was a tattoo — the U.S. Marine Corp insignia.

"Quite the place," I said.

"Yeah, just one big fuck fest," he shot back.

"A lot of them look like really nice girls," I added.

He turned and looked at me askance. "First time in Costa Rica?" he asked.

I nodded.

"Well, let me give you a little advice to keep you from making a fool of yourself. These girls all smile and make you think you're a king, acting all lovey-dovey . . . going gaga for you. They may seem sincere, but half of what they tell you is a lie and the other half is a line. Don't fool yourself into thinking any one of them really thinks you're something special. These girls are nothing but a bunch of whores."

"I'll keep that in mind."

"Look at them. Look at that one over there." He motioned with a beer bottle, pointing to a young woman in jeans and a yellow tank top. "I was here six months ago when she first hit the bar. She was sweet. I saw her with this guy . . . had to be three hundred and fifty pounds of whale blubber. He brings her a bag of goodies . . . make-up, perfume, chocolates, a stuffed teddy bear. Like he's going to somehow make her think he's a nice guy and maybe get better service. Look at her now. She's jaded. She has what I call fish eyes."

"Fish eyes?"

"That hardened, dead look. It's what happens to most of these whores after they've been humped by so many fat, sloppy, ugly guys."

"So there's no respecting these girls?"

"I don't respect whores. I don't get sucked into the whine about them having to feed their families. I pay to fuck them. That's why I come down here."

11

PREDATOR JOHNS

I think so much about what has happened to me.
Why these men did what they did to me. Old, disgusting men.
It was horrible. They knew I did not want to be there but they
paid their money. They used me. I was their property for the night.
They destroyed me.
—Fourteen-year-old girl at Casa Hogar,
a shelter in Costa Rica for children
rescued from the country's sex trade

She was a beautiful girl, small with flowing jet-black hair, dressed in a flowery blouse and denim skirt, standing alone. "She is the youngest right now," explained Maria Davilla, who ran Casa Hogar, a safe house for children rescued from the sex trade in Costa Rica. In 2004, Davilla very kindly agreed to be interviewed for my documentary on sex tourism, for the sake of her young charges.

The girl had been at the refuge for just three weeks. Maria

waved, but the girl didn't respond. She stared blankly into space, her eyes filled with fear.

"This girl lives in terror. Her mother was not only her facilitator [pimp] but also her instructor," Maria said. "She forced her daughter to have sex while she gave her instructions on what to do. Her mother found the sex tourists and introduced her daughter to these men. She even pushed the girl into group sex.

"Today, she has a strong aversion to anything that reminds her of semen. She can no longer drink milk or eat yoghurt or cheese . . . anything that reminds her of sperm. She was forced to give oral sex to as many as nine men a day and forced to drink the semen of these men."

"How is she doing now?" I asked, unable to take my eyes off the sad little girl.

"She is in a very difficult psychological situation. All this time, she has nightmares. She needs strong medication. This girl was used by many, many tourists." Tourists from Canada and the United States.

She was all of ten.

The refuge, near the Caribbean coast of Costa Rica, was home to thirty girls, aged ten to sixteen. All had been robbed of their innocence, forced to service men, most from abroad. In many cases, these were men who came to the country specifically to have sex with a child. "Many of the girls here have had sexual activity with around five, six, seven men a day," Maria explained. Three of them strolled around the grounds cradling their babies in their arms.

Maria noted that, for most of the girls there, the sexual abuse started long before they were put to work servicing tourists and locals. "It usually begins at home when they are four and five years of age. The girls do not have the strength to run away at that age."

Sadly, Casa Hogar was the one and only shelter in the country for girls rescued from the sex trade. Maria worked virtually for free. Her eyes reflected the love, warmth, and compassion she has for the children in her care. But they also betrayed intense frustration. "We have not received one penny from the government in the last six months," she said.

As it has emerged as the top destinations in the West for traveling johns in search of paid sex, Costa Rica has also become a magnet for men who want to have sex with children. The government knows this but has been embarrassingly ineffective at protecting its children or reversing the trend.

Ana León, the director of Patronato Nacional de la Infancia (PANI), the agency responsible for protecting children in Costa Rica, told me that the government had been working since 1998 on a plan to help children like those in Casa Hogar. Though she claimed the government was in the process of building another safe house, León acknowledged that Casa Hogar was still the only shelter of its kind.

"Just one home?" I prodded.

"Yes, because the issue is the numbers. . . . The numbers that are being handled are very confusing," she said. León then proceeded to venture a guess: "The number of cases identified in a year might reach one hundred fifty. No more than that." Children's-rights organizations would disagree. They estimated the number of children being abused in the country's prostitution racket to be as high as three thousand — a figure the government hotly denied, and still does.

Ana León pointed out that many of the rescued children have families, so there was no need to place them in a group home or treatment center.

"Even if you know a family is allowing — or even *forcing* — its child into prostitution?" I asked.

"We don't want to institutionalize these kids and they don't want to be institutionalized also. Under our laws, we cannot remove a child physically unless there is a court order or a situation that's very particular in which it is justified."

But surely if a child is being prostituted by her parents — sold to sex tourists or locals to bring in some cash — this would be justified, I insisted.

"Yes, but the International Convention on Children's Rights establishes that they have a right to move freely. Children have a right to move freely unless there is a reason . . ."

"*Rape* is a good reason!"

"Yes, but we cannot force them physically to go with us. The fact that they are involved in this business, that they are making money, that their families are being supported by that money, even if it's abuse, even if it's immoral, even if the money is coming from something that should never have happened —"

"This is really bizarre," I interjected, barely able to contain my anger. "If this were happening in the U.S. or Canada or most countries around the world, you could bet your life that the government — the police, the child welfare agencies — would step in and put a stop it."

"You can try to remove the child," she continued. "You can try to persuade her. You can work with her to convince her . . . but we cannot force a child, put her in a police car and take her away from her home. That is not allowed."

"So how do you deal with a child who is found in a brothel?"

"We try to convince her to leave the streets," León explained. "We take her back to her family, talk to her family about the risk their child is taking being out there or going into hotels." If the family is not willing to help, she added, "We try to convince the child to go into this home." There, "they are provided with the basic services. There is a school, and some activities to teach them certain abilities. It is an open place. It is not locked."

What she avoided mentioning was that Casa Hogar was surrounded by an eight-foot-high, chain-link fence and manned twenty-four hours a day by a uniformed security guard armed with a fully automatic assault rifle. He was there to protect the girls inside from being abducted by their parents or pimps and put back to work on the streets.

President Abel Pacheco de la Espriella was at the helm of Costa Rica's government when I was there. I took the opportunity to question him by barging into his monthly press conference. I wanted to ask the president about his government's commitment to stop the abuse of girls and do something about unbridled sex tourism. His phalanx of spin doctors was visibly rattled when I rose from my chair and put the following to their leader: "I would like you to comment on the shameful behavior of Canadian and American men who come to Costa Rica to sexually abuse young women and girls in this country."

President Pacheco's eyes narrowed. "This embarrasses us

terribly, but it should also embarrass those who come here to look for that. Those are the ones who should be embarrassed. Because as an old saint from our culture used to say: who is more at fault, the one who sins for the pay or the one who pays for the sin? And I think that at the hour of condemnation it seems to make much more sense to condemn those who pay to sin. Therefore, my criticism is absolutely of the tourists who come here in search of sexual pleasure."

When all else fails, cite God.

Pacheco finished his term as president in 2006, and little changed. Sex tourists continue to flood into the country, some hunting for child victims. Costa Rica remains ill-equipped to take on the problem. It does not have the infrastructure in place to investigate, let alone prosecute, these offenses. Computers are expensive, and most cops are technologically challenged. Authorities cite problems with access (not being able to find the girls), confusing numbers (not really knowing how many children are involved), and money complications (given the significant financial interests at stake). The list of problems — and excuses — goes on and on, and the men in search of children just keep on coming.

I DECIDED TO SEE FOR MYSELF just how easy it was to find child victims and headed back to the Del Rey Hotel. Lingering at the entrance, I took in the scene, amazed at how many North American men were drifting in and out. They went in alone and came out with pretty eighteen-year-olds on their arms. The "couples" were often giggling and laughing, but chances were that neither party had any idea what the other was saying.

I was accosted by a wiry doorman, who asked if I wanted to buy some marijuana, cocaine, or Viagra. I told him no. I hesitated for a moment, then lied. "I'm looking for some young chicks."

"Lots in the bar," he said with a wide grin as he motioned me inside. "The women at the Del Rey are the most gorgeous, best-looking working girls in all of Costa Rica. Beautiful women from Costa Rica, Nicaragua, El Salvador, Colombia, Honduras. For a hundred dollars, they will not only go to bed with you, they will be your escort for the day. And in the bed, I can guarantee you, they don't just jump on you and then they're out."

I pressed further. "I've been in the bar," I said, "and they're kind of old."

His eyes widened. "What? Most are like eighteen, nineteen, twenty years old."

"I'm kinda looking for something younger. Is there any way of, let's say, getting something around fourteen or fifteen, or is that a real problem?"

The doorman stared at me hard, trying to size me up. "Well, I'll tell you it's basically because of the fact that it's a crime here, sir. You could get arrested."

"Arrested?" I asked

"Oh, definitely."

"But . . . is it impossible?"

He looked around cautiously. "It's not impossible. I have two, three young girls that work with me that have given services to gentlemen," he confided. "It's not like they're novices. They've already been plugged."

"Plugged?"

"They're not virgins," he explained.

"What are the chances of getting caught?"

"One percent, so you don't have to worry. We watch out for you."

"How much will it cost?"

"Well, depending on the amount of time that you want to spend with her, usually it would be a hundred dollars."

"One of my buddies," I continued, "he really likes a little younger, you know?"

"OK."

"Would you be able to hook us up in a cab to go . . . wherever?"

"Yes, I will."

"So if I wanted to, say, film the fifteen-year-old with my buddy, would that cost a chunk more cash?" I asked.

"If you want to film, it's different. I had two guys from the U.S. A black guy — he was the banger. And a white guy who filmed. It cost them a hundred and fifty dollars."

I took in the information. "I'll get back to you on that."

"I'm always out here."

I was stunned. It took only five minutes to arrange to have sex with two minors and get permission to film.

I hailed a taxi for the short ride back to my hotel. I'd been told that taxi drivers are an important link in the sex trade here. Like doormen at bars, they are the middlemen. They know the sex scene and often drive clients to brothels — including those offering children.

Within seconds, the driver made an unsolicited offer.

"Are you looking for some action?" he asked with a Cheshire-cat grin.

"Always," I replied. "But very young."

"You like girls?" he asked, studying my face in his rearview mirror.

"Love them."

"I know a place with very young girls. Very sweet, very tasty."

"How old?"

"Twelve and thirteen."

"I don't know . . ." I played along. "What's the chance of me getting caught?"

"Not to worry," he assured me. "We will know if the police are coming."

"What does that mean?" I asked.

"Let me just say that the police take their cut."

"How much for a girl?"

"A hundred and fifty dollars. And another fifty for me because I wait for you," he said.

"Whoa, that's a little steep!"

"The girls are very beautiful," he insisted. "Very sweet. You won't be disappointed. I promise."

"Not tonight, man," I said, and our bargaining came to an end.

Several nights later, I headed to Morazán Park, an area notorious for men searching for young girls. I was with Bruce Harris, the Latin American director of Casa Alianza, an organization that provides services for many thousands of homeless children throughout Central America, with funding from the Catholic charity Covenant House, based in New York.

Just as we arrived, we noticed a police officer escorting a young girl to a patrol car. She was fourteen, tops. Clutched in her hands was a teddy bear. She was sobbing and blurting out her story to the officer. She had been raped by her stepfather, she said, and then thrown out of her home by her mother. "She said it was all my fault. She called me a whore and told me to get out." The girl told the cop that she had heard Morazán Park was a place where she could make a little money from sex tourists. "I am hungry, and I have no place to go."

She was fortunate that she was spotted by police before falling into the grip of a sex tourist or pimp. The police said they were going to take her to the authorities at PANI — the government ministry responsible for children — which would probably end up sending her home or, if she was lucky, to Casa Hogar. But the danger for this child might even be the cops themselves, explained Harris. Throughout Costa Rica, he said, children caught up in prostitution told authorities of incidents when they had been picked up by police and forced to give oral sex in the backseat of patrol cars. As the police car disappeared into the night, I wondered what would happen to this sad, defenseless child.

Against this bleak backdrop, it's difficult to remain hopeful. So thank goodness for the good guys. Costa Rica needs them. Bruce Harris, for one, had dedicated his life to helping poor and homeless children in Latin American. Harris was a world-renowned crusader and outspoken advocate for children's rights. The walls of his office were adorned with plaques and international awards honoring his work. British by birth, he was inducted into the Order of the British Empire by Queen Elizabeth in 2000. Among his prize mementoes was a photograph of himself with former president Bill Clinton.

When I met Harris in 2004, he was larger than life, a deadringer for British comedic actor John Cleese, and he made no attempt to hide his disdain for the men who preyed on his adopted country's children. "Sex tourist?" he exclaimed. "It's a very nice name for a bunch of perverts. These foreigners are mostly overweight fifty- or sixty-year-olds who couldn't get two looks from any woman in North America. So they come down here and think for thirty, forty, fifty dollars they can have sex with anyone they wish."

I sat down with Harris at his office in San José, and he gave me insight into the battle he waged every day. While he was disgusted by the sex tourists flocking to his country, his main concern was the men targeting children. "These are not prostitutes," he said firmly. "These are children who have been prostituted. These are children who are being sexually exploited by people who don't give a damn. . . . They just want to fulfill their perverted sense of pleasure, and they don't give a damn about the child, who is going to suffer permanent emotional damage."

Harris had been to the bars to listen to the incessant bravado of American and Canadian sex tourists. "These men are bragging about the fact that they spent a night with a fifteen- or sixteen-year-old, or they'll even talk about swapping victims. It's sick to listen to the conversation."

"What kind of world are we talking here?" I asked.

"A world where children become nothing more than part of a mercantile transaction. We're talking about a subworld full of pus where these perverts come and think they can get away with robbing the innocence of these children."

For fifteen years, Harris had been on a crusade to smash the cycle of sexual exploitation of children rampant in Costa Rica and the rest of Central and South America. "It's very difficult," he said. "It's an uphill battle, assuming that the police at the street level are honest. Unfortunately there are many examples we have where they are not honest and they often become just one more sexual abuser of the children."

Harris cited a brothel raid in which a highly visible madam was arrested and charged with pimping children in San José. In her possession was a client phone book. "A lot of the names in that book were people in the highest levels of government. They're significant political people in the country and well-known figures." None of the clients has ever been arrested.

"It shows you what level the corruption has reached," he continued. "It shows you the level of sexual exploitation of children. It has permeated the whole system here. And one of the most difficult hurdles is that, within the culture, people believe that it's OK to have sex with a thirteen- or fourteen-year-old kid."

Harris's disdain for the men who use his country's children was matched by his relentless efforts to protect the young victims. So when he abruptly announced his departure on September 15, 2004, the news sent his staff at Casa Alianza into a tailspin. Harris, who had just turned fifty, quietly resigned, citing personal reasons. In a prepared statement to his staff, he said he was worn out and wanted to spend more time with his wife and children.

Two days later, Covenant House announced in New York that Bruce Harris had been fired. One month earlier, Harris had gone on a business trip to Tegucigalpa, the capital of Honduras, and on the night of July 14 he was caught doing what he claimed to despise most. Around midnight, he strolled through a downtown park, picked up Carlos Alberto Ortiz, an eighteen-year-old street prostitute, took him to a nearby hotel, and paid him for sex. That very teenager had been rescued from the Honduran streets by Harris's own organization a few years earlier, when he was still a minor. Shortly after the act was consummated, Ortiz revealed all to a Honduran parliamentarian, who put the heat on Harris.

The day he was fired, Harris confessed in an e-mail to a number of news media outlets. "Sheltering behind a lie has never been my way, so I assume, as I always have done, responsibility for my actions, correct or incorrect. I do not want the children served by Casa Alianza to pay for my private life. I am being judged on my fifteen years of service to children for a specific fifteen-minute mistake. I do not deny that it was my mistake."

It was the ultimate betrayal. The scandal was too much for Casa Alianza. A few days later, the organization closed its doors in Costa Rica.

Six months later, four women, all former Casa Alianza employees, founded Alianza Por Tus Derechos (Covenant for Your Rights). They had no money, just their commitment and drive to save children from sexual abuse at the hands of sex tourists. In an interview in April 2008, Rocío Rodríguez García, executive director of the new children's organization, lamented that the problem of child sex tourism was as bad as ever. "The reality is that sex tourists continue to arrive to abuse children. Many factors make this happen, but the main one is impunity. The laws continue to be very weak to punish those abusers," she explained. "The pimps have become more resourceful in keeping a few steps ahead of the police.

"Another factor affecting the care of these children is the lack of funding and donations we receive. It is often more important for people to donate to keep the rainforest than to help girls and boys," Rodríguez observed.

And how goes the government's broader effort to provide the rescued children a safe place to stay? "There are no longer any specialized centers in the field to care for victims of sexual violence," she said. Casa Hogar, the only safe house in the country for children rescued from the sex trade, was shut down for lack of funding in 2005. As for Alianza Por Tus Derechos, it is barely a Band-Aid on a huge open wound.

SVAY PAK, A TINY VILLAGE IN CAMBODIA, lies a few miles outside the capital of Phnom Penh. Fragrant incense burns and bee's wax drips down flickering candles like golden teardrops. These miniature Buddhist shrines are perched outside battered cafés and shops along a dusty dirt road. It is dark, sweltering hot, and the humidity is oppressive.

From the shadows, four small figures emerge and approach a lone, middle-aged white man. A boy, no older than fourteen, asks the man in broken English, "You want girls? You want fuck girls?"

Standing beside him are three pubescent girls. They look around twelve years of age. They are wearing tight clothes, bright red lipstick, and they come on like seasoned hookers, licking their lips and slowly thrusting their tiny hips.

The man asks about younger girls.

The young hustler smiles knowingly. "You want small-small? I can get small-small."

The boy quickly leads him down a path past a warren of run-down clapboard and metal shacks. The man is ushered into one and introduced to the mamasan, who sizes him up and then calls out to three girls. They patter into the room in bare feet, wearing only paisley-print pajamas. They are between the ages of five and nine. They smile as if on command, but the deadness in their brown eyes is heart-wrenching. The cost is thirty dollars for "yum yum" (oral sex), the madam says, stressing, "No boom boom" (intercourse). The man points to his video camera and she nods her approval for him to record his sexual feats.

Svay Pak is notorious for its more than fifty brothels offering underage girls to legions of sex tourists from places like Britain, Japan, Canada, the United States, Australia, and Europe. It is a remote backwater where the prey is plentiful, extremely vulnerable, and very easy to stalk. Here desperate mothers sell the virginity of their daughters to the highest bidder. And it is a safe bet that virtually every john swilling beer at the roadside bars on any given day is in the village to rape children — children who should be in grade school, not a brothel.

On this particular evening, the man who has been propositioned is not here to use children. He's here to save them. He is an undercover investigator for the International Justice Mission, attempting to infiltrate the ring of child brothels and gather evidence to free the children. His assignment is dangerous because corruption here runs deep, and he knows corrupt police and government officials are directly profiting from the trade in child bodies. If he's found out, he could be killed.

The IJM is a Christian organization headquartered in Washington, D.C. It's a sort of A-Team for Jesus that kicks down doors and rescues children forced into sex. Its founder is Gary Haugen, a lawyer and former war-crimes investigator. He is also a modern-day warrior on what he describes as a God-inspired mission.

IJM's investigation in Svay Pak began in 2000 after rumors emerged of a small, lawless village composed almost entirely of brothels, where hundreds of very young girls were being sold for sex on the open market. For two years, its undercover team stealthily gathered evidence, including testimony from girls who had escaped from one of the brothels with the organization's aid. IJM investigators met with officials from the Cambodian government and the U.S. embassy in Phnom Penh, but the meetings were tense and inconclusive, with no one on the American side trusting anyone on the other. Corruption in Cambodia is a way of life that snakes its way up the chain of command, from the police to the top echelons of government power.

"The initial undercover operations left our investigators with nightmares but also grave concerns about the gunshots they heard in the streets," Haugen recalls. They were concerned too about "reports of top police officials who protected and profited from the brothels." The organization almost threw in the towel. "With limited resources and a sea of brutal injustice in the world, IJM can't be everywhere and can't do everything, and this just seemed like one of those hard situations where wisdom suggests we should pass," Haugen said. "There were at least fifteen reasons why tackling Svay Pak just seemed impossible. Cambodian authorities had been unmoved by IJM's irrefutable evidence of these atrocities for two years. The rumors of high-level police protection for the pimps and customers were true. Even if we could avoid a police tip-off and rescue some of these girls, who could provide aftercare for so many? And where would we find police willing to actually arrest and prosecute?"

All sound reasons to walk away, but Haugen was haunted by the image of a six-year-old girl captured on an IJM undercover video. "Jesus taught that we were to do for them what we would want done for ourselves, or our own daughters," he explained. So he came up with a plan to mount a daring, commando-style raid to bust open the brothels and rescue the children.

On a spring evening in March 2003, after an intense week of planning, IJM decided it was time to move mountains. Backed by a platoon of sixty hand-picked Cambodian cops and with NBC *Dateline* cameras in tow, IJM hit the brothels of Svay Pak, rescuing thirty-seven girls, nine between the ages of five and ten. More than a dozen pimps and madams were arrested and charged.

"I don't need many more gifts from God in my lifetime than the one I received when I visited the IJM safe house the day after the raid. There was that little six-year-old girl from the old undercover video," Haugen recalled. "She was smiling, laughing, and playing — in a safe place, away from abuse and terror."

NOON HOUR, TUESDAY, DECEMBER 2, 2003. Crab Park, on the seedy east side of downtown Vancouver, British Columbia. A city employee sits alone in his car eating lunch when he hears bone-chilling screams coming from a nearby clump of bushes. He calls 911. Moments later, a man and a woman emerge from the thicket as a police cruiser — roof lights flashing — pulls up to the scene.

The woman, looking distraught and clutching a twenty dollar bill, is native, a crack addict and a known street prostitute. The police ask if she is OK.

"He's one sick fuck!" she exclaims, gesturing toward the balding man walking several feet ahead of her. He is carrying a video camera and tells the officers that he was just doing some amateur photography.

The couple is placed in separate squad cars and taken to the station for questioning, but the woman isn't very cooperative. She is edgy and wants out, clearly desperate for a fix. The officers have a hard time keeping her on track. She tells them that she was approached by the suspect on the city's hooker drag and agreed to go with him to the park. Once there, he tied her up and did things to her that she had never agreed to.

The suspect, who is as nondescript as peeling wallpaper, sits motionless in another interview room, saying nothing. He is identified as forty-year-old Donald Michael Bakker, who, for the past sixteen years, has worked at a luxury hotel in Vancouver setting up chairs and tables for banquets. He has a wife and a child. In his spare time, he raises money for World Vision, an international children's charity.

During questioning, one of the officers rewinds the video and is surprised at what he sees. He calls in Detective Ron Bieg of Vancouver's sex-crimes unit. The two watch as Bakker is shown setting up the camera, tying up the woman who is now in an interview room in the station, and attaching clips to her nipples and vagina. The woman is shown begging and screaming for him to let her go, but instead of just removing the clips, he pulled them off with little tugs.

"He did some other things to her of a sexual nature, or at least for him they were, and when he was finished, he gave her twenty dollars for her efforts," Detective Bieg explains.

The detective, along with his partner, Mark Forshaw, then watches the entire videotape. They see seven other women, all victims of "gratuitous degradation and torture."

Bieg notes that the women were "all drug-sick prostitutes from the downtown east side." The detectives realize they had a lot more than a typical john. "This was no ordinary john. He was a predator, a sexual sadist, and we had a lot of other victims to identify."

Bakker is charged with assault and remanded into custody while a team of detectives goes to work to identify the other women. Five days later, a jailhouse informant tells them that Bakker had called his wife, instructing her to get rid of potentially damaging evidence. The police immediately secure a search warrant and seize three more videotapes from his home and another from the wheel-well of his car. The videotapes, self-made trophies of Bakker's sadistic conquests, reveal torture segments involving more than sixty women. Bakker's victims were tied on the floor or on a makeshift wall rack in a garage. He is shown kicking them with a steel-toed boot in the vagina and doing everything from whipping them with electrical cord to urinating and defecating in their mouths," Bieg explains. "We went from one known victim to seven unknown victims to potentially almost seventy."

But the depth of Bakker's depravity is yet to come. On the tape discovered in his car, the police find a segment showcasing children. The scenes show three very young Asian girls, each giving a man oral sex. At first blush, the detectives think Bakker is into child porn. Five minutes into the tape, a hand reaches over and tilts the camera upward toward his face.

"That was the million-dollar moment . . . when he zoomed out and we could actually see Bakker's ugly mug as he's being serviced by these five- and six-year-old kids," Bieg recounts. There are three segments featuring Bakker with three little girls, a total of seven different victims.

The investigation brings in another detective, Detective Benedikte (Ben) Wilkinson. "We were all floored seeing this kind of ugliness on the video," she noted. "It was incomprehensible. The children didn't look so much scared. It's almost like they shut themselves down. You could see the pain in their eyes. A child who is five who knows how to perform oral sex . . . It's all too much."

The investigation, at this stage, is split into two — one focusing on the Vancouver women, the other on the children. The detectives confront Bakker.

"During the interrogation, he was very flat. None of what he had done to these women seemed to bother him," Wilkinson recounts. "He had no remorse. The only time his interest sort of peaked is when we showed him the videos of him torturing the women."

When it comes to the children, however, Bakker shuts down. "He wouldn't speak to it, and he wouldn't confess."

The detectives quickly realize that prosecuting Bakker for assault against the women would pose a monumental challenge. Because of their severe drug addiction, the authorities felt the women would make very poor witnesses at trial. Moreover, the women "didn't want to come forward because he paid them," Wilkinson notes. "He paid them five dollars for each kick. Twenty dollars was the most . . . One of the women he abused was so hooked on heroin and crack cocaine, she was in very, very poor shape. She would do anything to get money for drugs."

The detectives decide that the only way to nail Bakker and put him behind bars is to build an ironclad case of sexual assault against the children. But although they have conclusive video-tape evidence, they have no idea who these young girls are or where they come from. All they know for certain is they appear to be Asian.

The police seize Bakker's passports. They contain numerous visa stamps, dating back to 1986, that chronicle journeys from Canada to the Philippines, Thailand, Cambodia, Myanmar, and Vietnam over the intervening years. Bakker's employers confirm that he was in the habit of taking the months of February and March for vacation in Southeast Asia.

The investigation explodes. More than eighty-five investigators are called in from across British Columbia. One officer with the Royal Canadian Mounted Police tells the Vancouver detectives about a civilian employee who works for the force as a forensic expert in firearms. Brian McConaghy, who runs a children's charity in Cambodia, is put forward as someone who might help identify where the girls are from.

McConaghy doesn't disappoint. Within a day of getting the call, he arrives and studies the video to try to pinpoint where they are. He notes that the girls are speaking mostly Vietnamese, with a little Khmer, which is the language in Cambodia. He also observes that one of the little girls is wearing a scarf called a Krama, which is very distinctive to Cambodia.

And then a breakthrough. On NBC that night, *Dateline* runs a segment entitled "Children for Sale." The investigation features the IJM raid on the brothels in Svay Pak, Cambodia. McConaghy phones Bieg at home, telling him to turn on his TV. They are stunned at what they see. The next day, they painstakingly pore over both the *Dateline* feature and Bakker's videos, playing them in slow motion side by side. The detectives note the same pictures and calendar on the walls. They immediately contact Bob Mosier, the lead IJM investigator on the Svay Pak raid.

Mosier agrees to look at background and facial stills of the girls on the Bakker video to see if he can tentatively identify the location and the children. Within two weeks, they have their answer. Four of the seven girls abused by Bakker had been rescued in the IJM raid eight months earlier and were now in a safe house in Phnom Penh.

The detectives switch into high gear. They begin to build a case against Bakker to charge him under Canada's child-sex-tourism law. Bieg, Wilkinson, and Forshaw head to Cambodia to gather more evidence. When they arrive in Svay Pak, the detectives are shocked at what they see.

"It was an absolutely disgusting, filthy place. It was bedlam in that village, like the Wild West. You don't know if somebody is going to knife you or shoot you in the back," Bieg recalls.

"It was a hell hole," Wilkinson adds.

They are taken into the shack where the girls were rescued.

The detectives feel like they've hit the jackpot. It is like stepping into one of Bakker's films. "All the images on the video were right there. The 2002 calendar was still hanging on the wall. The magazine photos on the wall were still there. It was bizarre," says Bieg.

Bieg and Forshaw are not allowed to see the rescued girls. They are white and they are men, and the more than fifty girls in the safe house would associate them with sex tourists — their abusers.

But Detective Wilkinson, a woman, is permitted to see them. "It was refreshing. It was enlightening. . . . I could see they had some hope. They had put on some weight. They were vibrant. There was light in their eyes. They were children again."

The detectives decide not to interview the girls. Their goal had been to confirm the where and when, and they'd succeeded.

Back in Vancouver, Bakker becomes the first and only person to be convicted under Canada's sex-tourism law, but only after arguing at his preliminary inquiry, in September 2004, that the federal government had no right to police Canadians while they were outside its jurisdiction and that Canada's sex-tourism law, enacted two years earlier, violated international law and offended the nation's Charter of Rights. Bakker pleads not guilty to twenty-two counts of assault involving prostituted women and sixteen counts related to children in a foreign country. A trial date is set for early June 2005. The day before trial, he accepts a plea bargain.

Bakker pleads guilty to three counts of sexual assault involving women and seven counts of sexual interference with children under the age of fourteen in Southeast Asia. He is sentenced to ten years in prison, but because he gets credited double time for the time he spent in prison awaiting trial, Bakker is due to be released from Mountain Institution — the medium security penitentiary where he is being held — in 2012. He claims to have found religion.

12

THE BROTHERHOOD
OF JOHNS

*We'd be labeled . . . twisted demons, even though most of us
are as mellow as can be and wouldn't harm a soul. We just
like to get laid and we realize we have to pay for it.*
—A JOHN WHO CALLS HIMSELF BEACH COMBER

Slickdickrick, Thickcane, Organgrinder, Manwhore.
Mobydick, Loverboy, Dickus, Dickyloong.
Caveman, Tigerwoody, Latinoheat69.
Anonymous, Asianhoneylover, Anon69.

No, THEY'RE NOT THE HANDLES OF AGING porn stars. But yes, most are
deliberately and ridiculously suggestive. That's part of the game.

So is sharing. Sharing photos, for instance, of their most
boast-worthy erotic conquests. Pictures of women sprawled out
on mattresses, close-ups of lips surrounding once-flaccid

members, photos of body parts and naked women's faces, wide-angle shots of awkward positions and penetrations.

But don't bet on seeing the man behind the camera. His face is well hidden or obscured by shadows.

Welcome to the brotherhood of johns—a secret fraternity where men boast yet cower . . . come out yet hide. It is the biggest support network on the planet for men who get off on paying for sex, and it is available 24-7 in every corner of the globe served by an Internet connection. It is not an exclusive club. Its members number in the millions. Entry is free on most sex sites, and any man with a predilection for prostituted women can join. That is, as long as he follows the brotherhood's rules, which means buying into the philosophy that man is hardwired to pay for play.

The prime objective of the brotherhood is to assist johns in achieving liftoff. It is a locker room, a travel agent, a tour guide, and a coach. For johns who congregate here, it is a candy store, but also a peep show and peddler of porn. For those who have paid for sex but are feeling pangs of remorse, it's a confession booth, a therapist, and "Dear Abby" rolled into one. For the john who is frugal, it's a financial advisor, and for the savvy consumer, it's a Frommer's. It is a veritable gold mine of information on the whos, hows, and why-nots of pay for play. There are even hints of a legal hotline with tips on how to avoid "LE"—law enforcement.

But it's also a powerful introduction service connecting johns with millions of others just like them. Some are novices, others veterans. Many offer advice. Some become mentors. Yet all have at least one thing in common—they are committed to their so-called hobby and no longer afraid to say it . . . at least online.

There are, of course, few consequences, as none of them ever uses his real name. They fondle their mice and tap away at their keyboards from the relative safety of cyberspace. The Internet has made for a remarkable transformation. The solitary john furtively gleaning the personal-services ads in the back pages of tabloids has been replaced by a technologically empowered breed imbued with bravado and worldly zeal.

"Dear John . . ."

Morris is a businessman from Toronto expecting a two-day lay-over in Frankfurt. He wants to know about German sauna clubs, otherwise known as FKKs (in German, *Freikorperkultur*, which translates to "free body culture," the term for a "naturist" nudist movement in Germany). Thousands of other men seek similar advice for layovers through Frankfurt, Munich, Hamburg, and Berlin. Layovers, in fact, are a common request for virtually every city on a major air traffic route.

The boards are virtually humming with recommendations and reviews. Every traveler, it seems, has a trusted favorite. One john, who calls himself Cucumber, raves about a popular club in Berlin. "If you're in Berlin, set aside 3 to 8 hours for Artemis FKK club. It is a must," he says. "Hordes of naked women, you choose what you like. After sex, you can relax in the pool area, take a hot sauna, or get a professional massage. Eat some food and have more sex. Fuck till you drop. And the price for this fantasy world is a bargain. I usually spend 250 euro per day."

Another traveler, Bananaman from Mauritius, cites a club

where the men can touch before they buy. "All the girls are beautiful and lovely," he says. "You have the right to talk with them, touch them, smell them, and finally choose what your BIG HEAD and SMALL HEAD want. SO GO THERE, SEE FOR YOURSELF, FOLLOW YOUR HEART . . . ENJOY."

A third, who calls himself Spike, speaks with rapture about a woman in his favorite place. "Check on a girl name Gabriella from Venezuela." She kisses with a passion "that will make you explode before you enter," he says.

Other men seek similar advice for longer stays, usually vacations. Brad, a forty-two-year-old high-school teacher from Philadelphia, is planning a weeklong holiday during spring break. He wants to learn everything about Colombia. By everything, he doesn't mean the historic sites, the rain forests, or the amazing expanse of the Amazon River. "Hey guys, I'm thinking of taking a trip to Colombia and was wondering what tips anyone could offer . . . such as where to pick up girls and prices?"

"Meeting chicks in Colombia? Man, it's like stealing candy from a baby," replies a john called Adam, literally within minutes. He recommends the city of Medellín: "You need a great taxi driver because Medellín is so spaced out and everything you want is all over the place. I stayed at the Casa Victoria Hotel. My amazing taxi driver was Jorge. He can pick you up at the airport and show you around . . . The guy rocks!" he says.

"Jorge knows where to take you. I went with him to a casa which was out of this world . . . a compound truly. A little bit of a drive with a gate and guards. . . . The girls pass through one by one, wearing bikini bottoms and introduce themselves, each hotter than the last. You see about 20 girls — all nines and tens, none over twenty-three," he recounts. "Then you pick (not an easy task). It runs about $80. Unreal." Adam offers a link to his Web site, which is packed with his travel photos.

Harry, from the UK, is intrigued by Russia and Ukraine: "I hear the women are drop-dead gorgeous, willing to please and the price is right. . . . I'm planning to go sometime in August for vacation. What's your experience been?" he asks. Martin, who has visited both, recommends Ukraine: "I had the time of my life in Kyiv. I signed up for a 'meet the future bride' tour," he says. "A lot of these outfits are nothing more than fronts for prostitution. I paid $1,000, was taken to a hotel where every day I met all these beautiful women looking for a 'husband.' It was seven days of laying seven different women." Russia, however, is a different story: "Stay away from Moscow. The women are cold, calculating bitches. They are always drunk or drugged and looking for ways to rip you off," he warns.

Most of the men seem to travel alone, but some prefer to head out with a friend. Paul, from Bucharest, describes himself as a "nice young man looking for a partner for hunting in Odessa." He receives two replies — one from an American going in February and another from an Australian, who calls himself Kievdream, heading there in June.

Another asks where he can go for an entire year on a budget of ten thousand dollars. One fellow traveler suggests Brazil. "I fucked a sweet ass girl there for $7 US, and there's so many of them there for that price." Another recommends Ecuador, noting that the price is seven dollars there too but the cost of living even lower. "You can live a comfortable life on $500 US a month. I know this for a fact," he attests. He also suggests Southeast Asia and offers this little travel gem: "If you're not going to look for work (doesn't sound like it) stay out of the big cities and go rural. Cheaper, and you won't have to share . . . with other foreigners."

Some johns also want to ensure that they're understood. Crazydaze, from Finland, seeks help in improving his linguistic skills. "I'm interested to know how to say 'I am coming' in different languages," he says. He gets fifteen replies covering fifteen languages: Greek, Icelandic, Danish, Spanish, French, Swedish, Estonian, Norwegian, German, Finnish, Cantonese, Mandarin, Japanese, Malaysian, and Russian. But that's not quite enough. He writes in again: "There are still some Western European languages missing. . . . Don't Italians come at all? What about the Portuguese?"

Closer to Home

Huge numbers of johns travel abroad, but even more seek paid sex closer to home. They too let their fingers do the walking, scouring local Web sites and discussion boards for ads and reviews. Most of the sites are free, but some are commercial, offering premium services for a fee.

Big Doggie, a favorite of *Playboy* magazine (which named it best escort site on the Web in 2001), boasts "43,000 reviews and growing daily." My Red Book, another popular site, had 123,000 reviews as of January 2008. And The Erotic Review, which in one month drew 323,000 "unique users," informs its clientele that "Life is an Erotic Highway. Sometimes, you just have to stop and ask for directions.

"If you are lost, let the Love Goddess be your backseat driver," it says. "This way, you'll really be in the know when you search the web for that special someone!" The Love Goddess, it explains, is "a licensed sex therapist" with a "very, very erotic streak" and — just in case a john's still in doubt — "a deep knowledge of huMAN nature."

The Erotic Review consists of a Web site, accessible to anyone, containing thumbnail sketches of thousands of women. But for twenty dollars a month it also offers a VIP membership that provides intelligence on local "providers." VIP members have access to physical details — like age, build, ethnicity, even breast size and information on whether the woman has implants — a description of her service, and the clichéd ten-point-scale rating.

Take Jacqueline, a provider from Chicago. One of her "date reviews" gives her nearly perfect scores. The reviewer rates her appearance a 9 ("model material") and her performance 10 ("once in a lifetime"). The atmosphere, he says, is "very classy," her attitude "terrific," and the cost five hundred dollars for an outcall. "After reading the other reviews," the date notes, "I couldn't resist calling Jacqueline. I was not disappointed. She is incredibly bright, beautiful and sensual beyond belief." There's a section of the review entitled "Juicy." This is where the date blows his own horn: "I called to set up an in-call a day in advance. . . . On the phone, she asked what I wanted her to wear. And boy did she deliver. . . ."

Such glowing reviews no doubt stoke the coals of many

passing johns. But what happens when a so-called date doesn't go as planned? Johns give bad reviews too. "She was all attitude," wrote an irate john in Chicago. "Thought she was doing me a favor. But what pissed me off when she got to my hotel room was she wasn't at all like her picture. At best a six in looks! I decided what the heck. What a mistake. Didn't even fake like she was enjoying herself. Don't waste your money on her. . . . She calls herself Elaina."

Performance aside, there is a troublesome issue that continually lights up the boards. While most johns are ruled by the stirring in their loins, many are astute enough to recognize that on the Internet — whether in chat rooms or on Web sites — things are not always as they seem. For instance, the hugely popular Craigslist, which connects buyers and sellers for every knickknack or service under the sun, advertises in more than 450 cities; its most popular offering is "erotic services." Look up New York's list and you'll come across a smorgasbord of suggestive headlines: "Expert tool handler" (from Westchester, charging "125 flowers an hour"), "Let me be your private plaything" (a twenty-two-year-old from Manhattan), "Hot chocolate bombshell" (Brooklyn), "Wet your whistle on this Asian temptress" (midtown Manhattan), "I'm so good with the 'tool' you'll think I was a female mechanic" (the Bronx). Look closer and you'll see that the services are offered by every kind of woman imaginable: blonde, redhead, brunette; full-figured, petite; regulars and those in town for the weekend. But while the ads may titillate and tantalize surfing johns, there is always the possibility of a very chilling downside.

"Hi, I'm Jasmine," says one ad. "Just flew in from New Orleans. . . . Call me. I do everything. You won't be disappointed."

These days, a john has no way of knowing what or who awaits on the other end. If he's lucky, he'll be greeted by Jasmine in a negligee. If he's not, he'll come face to face with Officer Jane.

Vice cops in North America have caught on to the trend and are following the trail of sex-for-money online, usually by posting salacious ads of their own and busting the deflated johns as soon as money changes hands. But the johns are equally savvy. They are posting questions about sudden newcomers and hoping that other johns will quickly reply with reviews, or at least verify that "Sexy Susan" is not a cop.

"Hot Cindy says she's in town for the weekend, anyone got any info on her? Don't want any surprises if you know what I mean," writes a cautious Captain Midnight. An hour later, Midnight gets the news he'd been hoping for: "She's legit!"

But it's not just online escorts who are risky. Cops also pose as working girls on the streets. Here too the brotherhood steps in, sharing tips on detecting possible stings. Some suggest circling the block a few times and looking for men in parked cars within view of the stroll. Some johns go even further, posting in real time what girls are working the hooker strolls, which are worth the price, and who to avoid, particularly if they see anyone new or suspiciously out of place.

Chester, a john who claims to be a former Chicago cop, speaks from experience. He has his own Web site, Chester's Sex Guide, which is like a buyer's-beware manual for johns. In it, he offers prudent counsel on how to stay safe. "If you know what to look for," the former cop writes, referring to street stings, "you'll never get busted this way. First of all, when you are looking for any hooker, always pay attention to the surroundings," he suggests, instructing that when a sting operation is taking place there are a number of telltale signs, such as suspicious cars parked nearby with people sitting in them.

He stresses that police officers patrolling a hooker stroll know the women working the streets, and if they detect one getting into a car, they will most likely pull the vehicle over. If this happens, Chester warns, "Whatever you do, don't be a smartass and they'll probably be cool about it. If you act like an asshole and tell them that you thought the girl wasn't a hooker, they may take you in just for being a dumb ass." He suggests playing it straight and, above all, remaining respectful.

Chester also offers a reality check for men who cruise the streets searching for the perfect Jacqueline. He wants them to recognize that this type of woman — beautiful, sensual, intelligent — will be nowhere in sight. Women working the strolls are usually in dire straits — addicted to drugs, suffering from mental health problems, and under the control of a violent pimp or abusive boyfriend. As a result, johns should not expect the women to be "well-mannered, well-educated, and patient. . . . The vast majority of the ones I've studied are of average to way below average intelligence, and are from tough backgrounds. If you assume the worst, you won't be so disappointed later on. Some of these girls have had the shit beat out of them for years, and are so hard and callous that not even Mother Teresa could get through."

Chester warns that prostituted women are adept at stringing naive johns a line, telling them they have a real day job and that they're only working the streets to live out a fantasy or to earn extra cash. What they won't tell tell you is that drug addiction is what drives them, or they have HIV/AIDS, "or that their life is total shit. Keep that in mind when you start laying down your lines of bullshit."

Bragging Rights

While all the advice and tips are roundly appreciated, the brotherhood fulfills another vital role. It offers the ultimate audience for kiss-and-tell. Particularly popular is the numbers game. One john by the name of Libertine says he wishes he "had the drive" to "handle ten to twelve girls a day" but adds, almost apologetically, "Most of us are in the range of one to three." Burrito, on the other hand, claims he has had sex with as many as seven women in one day, but, like Libertine, he admits his usual number is only "between two and three." Tigerwoody, whose name suggests his proficiency, claims to tally at least a dozen a week. But a twenty-one-year-old college student beats them all, boasting:

> Most guys who go to my college can only DREAM and BRAG of fucking more than one woman at the same time.
>
> I can legitimately say that I have fucked close to 100 different girls (having lost my virginity a little over a year ago), have been with more than 2+ women at the same time all night, have had many great, conscious-expanding ass tapping sessions, orgasmic screaming sessions, and [all] since my introduction [to mongering] a year ago.
>
> So not only do I receive a powerful reward of ecstatic vibrations from doing the sexual acts, but everlasting knowledge

is plucked from the vagina as well. Because I engage in p4p, the purest, quickest, and STRONGEST form of sexual gratification, I have attained the bliss of SEXUAL ENLIGHTENMENT!

His screen name? Diehard.

For certain johns, however, bragging isn't enough. They post trophies — photos and videos. The women in the pictures, mostly from Third World and Eastern European countries, are always featured naked, often performing oral sex. One john displays a photo of one of his conquests during a weeklong sex swing through the Philippines. "She is great in bed. She loves sex. She will suck you, fuck you and then she'll wash you . . . all for fifty dollars," he boasts. Hunter, an American, follows suit, chronicling a fourteen-day vacation in Thailand that he dubs a "fucking spree." This latter-day Don Juan posts photos, along with the names, descriptions, and locations of the women. As per protocol, he remains a blur in the shadows. "I was doing two to four chicks a day," he boasts. "It was nirvana."

Does Anyone Else Know?

While johns crow incessantly and strut around like virtual cocks in their cyberbarnyard, they do so under a cloak of anonymity. In the real world, it appears, most keep a tight lid on what even they see as their dirty little secret.

One john posts a question to a popular discussion board asking if any of the others have ever told anyone about their hobby.

He gets an avalanche of replies, most admitting that they keep their forays shrouded in silence.

"Far as I'm aware no one knows I holiday purely for sex," offers one.

"It's my business, and that's it," insists another. "I don't trust a bunch of nosey fuckers."

Apeman suggests, "Keep it quiet. If you have to talk, talk to a dog, cat or fish in a room where no one can hear you."

Some are more emphatic. "[A] big HELL NO!" replies one, going by the name Batman:

> As a matter of fact, I have my "normal" life so well worked out, that people actually believe I am one of the most naive of them all. Hehe. BJ? What's that? A big jar?
>
> Anyways, I trust no one [with] that kind of information and if they knew, who knows what could happen in the future. I mean, you could end up being bitter enemies or something trivial and he/she may now know more about you than you know about them. I say keep that info to yourself no matter how much you might want to brag about the numbers or trophy ho's you've had. I'll be the first to say that I am no saint and I sure as hell don't act that way at all. I am simply saying that I actively portray myself as a guy who looks but doesn't touch. But I just wanted to clarify that I too consider myself a good guy and place top priority on the values of a decent family.

Beach Comber, a regular, offers a similar story, noting that the people he knows would be horrified if they ever found out. "'That nice young man, Beach? No way!' We'd be labeled . . .

twisted demons, even though most of us are as mellow as can be and wouldn't harm a soul. We just like to get laid and we realize we have to pay for it."

Only one john claims to brag about his hobby to anyone who will listen, online or off. "I'm quite proud of my activities and even boast of them in front of people. I guess I just like to rub it everybody's face so I can make them upset. They're so religious, moralistic and uptight about everything. The more I get them upset, the more entertaining it is." Ironically, this out-of-the-closet john uses the screen name Anonymous 666.

Johns preoccupied with keeping their antics hidden are a fertile source of pretexts and excuses. One john interested in foreign sex haunts seeks advice on the kinds of jobs that would provide extended assignments in Third World sex pits.

The brotherhood comes through.

A john called Prolong says that, if he could pick anything, he'd choose to be a *National Geographic* photographer. "'Hello, I'm here to photograph your tribeswomen . . . naked.'"

Another recommends teaching English as a second language.

A third suggests volunteer work: "Find a job as an aid worker for some UN aid agency. Everyone will think you're a saint for doing this work and you'll be scoring all kinds of women."

And a fourth offers an unsettling personal example. "I work in Higher Education, and many years ago did a brief leadership development lecture in Myanmar. That is now my cover. I travel every year to 'teach' in some third world country, where UN-FORTUNATELY there is no telephone service and very little Internet service. In other words, I cannot be reached. Not only do I have the perfect cover for a spouse, but co-workers think I am a saint for volunteering in third world countries."

"He paid how much?"

On March 12, 2008, the public got an unexpected glimpse at the present-day sex trade with the revelation that New York governor Eliot Spitzer frequented a high-priced call girl through a prostitution ring he found online. The media focused on Spitzer's personal and political downfall, devouring every juicy detail and irony with zeal, but it was the aftermath of the scandal that provided a view into the minds of regular johns.

To many in the brotherhood, Spitzer was a martyr of sorts, and he quickly became a rallying cry for the legalization of prostitution. On numerous online discussion forums, johns wondered incredulously why the news media had made such a big deal about a private matter.

"Men go to prostitutes all the time," said one. "It's a simple consumer transaction, and it's no one's business." Another noted that the "ridiculous thing" about the Spitzer case is "the fact that having sex is a crime."

"Who cares if someone wants to pay for it?" wrote another. "We are men. We NEED to GET LAID! I could just punch anybody in the face that thinks fucking should be a crime, for whatever reason." And a third speculated that Spitzer "just could not resist the 'natural' urge," noting that "the urge is overpowering, just like we fall victim . . . sometimes!"

A john calling himself Stallion had a different take, pointing out that "Spitzer's problem is he got caught. Other countries are probably wondering what the fuss is all about. One of my co-workers suggested why not take the $80K he blew and set up a mistress. That would also be acceptable elsewhere around the world."

Not surprisingly, some in the brotherhood took aim at Spitzer's wife, blaming her for his spectacular downfall. "Too bad she slacked off her only job, too little too late," wrote Dino. "A man will always take care of his sexual needs . . . if only his significant other had been doing her job." Another concurred: "[S]he has a cook to prepare meals — when not eating out; a maid to clean house, and a nanny for the kids. There is nothing else for her to do in the marriage but screw her husband . . ." As did a third: "This is so true! Never thought about it, but when you have all those servants, all you really have left is to look after your husband's sexual needs!"

But Spitzer wasn't off the hook — not by a long shot. The Internet may be a haven for johns — providing a safe place to share and find encouragement and support — but there are limits even to what the community of johns will accept when one of its own does something it considers really, really dumb.

Many were outraged, not because he got caught or because of the reaction by the media and public, but by the fact that he had had the temerity to pay up to $4,300 for an hour of sex.

"Obviously that's a ridiculous rate," one john exclaimed, fuming over Spitzer's fiscal irresponsibility. "I wonder if she even kissed him, blew him BBBJ [bare back blow job] or let him get anywhere near her ass? The only reason to pay that much would be if you were stupidly rich and in a position (like him as a politician) where

ABSOLUTE discretion/secrecy must be GUARANTEED. Well, there are no guarantees when more than one person is involved. So what's the point of paying such a horrendous sum?"

Many agreed. "I am just shocked that he spent over four grand on a hooker," said a john called Keith. "That is amazing to me. Sure these aren't typical crack whores we are talking about. He probably isn't going to catch a STD and the girls look like models. Alright so she doesn't have chapped lips, a c-section scar, and she has all of her teeth but really four grand?"

"In all honesty," offered one traveling john, "for $4,300 you could get laid 100 times overseas."

Others saw it as a sign of fiscal irresponsibility in his public life. "He is showing bad judgment paying that much money for a few hours work that requires no training or capital investment. I can imagine how he spends taxpayers' money," speculated a john who calls himself Johnson.

And still others in the brotherhood felt no pity for Spitzer because of what he purported to represent. Before his election as governor, Spitzer was attorney general of New York, and as attorney general he had taken a tough stance against prostitution. "The issue here isn't the actual act of the Governor paying for sex but the fact that he took a hard line against prostitution and even closed one operation down when he was an AG," wrote one. "So he is a big hypocrite, he's against the trade professionally but then on other hand he uses the service himself."

"I guess my big issue with Spitzer is that this man sent people to jail for the same exact thing he was doing behind closed doors," remarked another. "I doubt Spitzer started visiting prostitutes just this week. He's probably been doing so for awhile.

During a typical day, he may as well have finished prosecuting a prostitution case at 3 pm, then met his hooker at 6 pm. So since there are people sitting in jail for prostitution that Spitzer put there, he should also follow suit."

Others agreed. "Here's a guy vowing to clean up all the evil mongering in NY and then goes out and overpays for it himself. STUPID SOB deserves to rot in a jail cell for what he paid this whore. It's guys like this that want to tell everyone else they can't have P4P here in the USA and send out the police to bust all the good places in order to get votes but its ok for them to do it. I say tattoo some tits on this piece of shits back and toss him in prison so Bubba can get him some booty too."

Yet another exclaimed that he was "sick and tired of all the hype" on Spitzer. "I admit that karma came at him for taking down prostitution organizations and making pussy around my area very pricy."

THE INTERNET IS THE MATCH that has set the flesh trade ablaze, making shopping for body rentals a cakewalk. But it is the brotherhood — the online community of johns — that has fanned the flames into a raging inferno. Putting johns in instant touch with one another in every country around the world, the Internet has taken much of the shame out of mongering by showing these men that their desires are shared by millions of others. No longer is buying sex an unspoken vice. There's no need anymore to keep it deeply hidden. The Internet has allowed these men to create communities of support where they can share not only their urges but also their doubts. In the process, it has given them a way to talk themselves out of any uncomfortable emotions.

Without these high-speed connections and the validation they bring, men buying sex would still be cowering in the closet. Instead, they trade fantasies, queries, and reviews, rally around one another when the need arises, and perpetuate the myth that buying sex is as natural as going to the grocer for a carton of milk. But what johns blithely forget — or willfully ignore — is that they're not just procuring another good or service. They may like to think that all they're doing is feeding fantasies, but the reality remains: they're buying and trading in human beings.

13

SEX EDUCATION
101

*Many times in my life I start out watching porn, next thing I
know I am in my car looking for the real thing.*
—A john called Bull Rider

VOLUMES HAVE BEEN WRITTEN for and against pornography. This is
a book about johns. So what's the connection? Porn and johns go
hand in hand. Porn is often what turns the men on, revs up their
sex drive, and sends them out into the night. It is the halftime
show between sex junkets abroad, something to tide the travelers
over until they can head out again. It is the poor cousin of prostitution — a man's surrogate for the kind of sex he craves but can't
easily get or afford. And while the porn industry tries to sell its
product as a form of sexual liberation, free speech, and artistic
expression, pornography is in essence prostitution, because it

involves the purchase of another person's body for sexual gratification. Therefore, the men who buy and watch porn are themselves johns.

The Internet is rife with postings by johns admitting their addiction to or love of porn, and would-be johns who indulge in porn as a substitute for the real thing. One john, tagged Plumber, notes, "Hey, when you've got no cash, at least you've got your right hand and a whole mess of porn on the Internet, and the great thing about it — it's FREE!"

"I would rather have sex with a woman," says Rod, "but it costs money — whether you go to hookers like I do or go on dates where you pay, pay and pay in the hopes of getting laid. So when I have no cash, I hit the free porn sites on the Internet."

"Some of us travel, and for the rest of the time between trips we don't get much action in the USA, so we end up just watching porn," says a third.

Snake, who would prefer to go abroad for sex, describes porn as a consolation prize: "Having sex with AWs [American Women] is very difficult so we have nothing better to do than to fantasize about it with porn. Most of us cannot afford to travel and fuck foreign women so those of us in this situation are forced into this. . . ."

Some men, like Prowler, see it, then want it: "You cannot deny for a second that when you see a porn and focus the attention on the women you say to yourself man I wish that could be me hittin' that."

For Bull Rider, "porn and mongering go together like peas and carrots. Many times in my life I start out watching porn, next thing I know I am in my car looking for the real thing."

A john called The Man says he only watches porn when he's planning a paid encounter. "I watch the positions; find a girl who looks like one of the performers and make porn the build up to the planned party."

For those who do take the next step — pay their way to sex — what they demand behind closed doors is often what's portrayed on the screen. One john, who goes by the name X-rated, writes, "I've watched a lot of porn and I jerk off to it. But in the end, there's no great orgasm. I just come. Every once in a while, when I have some spare cash, I go out and hire a hooker . . . been doing that for over 20 years. When I pay for it, there's no way I'm going to settle for the missionary position. What I get is hardcore. It's around the world sex. If the whore gives me attitude about it, I show her the door. I'm paying, so I call the shots, not the whore."

X-rated isn't alone. A 1990 study by the organization WHIS-PER (Women Hurt in Systems of Prostitution Engaged in Revolt) revealed that 52 percent of women interviewed said that porn played a significant role in teaching them what was expected of them as prostitutes, 30 percent reported that their pimps regularly exposed them to pornography to get them to accept the sex acts shown there, and 80 percent said that johns showed them porn in order to illustrate specific acts they wanted performed. Melissa Farley, a leading researcher on prostitution, found a similar link between what johns see and what they seek. In interviews with 854 women in prostitution in nine countries, 47 percent were upset by their johns' attempts to make them do what they had seen in pornography.

And the johns' interest isn't lost on those hoping to sell their services. Ads placed by "call girls" on Craigslist now tempt prospective johns with promises of the "PSE" — porn-star experience.

The message is clear: if prostitution is the main act, porn is the dress rehearsal.

So What Are They Watching?

If johns are requesting what they're seeing in porn — or nurturing fantasies on what they would do with a women based on what they see on the screen — it becomes all the more important to understand what they're watching and how it's shaping their perceptions of women.

The answer may shock you. The reality of today's pornography is that it does not even remotely resemble the porn of old — the soft-core erotica involving repairmen, door-to-door salesmen, and silly B-line plots.

Gail Dines, a professor of sociology and women's studies at Wheelock College in Boston and one of the founding members of Stop Porn Culture, a national antipornography movement, argues that over the past twenty years the porn industry has become more misogynistic, more violent, and more criminal. "Our lives are being overwhelmed by images that scream misogyny.

"The old distinction between soft-core and hard-core is over. The reason is, all the soft-core porn has migrated into pop culture. That's where it sits today. When you go on the Internet, the vast majority of the pornography that is accessible is hard-core. The distinction in porn is no longer between soft-core and hard-core. It's between features and Gonzo."

A feature tries to mirror a low-budget Hollywood film. It has a bit of a plot and some dialogue, but its enticement is body-punishing sex. In Gonzo, however, there is no story line. It is just body-punishing sex.

Sex in Gonzo, Dines points out, is not merely sex, and women in Gonzo are never just women. "In Gonzo, women are pathetic bitches, slut sandwiches, cum buckets, whores, and squirting skanks. The premise of Gonzo is that women are meant to be fucked, dominated, made to suffer, and be humiliated."

To illustrate, Dines shows some of the provocative and graphic images she downloaded free from the Internet. Each of these, she points out, was found through a five-to-ten-second search on Google. "Sometimes a woman's face is a canvas . . . there is no pretense that she likes it," she says. "On the whole, [the porn producers] are letting you know how she feels." She points to one. "Look at her mascara running down her eyes. She's crying. And they don't wipe it away. Why not? Because part of the thrill of this is that it hurts and she hates it. There is no attempt to make out that this is pleasurable to her."

The latest craze in Gonzo, Dines says, is ATM (ass to mouth): a man rams his penis into a woman anally and then puts his penis straight into her mouth. The message is "Eat shit!" Also popular is gaggle, or "throat fucking" — shoving a penis so far down a woman's throat that she gags and vomits. For variety, three men at once: in a woman's mouth, vagina, and anus. Then they withdraw and ejaculate onto her face or, in a scene called pink eye, into her eyes.

Some scenes in Gonzo are so vile that they don't even resemble what we know as sex. One of the most incomprehensible

acts in Gonzo is "gaping" — the use of dental and medical equipment (such as a speculum) to spread open the vagina or anus to
give the camera and the viewer a look inside.

"What you are looking at here is torture," Dines maintains.

The godfather of Gonzo is an aging porn star who goes by the
name Max Hardcore but whose real name is Paul F. Little, aka
Max Steiner. Max, often seen in a white cowboy hat and sporting a cheesy grin, is a man of many pornographic talents: he pro-
duces it, stars in it, and, on June 7, 2008, was convicted of
obscenity in Florida for distributing it. Max's Web site promo offers a glimpse into his soul: "I force girls to drink my piss, fist-
fuck them, ream their asses and drill their throats until they
puke."

Probably the most vile sex videos made by Max Hardcore are
what he calls Cherry Poppers. In effect, they are instructional
tapes for pedophiles on how to rape a child. "They help the pe-
dophile to get ready to season the victim," Dines explains. "They
normalize pedophilia. They provide ideas. This is so specific that
at the end of one of these segments, Max Hardcore . . . takes a
camera and takes a picture of the girl. And he says, 'Listen honey,
if you tell anyone, I'm taking this picture to school and I'm going
to show all your friends exactly what you do.'"

Incredibly, Max has a huge and growing fan base. They idol-
ize him. They speak glowingly of this man who brought them
Gonzo, using words like "hero" and "icon." Some have set up
blog sites in his honor, lauding his particular form of "art." Others share their passion on discussion boards, including the forum
on maxhardcore.com.

Says one fan, who goes by the name Charger, "I've always

been a Max Hardcore fan because he pushes the limits in ways that even I can't stomach sometimes. . . . I'm glad he has the freedom to make his disgusting filth, and I'm glad I have the freedom to buy every second of it."

Another, who calls himself Ramsey, enthuses, "For me, Max Hardcore is an icon because he revolutionized porn. . . . Max changed porn big time when he first started with 'The Anal Adventures of Max Hardcore' and we hardcore porn fans should thank him for that because until then there was hardly any hardcore stuff like that on the market. Max is a hero."

And Big Bopper from the U.K. offers this: "A few years ago, I joined maxhardcore.com to see what all the fuss was about and, while I found a lot of the girls really hot in their teeny outfits, Max's attitude and actions in a lot of the clips left me feeling shellshocked, sickened and dirty. But, just as porn moves on, so did my tastes, and gradually I realized I was enjoying Max's extreme scenes more and more — whether that's corruption or desensitization, I don't know. All I do know is that I've gone from being a one time Max hater to a Max Hardcore fan."

So what effect is hard-core porn having on the men who watch it? "I say this to men over and over again," Dines says. "You might not go to porn hating women, but you sure as hell are going to come away with that feeling. You get much more than you bargained for with porn, and that's the problem with it.

"The other problem with porn is that it sexualizes the violence and degradation against women. And when you sexualize that violence, you render that violence invisible because when men see that they can't sit back and critique it. Have you ever sat back with men who watch porn? You're going to basically have a conversation with an erection and it doesn't work. Erections are not known for their rational understanding."

Robert Jensen, author of *Getting Off: Pornography and the End of Masculinity*, maintains that one of the most damaging aspects of pornography "is not only that it objectifies women but that it also encourages men to objectify ourselves, to cut ourselves off from the rich, complex experience of sexuality and intimacy.

"Pornography provides men a quick and easy orgasm, producing physical pleasure with little or no emotional engagement. But to do that, what are we doing to ourselves?" Jensen says that in hundreds of formal interviews and informal discussions he has had with men who use porn, "I repeatedly hear them describe going emotionally numb when viewing pornography and masturbating, a state of being 'checked out.'

"So, to enter into the pornographic world and experience that intense sexual rush, many men have to turn off some of the emotional reactions typically connected to a sexual experience with a real person — a sense of the other's humanity, an awareness of being present with another person, the recognition of something outside our own bodies, as well as a deeper connection to oneself.

"In short, pornography helps train men not to feel during an experience that is mostly about feeling," Jensen says.

Jensen argues that pornography is not only destructive for men "but dangerous for women. Because sex is always more than a physical act, men seeking this split-off state often find themselves having uncontrollable emotional reactions that can get channeled easily into violence and cruelty, increasing the risk to women.

"Despite this, the pornography industry continues to tell us that their products represent the ultimate in sexual liberation. But the only thing that is being liberated is our cash, into their pockets."

And liberate cash it does, by the truckload. In 2008 the porn industry generated an estimated sixty billion dollars worldwide, almost fifteen billion dollars in the United States. Porn revenue is larger than the combined revenues of all professional baseball, basketball, and football franchises in the United States, and exceeds the combined revenues of television networks ABC, CBS, and NBC.

Dines shakes her head and wonders aloud who it was that "decided that these white pimps should control what sex is in this culture. The truth is they will do to sex what McDonald's does to food. They strip it down, they turn it into a plasticized formulaic way of living, and they destroy the creative and life-loving experience these things can bring. And then if we stand up to them, we are demonized. We are mocked out there. The media never come to us anymore. We have been basically closed out."

Dines warns that society is "very, very close to losing it all. There is a point at which it is very hard to pull back. What's going on in environmental destruction is similar to cultural destruction. There is a point where it is all over. People are very robotic. They have lost what it means to be human and they are fully colonized by the corporate pimps. This has to stop. We have to fight back."

Make Your Own Porn

Incredible as it may seem, even Gonzo fans may eventually get bored with what the producers and peddlers of porn have to offer.

Others may grow weary of the standard positions and story lines so predictably packaged as soft- or hard-core and yearn for something more engaging than passively watching the director's cut. These porn addicts may want to sit in the director's chair themselves, but most will never have the opportunity or means. They may also be tempted to play the starring role but lack the money or nerve to seek out the PSE (Porn Star Experience).

What's their solution? Web cams. A new breed of johns — cyberjohns — are investing in Web cams by the hundreds of thousands and seeking out Web sites that let them create XXX from afar. They sit alone in dark rooms in cities like New York, Toronto, Dallas, and Miami and order up a woman in Kyiv, São Paulo, Bucharest, and Manila. They direct the woman to perform sex acts on command, in real time.

For the uninitiated, there is a plethora of online sites singing the praises of cybersex. One of the more popular is Sex Cams 101, a site that explains the process and offers reviews. "The guts of all cam sites are their private sex shows," it explains, where women play out johns' fantasies live. The private sessions are billed by the minute at rates from $0.99 to $5.99. Some even offer a free "teaser chat" beforehand where the men can plan the performance.

"Think of it as a strip club that [lets you] see things you otherwise might not be able to see," Sex Cams suggests. "You'll be able to enjoy the privacy of your own home as well as to do as you please. Don't be shy! The beauty of cam shows is that you can live out some of your fantasies that you may otherwise be too shy to ask for in the outside world. These girls have heard it all, so don't be ashamed to ask them whether they do something or not. Get the most out of your time and money."

For the novice john, Sex Cams summarizes the advantages of one popular site, LiveJasmin.com. "You can get a good 15 minute session in for under $30, which gives you about three times the time you'd get for a lap dance at your local titty bar."

Another popular site is Webcam.com. It cites a virtual smorgasbord of offerings: "Teen Cams, Couples fucking on cam, Lesbian cams, Black girl cams, Asian cams, Indian cams, Latina cams." It also offers "hardcore cams" such as anal, bondage, double penetration, and even "pregnant girls get fucked on cam." Yet another site, which has been dubbed "the true king" of sex cams, is iFriends — the originators of the adult Web cam world. Here, too, fetishes are popular: bondage, discipline, dominance and submission, sadism and masochism, pregnant women, and, according to a Sex Cams review, "a whole slew of alternative options that the other cam networks can't even touch." iFriends boasts more than five hundred thousand registered cams and eight million members worldwide.

As for the women in front of the cameras, Sex Cams touts that "cam girls come from all across the world," signing up at various sites "to be able to perform live for you" for a "nominal" fee. Many, however, are from impoverished regions of the world. LiveJasmin, it notes, boasts "hundreds of sexy Eastern European girls," while iFriends is "filled predominantly with Eastern European girls and some Asian babes." In fact, "[t]his seems to be a staple of the live cam industry as these girls work for much less than American chicks."

So what is this phenomenon? Just another Internet fancy? Without a doubt, it is an extension of prostitution. These men are paying to use women for their own sexual pleasure and perversion. The women may or may not be willing participants, but the preponderance of Eastern European and Asian women — typical targets for traffickers — should set off alarms. What woman wants to expose herself, be subject to double penetration, perversion, or bondage at the command of a disembodied voice in some far-off corner of the globe? Cyberprostitution — if it needs a name — is just as harmful as the traditional kind, and any man who orders up these women online is just as much a john as the ones prowling the streets or scurrying into brothels.

Johns in Training

As disturbing as these trends are, there is another, more troubling aspect of pornography: it is a training school for johns. It's their unofficial Sex Ed 101. Boys are naturally curious. They want to know what sex is about. For many, soft-core porn introduces them to the basics. The prevailing wisdom has been that porn is relatively harmless. A rite of passage, some might say. A way to relieve the constant tingling in their jeans. But today's teens don't have to pass around *Playboy* in secret or rifle through the stash of skin magazines under their father's mattress. In fact, there's no need to go looking for it at all. Like it or not, porn finds them.

Porn pops up on the Internet without the slightest provocation. Young children are assaulted by it as soon as their little fingers are able to start typing. Computer users are accosted by porn-video trailers and explicit photographs on music and movie download sites.

While the research on the effects of porn on children is not as extensive as it could be, there are signs that it is making an arresting appearance in their young lives. Studies show the average age of the first online exposure to porn is eleven. Ninety percent of eight- to sixteen-year-olds in the U.S., Canada, Britain, Europe, Japan, and Australia have viewed porn online while doing homework. Eighty percent of fifteen- to seventeen-year-olds have had multiple hard-core exposures. One study of thirteen- and fourteen-year-olds by the University of Alberta found that one-third of boys viewing porn did so "too many times to count."

A study published in the April 2008 issue of *CyberPsychology & Behavior* found that the Internet is having an accelerant effect. The study, by Shane Kraus, a psychologist from Castleton State College in Vermont, found that boys aged twelve to seventeen who regularly view pornography are having oral sex and losing their virginity much younger, "sometimes by a good three to four years for oral sex and two years for their virginity." It also noted the boys are more likely to initiate oral sex, apparently imitating what they have watched.

At fourteen, Jason from Toronto says he's seen everything there is to see on porn. "Guys urinating and defecating on women; women with animals; men torturing and raping women . . . I've seen it all, and so have a lot of my friends. We started off right away with hardcore. It's right there always in your face when you go to a lot of these movie download sites on the Internet like Torrents."

Jason says he and his friends kind of understand that porn is not about real relationships and that the people are acting, but he grudgingly admits that they are all having trouble figuring out what is normal in a sexual relationship. "We look at girls in school and talk about what we would do to them, but everything we say comes from porn and it's the real dirty stuff. I know it's not healthy and I know the girls would be disgusted if they knew what we fantasize about doing to them. It's pretty sick."

Jason's father eventually discovered what he was doing all those hours alone in his bedroom. "He tapped into my toolbox, hit history, and I was in big trouble. We had the talk . . . a long talk and he got me into therapy. The sad thing is I know a lot of my friends are in big trouble. They are totally hooked . . . and their views on girls and sex are screwed up big time. Trouble is they don't have anyone to talk to. They don't have a father like mine who took the time to really deal with it rather than freaking out on me, and you can't really go to your teacher. Then you'll be known as a perv."

Children and teens who are exposed to the unrelenting assault of hard-core on the Internet are being drawn into a very confusing and frightening world where women are treated worse than beasts, violence is associated with manhood and glamour, and sex has nothing at all to do with intimacy or love. If their vision of sex is what they're seeing on the screen, how is this shaping their views of women, gender roles, power, sexuality, and relationships? How are these boys going to treat girls when they start dating? What will they expect from the girls they go to school with, and later from women? How will they deal with the disappointment and rejection when they ask for or attempt to act out some of the porn themes they've viewed online?

Research on the effects of repeated exposure to hard-core is virtually unanimous in its findings: men soon lose respect for women and develop an increased sexual callousness toward them. As they progress to more deviant, bizarre, or violent porn, they begin to trivialize rape and form distorted views of women, sexuality, dating, and marriage. These are the findings on adults, who supposedly have the capacity to make sound and informed decisions. Imagine the effect on teens and children.

14

A GIFT
TO JOHNS

*Make sure that the place has panic or duress alarms in all the
rooms, with buttons or buzzers that are accessible.*
—Safety advice to prostituted women
working in Australian brothels

"Plan an escape line before any job, before every job!"

"Don't wear chains or jewelry you can be strangled with."

"Get your eye level down to their genitals so that you can
have a good look. Just opening the fly of his pants is not good
enough. It's best to have his pants right off so that you can
look at the balls, between his legs, and anal area."

"Part the pubic hair and look for crabs and their eggs. Pull
gently along the hair with your fingernails and look for lice
or anything that moves."

"Putting on a condom with your mouth is useful if the client does not want to use them. This can eroticize condoms."

THESE ARE JUST A FEW of the many occupational health and safety tips developed by state governments and sex-worker-rights organizations in Australia. They are enough to rattle the common senses of ordinary people.

A sex-worker pamphlet strongly recommends checking every john for sexually transmitted diseases (STDs). "Even if you use a condom every time a penis enters your mouth, vagina, or anus, you can still be exposed to STDs . . . especially crabs, herpes, and genital warts, which can be transmitted from the uncovered genital area."

Another glossy brochure warns that condoms sometimes break or slip off. In these cases, Australia's national prostitutes'-rights organization — the Scarlet Alliance — suggests that all the semen be scooped out from inside, with care being taken "to avoid scratching the lining of the vagina with fingernails."

The brochure details several strategies for dealing with rough and rowdy clients, but the onus remains on the woman to convince a protesting john to wear a condom or to calm him down when he gets too demanding or abusive. It strongly recommends that women entering prostitution take classes in hostage negotiation skills.

Here's one bit of advice: "If a client has gone past your limits, you need to be able to bring him back without causing too many issues such as him losing his momentum (or hard on)." For women working the streets, it warns, "If you think things could turn dirty, let him think you could throw up in his car." If the situation escalates, "Leave your mark in the car. Leave fin-gerprints. Leave DNA (hair, a bit of fingernail)."

For escorts heading off for a rendezvous in a hotel or home, a South African sex-workers' organization strongly advises women to "accidentally" kick a shoe under the bed and, while retrieving it, to check for knives, handcuffs, or rope.

The Australian Scarlet Alliance also recommends, "If you feel in danger do what you need to get out safely, regardless of any re-fund you may have to give. An assault leaving bruising can force you into having time off work, in turn losing more money than the client's booking fees."

As for women working in legal brothels, the advice is to keep within close striking distance of the panic button: "Make sure that the place has panic or duress alarms in all the rooms, with buttons or buzzers that are accessible."

Finally, this stern warning: "Don't relax after the job's done — that can be the time he'll assault you. Relax after he's gone!"

One touchy-feely section of the Australian occupational health and safety guidelines deals with the physical and mental well-being of women in prostitution: "Feeling disillusioned with work and life in general? Adopting a sarcastic and cynical atti-tude towards work and clients? Finding it increasingly difficult to see the positive aspects of work where even the money doesn't make you feel better? Feeling physically sick at the thought of seeing another client? Your whole day is miserable if you know you are working that night? You stop making an effort to look good? If so, you could be suffering from BURNOUT!"

The brochure offers a few ideas on how to prevent and treat this mental-health affliction. It suggests a warm bath, a manicure, aromatherapy, meditation, yoga, walking, swimming, and "even macramé and laughing."

What these tips graphically illustrate is just how risky and dehumanizing the sex industry is. What legitimate employment requires a panic button, aside from a maximum security penitentiary or a nuclear power plant? What occupation urges its employees to take a course in hostage negotiation? These tips confirm that, in the world of prostitution, there is no such thing as safe sex. It is a world prone to violence, drug addiction, degradation, disease, depression, vulnerability. Survival means being on guard at all times. This is not a glamorous occupation. It is outright dangerous in so many ways.

That, however, is not how it's presented by the lobby pressing for legalization. To the contrary, advocates of legalization present prostitution as a career choice. They speak of "empowerment," "financial rewards," "harm reduction," "health safety," and the benefits of a life selling sex to men. They bemoan the fact that prostitution is not recognized with the full rights and respect that the "profession" deserves. But who are these advocates who so staunchly defend women's right to sell their bodies and men's right to buy them?

The Happy Hooker Lobby

Their slogans are catchy: "Legalize and decriminalize!" "It's all about choice!" "Give women the right to sell their bodies!" "Prostitution can be a rewarding and fulfilling occupation!" And the clincher: "Hookers and Housewives unite!"

These women — like Carol Leigh, aka the Scarlet Harlot,

who heads COYOTE (Call Off Your Old Tired Ethics), Robyn Few, a former prostitute and executive director of SWOP-USA (Sex Workers Outreach Project), and Maxine Doogan, founder of Erotic Service Providers Union — all from San Francisco; Stacey Swimme, a self-described sex worker and founder of the Desiree Alliance in Henderson, Nevada; Valerie Scott of SPOC (Sex Professionals of Canada); and Elena Jeffreys, president of Scarlet Alliance — are a powerful voice for the happy-hooker lobby. They profess that once prostitution is legalized or decriminalized and recognized as a legitimate career path, all will be well with this maligned segment of society.

Prostitution, they insist, will become a job like any other. Johns will no longer skulk down dark alleys. The centuries-old stigma will become an anachronism. The demeaning label "whore" will be replaced with gentler terms — "sex worker," perhaps, or "provider." This new generation of sex workers will be able to hold their heads high, while ordinary men will strut into brothels on Main Street unencumbered by lingering vestiges of shame. More importantly, the lobby contends, legalization will put an end to the inherent violence, the toll of rape and even murder that remains an occupational hazard. It will save women from having to endure what they currently tolerate because they have no rights at work. In short, it will transform prostitution into a cleaner, kinder, and safer job.

But that's the extent of what they volunteer. There are many aspects of the trade that they deliberately avoid discussing publicly. They don't speak, for example, of the tragic histories of the majority of prostituted women, of how and why they ended up selling sex in the first place. There are reams of research showing that most women in prostitution were sexually and physically abused as children, that they have suffered a host of other deprivations, and that they were pushed into the flesh trade very young—on average, at fourteen.

The advocates also gloss over the undeniable links to poverty. Foreign women, especially in countries like Thailand, Cambodia, Costa Rica, Brazil, and Russia, are in the sex trade not because it's a rewarding profession or something they've aspired to as young girls. Millions of women and girls are in it because they face the crushing burden of supporting families—brothers, sisters, children, aging mothers and fathers—in nations that offer them no chance at real work and little prospects of survival if they choose to do nothing. Hundreds of thousands of women are trafficked into the sex trade every year. They are conned into believing that the jobs they've been offered in foreign lands are legitimate, only to be sucked into a dehumanizing world of slavery. The legalization camp maintains that it takes a strong stand against trafficking, but at the same time it blithely asserts that most women choose to work as prostitutes . . . that they rush into the sex trade with eyes wide open.

In truth, most women do not choose prostitution. Often, trafficked women don't speak the language of the countries where they work. The only local language they've been taught may be phrases like "sex, one hundred," "blow job, fifty." These women live in perpetual fear. They trust no one, male or female. They have been broken in—their spirits crushed—through violence, intimidation, and ever-present threats. They have been trained to smile and feign pleasure, so even if asked if they are selling sex freely, most would probably nod vigorously and lie. They also have very little contact with the outside world beyond the club, brothel, or apartment where they work, and they are usually under guard. On what basis, then, does the happy-hooker crowd conclude that these women ever had a choice?

The happy hookers don't have the answers. In fact, they often come across as glib. In an interview, Carol Leigh of COYOTE admitted that most women enter prostitution out of desperation. "Poverty, homelessness, drug addiction, not having a job opportunity, paying medical bills, paying their way through school," are some reasons she offered, as well as "curiosity." But, Leigh noted, choosing prostitution for many women is much better than flipping burgers in a fast-food joint. "Who chooses to work in McDonald's? Who chooses to work in a factory? I think this question of choice is a specious argument. It's a red herring. It holds prostitution up to a different standard than other kinds of work." Asked why she works in prostitution, Leigh said, "I basically do it to supplement my work as an artist."

The legalization lobby avoids talking about the debilitating effects of prostitution, and it steers clear of eye-opening research, such as that by Dr. Melissa Farley, a psychologist who is director of Prostitution Research and Education, a nonprofit in San Francisco. Her groundbreaking study, published in the *Journal of Trauma Practice* in 2003, was based on interviews with 854 prostituted women in nine countries — Canada, Colombia, Germany, Mexico, South Africa, Thailand, Turkey, the United States, and Zambia. Farley found that 68 percent of these women met the criteria for posttraumatic stress disorder.

"It took me many years of listening to women in prostitution to understand that the most severe damage of prostitution is not physical, it's psychological. The rates of posttraumatic stress disorder are among the highest of any group of people ever studied," Farley says. "Women in prostitution suffer extremely high rates of depression, substance abuse, dissociation, head injury, and suicide attempts." Farley also found that 89 percent wanted to escape prostitution but were forced to remain in it because they had no other options for survival.

Virtually all other research on women in prostitution — and every single interview I've had with women caught in the trade — reinforces this stark reality: most truly want to leave but can't. They believe they have no other options. Many are shackled by drug addiction, poverty, hunger, and despair. They are trapped by violence and intimidation. They despise the men they service and the pimps who control them. And they would never wish their tragic lot in life on any other woman or girl.

When the pimps are out of earshot, most prostituted women don't sugarcoat their existence. They tell it like it is. For the majority, prostitution isn't a profession, it's a prison sentence. Their lives aren't fairy tales, they're nightmares. These women pray that their next john, and the one after him, will not be a sadist, that they will not be infected with a fatal disease. They pray that one day they will escape from their hell.

Sadly, very few social commentators and journalists bother to look critically at what the happy hookers proffer. They simply fall for the spin, hook, line, and sinker. These happy hookers have had years of experience fabricating alternate realities for their clients.

Unfortunately, most pro-prostitution pundits have never visited the streets, massage parlors, or brothels to talk directly to the women the happy hookers purport to represent. They seem to buy into the romanticized version — Julia Roberts in *Pretty Woman*. Real women in prostitution know that the movie is a pathetic farce. There is no romantic side to prostitution.

Who Is Behind It?

The organizations and groups worldwide advocating legalized prostitution may be small in number, but they are unrelenting and vociferous shills for the sex industry. There are the well-known groups: COYOTE in San Francisco; SWOP in nine U.S. states; SPOC in Toronto; Scarlet Alliance in Australia; and the Red Thread in Amsterdam. But that's just the tip of the iceberg. There are also numerous pro-prostitution groups whose names give the impression that their raison d'être is health or human rights, but legalization of prostitution is one of their key objectives. There's PACE (Prostitution Alternative Counseling and Education) in Vancouver; CARAM (Coordination of Action Research on AIDS and Mobility) in Cambodia; TAMPEP (European Network for HIV/STI Prevention and Health Promotion among Migrant Sex Workers) in Austria, Italy, Germany, and the Netherlands; and GAATW (Global Alliance Against Traffic in Women), which boasts a worldwide network of ninety non-governmental organizations and is headquartered in Thailand.

Although these groups speak loudly advocating for the legalization of prostitution and garner a great deal of the media attention, the truth is they represent a very small minority of prostituted women. The vast majority of those caught up in the flesh trade have no voice. They have been made well aware of the consequence of daring to speak out.

There is another huge pro-prostitution group that is too timid to speak out, but for good reason. Conspicuously absent at media events where the happy hookers strut their stuff is the force at the epicenter of the trade — the johns who drive it. Where are the men who are the sole reason for the existence of prostitution? Where are the johns on whose account the flesh trade is flourishing, like at no other time in history? Why are they not out in public presenting their case? They are, after all, the ones who expect the unfettered right to rent women's bodies. Why are they hiding behind the (mini)skirts of the happy hookers?

That there is no lobby of johns suits them just fine. They prefer anonymity. They know full well that their hobby is not universally accepted, and that coming out of the johns' closet is risky. If someone else — preferably women — shoulders the burden of the fight for legalization, then so much the better. Johns recognize a gift when they see one — and that's exactly what they're getting, on a platinum platter.

So who is behind the legalization lobby? Who is financing their organizations? Who is pulling their strings, and why? Take a peek into the shadows and you find pimps, strip club owners, princes of porn. They salivate for the day when, with the swift slam of a gavel, legalization will give legitimacy to their work. They are the ones making truckloads of cash on the backs of prostituted women, and they stand to profit even more wherever and whenever legalization takes hold. Once the floodgates are thrown open, these sleazy bottom feeders plan to morph into respectable entrepreneurs, operating legitimate business venues with no more worry of prosecution or arrest.

Legalized Bliss

In its attempts to persuade decision makers, the pro-prostitution lobby loves to talk about any country or state that has legalized the sex trade. The proponents frequently cite Germany, the Netherlands, and several states in Australia, painting them as sexual nirvanas. The benefits are plenty, the happy hookers insist: harm reduction, health safety, better working conditions, even unions. They credit legalization with cleaning up the trade, causing the extinction of the reviled pimp and the exodus of organized crime, and they rave about how it has put an end to the risky street scene by creating legal brothels that are better able to protect prostituted women. Most importantly, they laud legalization for bringing *dignity* to women in the trade.

The reality, however, is quite different. In every country that has legalized prostitution, the experiment has been a colossal failure. All legalization has done is exacerbate every despicable and dangerous facet of the industry.

Legalization has led to a dramatic increase — not decrease — in the involvement of organized crime. Prostitution is a multi-billion-dollar-a-year enterprise, and organized crime syndicates are not about to jump ship when a government decides to make their once-nefarious endeavors legal. In Germany, the Netherlands, and Australia, police have confirmed that organized crime is still heavily involved in the trade. Nor are the pimps about to pack up their bags and search for another line of work. They still control most of the women and girls. The only difference is that they are now legitimate "sex facilitators."

In fact, the situation in Amsterdam — often vaunted as a fairy tale sexual paradise — has turned into a fiasco. Seven years after legalization, Mayor Job Cohen lamented that a key aim of the policy — ridding the sex trade of criminals — has turned out to be a miserable failure. "The legalization of prostitution did not bring about what many had hoped," Cohen admitted at a press conference in the red-light district in December 2007. "We are still faced with distressing situations in which women are being exploited. It is high time for a thorough evaluation of the Prostitution Act."

Cohen conceded that the sex industry continues to be dominated by organized crime and rife with money laundering, trafficking, exploitation, and drug abuse. "We want in part to reverse it, especially in regard to the exploitation of women in the sex industry. We have seen in the last years that trafficking in women is becoming more, so in this respect the legalizing of prostitution didn't work out." The mayor also announced that he had ordered the curtain drawn on fifty-one of the infamous windows where prostituted women are put on display, nearly naked, for all to ogle as they walk down the street. And several sex clubs and brothels were closed because of direct links to organized crime.

Also in December 2007, the Dutch government offered a verdict of its own in the form of a disquieting report, *Prostitution in the Netherlands since the Lifting of the Brothel Ban on Oct. 1, 2000*. Researchers interviewed 354 prostituted women and found that their "emotional well-being . . . has declined between 2001 and 2006 with regard to all measured aspects." According to the study, "the extent of distress has become higher, and the use of sedatives has increased." The study found that forced prostitution, while difficult to quantify, is still a chilling fact of life in the Netherlands, and noted that, while it is possible that brothel operators use coercion, "it is mainly used by pimps operating in the background shadows.

"Pimps are still a very common phenomenon," the study acknowledged. "Prostitutes with pimps are primarily working behind windows, as escorts, and from home. These are the easiest sectors for pimps to keep an eye on prostitutes. In the context of the combat against the exploitation of involuntary prostitution, it is worrisome that there seems to be no decrease in the number of prostitutes with pimps."

Three months later, the Dutch government announced a series of measures to better control the trade. One key move is the criminalization of "visiting prostitutes" who are not officially licensed as sex workers. Even more controversial is its policy to compel prostitutes to be registered in a national database "before they may offer sexual services." According to a statement released by the Ministry of Justice, "There are still too many problems in the prostitution sector, including human trafficking." Women in the trade will now need to provide authorities with a phone number and fixed address. Johns, for their part, will be required to ask for proof of registration before paying for a service in order to avoid prosecution for purchasing sex from an unregistered prostitute.

In December 2008, Dutch authorities announced that they were shutting down half the brothels in Amsterdam in a bid to drive organized crime from the city center. Deputy Mayor

Lodewijk Asscher said the move was taken to stop the city from being a "free zone" for criminals. "Money laundering, extortion, and human trafficking are things you do not see on the surface, but they are hurting people and the city. We want to fight this." The city council cited indications that some red light businesses serve as a cover for organized crime, involving drugs and the forcible trafficking of women into the sex trade. The new measures aim to reduce the number of sex windows from 482 to 243, along with a number of peep show and sex show venues.

The Netherlands is not alone. Germany is also reevaluating its 2002 move to legalize prostitution. The government now admits that legalization has created a minefield for police in investigating and prosecuting trafficking. In early 2007, Ursula von der Leyen, Federal Minister for Family Affairs, Senior Citizens, Women and Youth in the cabinet of Chancellor Angela Merkel, conceded that attempts to improve the lives of prostituted women by giving them access to health care, social security, and pensions were floundering badly. "The possibilities in practice are almost never used," she told reporters. "The prostitution law has only achieved part of its goal," she said, adding that health and hygiene conditions have not improved.

But von der Leyen, a member of the conservative Christian Democratic Party, asserted that the government was not about to turn back the clock and make prostitution illegal. "We want to rigorously go after the criminal element surrounding prostitution." That includes prosecuting johns who use women that have been forced into prostitution, she said. "If the prostitute speaks no German and has bruises on her body then the client has to assume this is forced prostitution. He can no longer say, 'I didn't notice.'"

In May 2008, a German Ministry of Justice spokesperson confirmed that the government was drafting a law to clamp down on forced prostitution. The new regulations would make it a crime for a john to ignore signs of duress on a woman he pays for sex.

Another concern voiced by von der Leyen was that leaving the trade is still too difficult for women who want to do so. She stressed that a major goal of the government must be to "encourage prostitutes to get out of the field." Like the Netherlands and Australia, Germany promised to offer an exit strategy for women who want out. In all three countries, however, the offer never materialized in any remotely significant way. In the Netherlands, the government was urged by parliament in 2004 "to stimulate or facilitate exit programs," but three years later only 6 percent of municipalities confirmed that "attention was being given to the possibilities for prostitutes to get out of prostitution."

Far more troubling is the fact that in each of these nations, despite legalization, illegal brothels sprouted like mushrooms after a summer rain and quickly outnumbered legal establishments by a ratio of three and four to one. In 1984 the Victoria state government in Australia legalized brothels in an effort to regulate the industry. Mayhem ensued. Peter Richardson, president of the brothel-owners association in Victoria, complained at a sex-industry conference in May 1991 that legal brothels "have come under enormous financial pressure — all sixty-four of them — through taxation, health regulations, work care, payroll tax, insurance, and a myriad of other charges." According to Richardson, "Legalization introduced trading hour restrictions, room controls and a cap on the number of employees that could be on the premises at any one time. This has created a . . . situation where there are sixty-four permits, an estimated 6,000 sex workers in Melbourne and only 2,000 sex workers . . . required in legal brothels. The remaining 4,000 sex workers are now seeking employment within the illegal sex industry where there are no health restrictions, age restrictions or working permit restrictions. Illegal brothels, massage parlors and hand relief joints have been allowed to trade with impunity."

More than a decade later, the situation had deteriorated even further. An investigative media report by Victoria's *Age* cited police and the legal brothel industry as putting the number of illegal brothels in Melbourne at four hundred — compared to one hundred legal — in 2002.

In the Netherlands, as well, much of the trade has gone underground, often through escorts working out of hotel and motel rooms, and private and mobile homes. The trade has also gotten more creative. The 2007 Dutch study notes that there are a number of other sectors that are virtually impossible to police, such as couples clubs, sauna clubs, and massage parlors. What the couples clubs and sauna clubs have in common, it says, is that "Prostitution services are often not officially provided in these businesses. Both prostitutes and prostitute's clients officially enter as paying visitors of the club, and the operator has no involvement whatsoever with what the visitors then agree and do with one another. The enforcement agencies have no grounds whatsoever to check, for example, the documents of the prostitutes who have entered the club as a sauna visitor."

The Link to Trafficking

Perhaps the most disturbing lesson is that wherever prostitution has been legalized, the trafficking of women and girls has continued unabated or increased. Police raids on legal and illegal brothels, crackdowns on escort services, and street sweeps have borne this out time and time again. Meanwhile, the international debate on trafficking rages on, and in a calculated move to deflect international concern over the growing global crisis of trafficking in human beings, proponents of legalization, spearheaded by GAATW, began pushing for trafficking and migration for work — specifically, prostitution — to be dealt with as totally separate issues.

Yet study after study unequivocally demonstrates that trafficking in humans and prostitution are inextricably entwined. The U.S. State Department estimates that eight hundred thousand people are trafficked around the world every year. Upwards of 80 percent of those are women and girls, and the vast majority is targeted for the flesh trade.

Moreover, far from stemming the flow of trafficked women into prostitution, legalization has led to a stunning escalation in the number of foreign women shipped into the sex trade in Germany, the Netherlands, and Australia, and dozens of other prostitution-tolerant nations around the globe. A 2000 study by the Dutch government found that a staggering 80 percent of the twenty-five thousand sex workers in the tiny nation were foreigners. In Germany, which boasts more than two hundred thousand sex workers, foreigners make up more than 85 percent. Most of the women are imported from Russia, Ukraine, Romania, and Moldova. Huge numbers of young women are shipped from Thailand and the Philippines to Australia to meet its burgeoning demand for more and more female bodies. These numbers should trigger alarm bells. Most women from impoverished nations cannot afford the airfare or documentation to travel abroad, nor do they have the business acumen or language skills to set themselves up as independent sex workers in foreign countries. It should be obvious that they have not chosen their lot.

There is only one reason for the explosion of trafficked women and girls into the flesh markets of these well-heeled nations: brothel owners can't find enough local women to supply the ever-increasing demand. German, Dutch, and Australian women are not lining up in droves to enter the trade. Most have real jobs. They don't want to shed their clothes for up to a dozen men a day. They prefer to focus on careers in the true sense of the word, not on some fantasy dreamed up by a drove of happy hookers who now make a better living peddling deception.

Child Prostitution

Another ill-kept promise of legalization is the protection it claims it would offer to the most vulnerable children. Legalization was supposed to deal a decisive blow to child prostitution. Instead it has led to an alarming spike in the number of children trafficked or forced into the sex trade in all countries where prostitution is legal or accepted. In 1998, an organization called ECPAT (End

Child Prostitution, Child Pornography and Trafficking of Children for Sexual Purposes) collected information from 471 government and nongovernment agencies working with children in Australia. The findings were shocking. More than 3,100 Australian children aged twelve to eighteen had sold sex to survive, and Victoria, the first state to legalize prostitution, had the highest number in the nation at 1,200.

In the Netherlands, which has become an international hotbed for pedophiles and producers of porn, police believe the number of minors involved in prostitution is about two thousand, the majority from Eastern Europe and Africa.

Just about anything goes in the booming sex market of Germany — except children. However, German sex tourists simply take a short car ride to the Czech Republic. The Czech-German border region is reputed as Europe's biggest brothel. Along the Czech motorways, children wait by supermarkets, restaurants, and gas stations to be rented for sex; often their pimps are their parents or older siblings.

Why the trend? Because of an escalation in demand. And why the demand? Out of concern for health — the john's health. A segment of the johns who seek out children do so because of pedophilic fantasies. But many who seek out children aren't pedophiles. They just believe that the younger the child, the less chance they have of contracting HIV/AIDS.

Off the Mean Streets

The pro-legalization lobby maintains that a legal sex trade will dramatically reduce violence against the women in prostitution —

their term, "harm reduction." If there's any job in desperate need of "harm reduction," it is prostitution. There is no other activity — other than war — in which so many women are routinely beaten, raped, maimed, and killed each and every year. In 1985, the Fraser Committee report on prostitution and pornography found that women in prostitution in Canada suffered a mortality rate forty times the national average. A comprehensive U.S. study in 2004 funded by the National Institutes of Health and conducted by the *American Journal of Epidemiology* found that prostitution had a homicide rate higher than that of any other occupation. In fact, the study concluded these women are fifty-one times more likely to be killed than women in the second most dangerous job — working in a liquor store.

It's no secret that prostituted women are easy targets for violent johns worldwide. However, the prostitution lobby professes that, if legalized and done right, selling sex to total strangers can be a much safer endeavor. Advocates claim that legalization will remove women from the streets — where the risk is greatest — and shuffle them into a more civil environment: regulated brothels.

Yet although it is true that women working in brothels don't face as great a risk of being killed as those working the streets, several international studies clearly show that women in brothels are routinely beaten and forced into performing unwanted sexual acts. This is true regardless of whether the brothels are legal or underground. Why else would Australia's health and safety authorities advise women working there to ensure that they have easy access to panic buttons?

Just as importantly, the argument that legalization improves safety hinges on the assumption that the street scene will abate.

Yet in Germany, the Netherlands, and Australia, street prostitution — legal and illegal — flourishes like never before. The pimps who control the strolls quickly realized that the police were disinclined to investigate complaints once the government legalized the trade. For cops, it's not worth the effort to wade through the quagmire of figuring out what is legal and what is not, whether a woman is trafficked or otherwise forced, and the nature of the agreement between the provider and her client. As legalization confusion sets in, the only dilemma for the pimps is how to replenish the supply for the johns.

The harm-reduction argument also assumes that the women working the streets can simply be absorbed by the brothels — another fallacy. Many women on the streets are homeless and addicted to drugs; owners of legalized brothels are not about to touch them. The brothels are now required to ensure that the women they hire produce a valid health card showing that they are registered and medically fit. And many of these women are not women at all, but girls who have been pressed into service at a young age. The owners of legalized brothels avoid them as well. Finally, there are simply not enough spaces in legalized brothels to accommodate the women out on the streets. Those who do get in — taking the happy hooker's line at face value — are among the lucky few.

What is far more disconcerting is that the legalization forces seem satisfied with reduction in harm. The reality is that their solutions are like putting a wad of gum on a broken water main. Why are they not demanding the *elimination* of harm? Because the advocates know full well that women in prostitution will never be free from violence and abuse. The flesh trade is a dangerous business. If politicians and human-rights workers are really committed to reducing harm, why don't they support programs that help women get out of prostitution and into jobs where they won't have to fear the constant threat of being assaulted, raped, maimed, or murdered?

The Condom Solution

Safeguarding public health is the number-one hot button legalization proponents use to solicit support for their cause. What better way to get the stamp of approval from a frightened public than to scare them into action by invoking the scourge of HIV/AIDS?

These advocates praise the health systems of Germany and the Netherlands for carrying out routine medical checks on women in prostitution. Yet the check-ups are carried out only on the women, not on the johns, who may themselves be infected. Why don't the legalization forces demand that johns be required to undergo monthly health tests and carry a medical card declaring them free of STDs? Why should women be the ones forced to play Russian roulette every time a john struts in for servicing? The legalization lobby professes that they want to empower women in prostitution. So why do the johns continue to hold the reigns by remaining socially and legally invisible — and unaccountable? What the health push is really about is cleaning up the sex industry for the clients. No john wants to contract a disease, and certainly no husband or boyfriend wants to pass on gonorrhea or crabs to his partner. No, indeed. Sexually transmitted diseases — and the fear of contracting them — are bad for business.

But the health checks are only for the *legal* side of the trade. The illegal market, which is up to four times larger, is not subject to any kind of inspection, health or otherwise. With sex available so freely, the competition for clients is fierce; for pimps, health issues are secondary to profit. Moreover, a john is not likely to stand at a door with his pants around his ankles waiting to be inspected by a "sex provider" with a flashlight. He will take his erection and his money elsewhere. Those controlling the trade understand this. In fact, skimping on health care gives them a competitive edge.

How, then, does legalization improve health and safety for prostituted women and the public at large? So far, the advocates have offered nothing more than lip service; they have yet to offer a convincing answer.

With a Little Help from the United Nations

On August 13, 2001, the World Health Organization waded into the highly charged public-health debate on HIV/AIDS with a stunning announcement on prostitution. At an international conference in Vietnam, the WHO recommended that prostitution be decriminalized as a way to stem the tide of HIV/AIDS infections worldwide. In a statement, the UN-funded organization noted as part of its reasoning that the sex industry in Asia was expanding rapidly and that most commercial sex in the region was believed to be taking place without condoms.

Dr. Gilles Poumerol, the WHO's regional adviser on sexually transmitted diseases and AIDS in Manila, explained at a
1999 news conference that decriminalization of prostitution and
drug use would make prevention easier by not driving high-risk
behavior underground. "We think it's time to introduce this
effective intervention all over Asia. It is certainly an emergency
. . . men who visit sex workers should have no choice — they
should wear condoms."

WHO heavyweights effectively wrote off as nothing more
than whores the hundreds of thousands of women and girls
forced every year into the sex trade in the impoverished nations
of Asia and Africa. They saw the solution as no more complicated than dispensing packets of condoms. They would leave it
up to the women to convince the testosterone-driven johns who
used and abused them to don the latex. The WHO brass went so
far as to suggest that prostituted Asian and African women use
their feminine wiles to convince their clients that wearing a condom is erotic and sexy.

The WHO failed to understand that the very request to wear
a condom can get a woman beaten or even killed. A lot of johns
don't like wearing condoms. They boast about going "bare back."
The pressure on women to go without is unrelenting. In one U.S.
study, almost half of the women reported that men frequently
demanded sex without condoms, and almost 75 percent said that
johns offered to pay more if they didn't have to wear latex. And
extra money is a tremendous incentive for pimps.

The WHO, whose objective should be to get these women
the resources and training they need to obtain good jobs, was instead following in the footsteps of a sister agency, the Interna-

tional Labor Organization. In 1998 the ILO, the labor arm of the UN, had called for the recognition of the sex industry as legitimate employment on the grounds that prostituted women would benefit from the workers' rights and improved working conditions that it assumed would follow. The ILO's recommendations, set out in a report entitled *The Sex Sector: The Economic and Social Bases of Prostitution in Southeast Asia*, covered Indonesia, Malaysia, the Philippines, and Thailand — four impoverished nations that are prime targets of international sex tourists. The ILO noted that prostitution in the region has developed into a highly lucrative business that not only offers considerable employment but also contributes significantly to economic growth.

"The scale of prostitution has been enlarged to an extent where we can justifiably speak of a commercial sex sector that is integrated into the economic, social and political life of these countries," the ILO study asserted, adding that "the sex business has assumed the dimensions of an industry and has directly or indirectly contributed in no small measure to employment, national income, and economic growth."

The report estimated that the sex industry's contribution to these countries' gross domestic product ranges from 2 percent in Indonesia to 14 percent in Thailand. It also estimated that Thai sex workers in the cities remit nearly $300 million annually to families in rural areas. Prostitution in Thailand, it found, had produced between $22.5 and $27 billion in income from 1993 to 1995. In Indonesia, where brothels are tolerated by officials, the yearly income from the sex sector ranges from $1.2 to $3.3 billion. As to the number of women in the trade, the report estimated that, in Thailand, it was 200,000 to 300,000; in

Indonesia 140,000 to 230,000; in Malaysia 43,000 to 142,000; and in the Philippines 400,000 to 500,000.

The ILO maintained that not only would the recognition of prostitution lead to improved working conditions, it would improve the health of women in the trade and offer them the opportunity to form unions. However, the UN agency craftily straddled the fence as to whether these countries should legalize prostitution, which begs the question: how can prostitution be recognized as legitimate work without legal recognition?

Within minutes of its release, the report was slammed by many women's organizations as a demeaning blow to the dignity of women. For decades, unions and women's-rights groups have battled for gender equality and fought tirelessly to put a stop to sexual harassment in the workplace. Clearly, what happens in prostitution is sexual harassment at its toxic worse. Yet here was the ILO recommending that the flesh trade be recognized officially as legitimate work in a corner of the world where the effects of globalization have had a particularly devastating effect on the women and children forced into prostitution.

For the worldwide push by the sex industry to legalize prostitution, the WHO and ILO recommendations are worth their weight in gold.

Decriminalization vs Legalization

Thankfully, there are a handful of nations where the legalization camp is facing tough resistance — Canada, the United States, Norway, and the United Kingdom, to name a few. In these countries, the lobbyists change their vocabulary. They replace "legalization" with the more benign "decriminalization." They argue that prostituted women are victims and should not be treated as the perpetrators of crimes.

I agree with that.

They also argue that prostituted women are targeted by police and revictimized time and time again by an unfair and biased justice system, while most johns get to zip up their pants and disappear into the night.

I agree with that as well.

Studies across North America show that of the more than one hundred thousand prostitution-related arrests each year, 90 percent of them are of women and girls. In Boston, eleven women in prostitution are arrested for every one john. In Chicago, nine women are arrested for every client, and in New York City the ratio is six to one. It's as if there is a conspiracy of silence among men — a brotherhood — to let each other off the hook. But slowly, very slowly, that projohn bias is showing signs of weakening in places where authorities are educated and sensitized to the real issues in prostitution.

Yet the decriminalization proposal put forward by the legalization camp is nothing more than a smoke screen — deliberate obfuscation. Decriminalization without consequences for johns is de facto legalization. The consequence strongly supported by those who oppose prostitution is to criminalize only the john's side of the transaction — the act of buying sex. This approach could be what finally deals a serious blow to the global market in women's bodies. But that is the last thing the legalization advocates want, because it is the one thing that could hurt them — and the sex industry they represent — the most.

*   *   *

UNDER ANY GUISE, the negatives of legalization far outweigh the positives. Given the inherent violence in prostitution and the degradation and humiliation visited daily on vast numbers of prostituted women and girls, it is difficult to fathom why anyone—indeed any government—would support legalizing a trade for the few who purportedly choose it when the overwhelming majority never chose it, definitely don't want it, and desperately want out of it.

It is folly to buy into the argument that prostitution empowers women. If anything, it imprisons them, and legalization will exploit even more women and girls. Legalization guarantees that those who control the trade will hunt down more unwilling bodies to satisfy a demand that appears insatiable. It will empower men more than ever. Legalization sends a message that it's okay to purchase women for sex, to impose their sexual will via the almighty dollar. With legalization, the state effectively becomes a pimp, padding the nation's coffers with proceeds from sex tourism and taxation of exploited women. Real empowerment will occur when women do not have to rent any part of their bodies to survive. The legalization of prostitution is in fact a gift to johns.

15

CHARGE
THE JOHNS

The law is a concrete and tangible expression of the belief that in Sweden women and children are not for sale.
—GUNILLA EKBERG, SPECIAL ADVISOR ON PROSTITUTION AND
TRAFFICKING FOR THE GOVERNMENT OF SWEDEN

NIGHT, AND ONLY FOUR WOMEN are lurking in the lonely shadows of Stockholm's notorious main drag for prostitution. For decades, Malmskillnadsgatan, a street in the heart of Stockholm, Sweden's capital, flashed red when the sun set. Scores of women in microminis, plunging necklines, and stiletto heels paced up and down while platoons of johns cruised by. But with the toll of the clock ushering in New Year's Day 1999, all that changed. Now most men glance furtively at the few streetwalkers, too afraid to even ask, How much? These days, the best policy for men on the prowl for sex is to get a new girlfriend or reignite an old flame.

In a world where nation after nation is contemplating legalization as a quick fix for the myriad ills that plague prostitution,
Sweden was the first country to have had the courage and resolve
to turn against the tide. After years of research, study, and sometimes acrimonious debate, the Swedish government flatly rejected
the notion that prostitution is a choice, that it is legitimate work,
and that it is something women, girls, and boys *want* to do. It
concluded that the majority of people caught up in the flesh trade
are victims who are economically, racially, or ethnically marginalized and oppressed.

So in 1999 Sweden embarked on a daring course in an effort
to curb prostitution and stem trafficking from nearby Russia,
Lithuania, and Estonia. The government decriminalized the selling of sex, ensuring that women would no longer face arrest and
prosecution for prostitution. At the same time, it made buying
sex a crime, thereby holding johns criminally responsible for the
sexual exploitation of women in prostitution.

According to Jonas Trolle, an inspector with the Stockholm
police unit charged with combating prostitution, "The goal is to
criminalize the demand side of the equation, the johns, rather
than put emotionally and physically imperiled women behind
bars." Detective inspector Kajsa Wahlberg, head of the national
unit charged with combating trafficking of women, adds, "We
don't have a problem with prostitutes. We have a problem with
men who buy sex."

Sweden's Sex Purchase Law, or *Sexkopslagen*, doesn't mince
words. The preamble clearly states that "In Sweden prostitution
is regarded as an aspect of male violence against women and
children. It is officially acknowledged as a form of exploitation

of women and children and constitutes a significant social problem. . . . Gender equality will remain unattainable so long as men buy, sell, and exploit women and children by prostituting them."

To make matters more difficult for johns — known in Sweden as *torsks*, which translates literally as "cod" and is also slang for "loser" — the government decided in 2001 to get even tougher. The Parliamentary Sexual Crimes Committee discovered that a loophole in the law was being exploited. Guys getting together for a stag party would rent a hooker as a send-off for the groom, and corporate executives were occasionally providing an escort for preferred, out-of-town clients or business associates. Since the beneficiary of these services was not the purchaser, they escaped prosecution, as did their sponsors, who weren't purchasing sex for themselves. So Sweden cracked down on these situations. The middlemen who purchase a sexual service for someone else now face a fine and a possible jail term of up to six months.

When Sweden first began researching prostitution, it discovered that every eighth man older than eighteen had purchased sex at home or abroad. Studies also found that Swedish johns came from all income classes. Most were or had once been legally married or living in common-law relationships, and they were often fathers.

In determining how to respond to the problem, the government and public considered what kind of society they wanted. Two competing visions emerged. The first was legalization. The government could have "succumbed to resignation" and accepted the proposition that prostitution is "inevitable, inescapable, and necessary," Gunilla Ekberg recalls, "something that always will exist and therefore should be accepted, because men need it, or women choose it, or because prostitution is the 'oldest profession.'" This is a vision that "calls for women to be licensed as 'sex workers,' forces them to undergo health checks . . . allows for procuring and legal brothels, and assumes we can reduce the harm through tolerance zones, safe-sex programs, and safer streets."

The second vision called for the complete rejection of the notion that some women and children should be used as commodities that can be bought and sold.

Sweden opted for the latter, deciding that the only correct course was to work toward eliminating prostitution and creating a society based on gender equality, a society in which prostitution is seen as incompatible with the dignity and worth of the human being and the equal rights of women and men. "The law is a concrete and tangible expression of the belief that in Sweden women and children are not for sale," Ekberg explains. "It effectively dispels men's self-assumed right to buy women and children for prostitution and questions the idea that men should be able to express their sexuality in any form and anytime."

Ekberg, a former social worker and now special advisor on prostitution and trafficking for the Swedish government, has worked with women in prostitution for more than fifteen years. For her, prostitution demanded firm action; there is no doubt in her mind that most women caught up in the sex trade are not there by choice. "The situation of being in prostitution is the same as being a battered woman. The violence that she experiences is normalized. To live in that situation and to find dignity in being abused, many women will of course say that they have chosen this and that it's work. I have met many women in many countries who have claimed that, but when they were given the option of leaving prostitution and had a chance to look back, they could see what other life they had a right to. I think the best thing we can do for our sisters . . . is to support them to get out of it, not to reduce the harm and try to pretend that one of the worst forms of sexual violence in the world is something that is benign and something a woman chooses."

It has been a decade since Sweden passed the Sex Purchase Law, and results have been impressive. "Criminalization has meant the number of men who buy sexual services has fallen, along with the recruitment of women and girls," says Ekberg. That's because johns know the consequences. This, in turn, has led to what Swedish authorities describe as a dramatic drop in the number of people involved in prostitution. The government estimates that around three thousand women were involved in the sex trade before the law. Within four years that number more than halved. Street prostitution, as reflected in the meager action on Malmskillnadsgatan, is only 60 percent of what it used to be.

And there are clear indications that the law is having a direct effect on the trafficking of women into Sweden. According to the Swedish national police, the number of trafficked women is now as low as five hundred, quite a small number when compared to Sweden's Scandinavian neighbors. In Norway, Denmark, and Finland, which each have half the population of Sweden, it is estimated that the number of trafficking victims are 5,000, 7,000, and 12,000 a year, respectively.

The result of this dramatic drop, Detective Wahlberg notes,

is that organized crime has decided that Sweden is simply not worth the hassle. "They are calculating profits, costs, and marketing, and the risk of getting caught," she explains. "We're trying to create a bad market for these activities."

Police witnessed the frustration firsthand in wiretapped conversations recorded during criminal investigations, in which pimps and traffickers repeatedly expressed dismay over the difficulty of setting up shop in Sweden. One of the key reasons cited: Swedish men who want to purchase sex are too afraid of being arrested. To compensate, traffickers have increased their operations in neighboring countries.

But change in Sweden wasn't quick or easy. As with many laws, implementation was a challenge. It became obvious after the law's first anniversary that not much had really changed. The police — most staunch believers in the boys' club — weren't keen on enforcing legislation that threatened traditional male values. The same held true for prosecutors and judges. Chasing down johns simply wasn't a priority.

"Initially, when the law came into force, these groups were very critical of the legislation, saying it was impossible to find evidence, asking how they should prosecute, and so forth," Ekberg recounted.

In response, the government initiated a series of intensive workshops in 2003 aimed at educating cops, prosecutors, and judges about prostitution, the victims, the rationale behind the legislation, and how to implement the law. Within a year, there was a 300 percent increase in arrests. From January 1999 to December 2007, the country saw 1,648 men arrested and charged. As of 2006, more than 500 have been convicted or have pleaded guilty to purchasing sex. The oldest john collared under the law was seventy-two, and the youngest a mere sixteen. Only one man, a repeat offender, has been sentenced to prison. Fines under *Sexkopslagen* are based on the income of a john. The largest — $11,750 — was handed out to a CEO who had an annual salary of $241,700.

Some of the johns were captured on surveillance cameras as they entered and left apartments being used for prostitution. Within weeks of the visit, police would fire off a letter to the *torsk*. Those letters — stuffed in envelopes embossed with the police logo — have triggered fierce family confrontations and have led to some humiliating face time before the country's no-nonsense judges.

An apartment building in a suburb of Stockholm was placed under surveillance as part of an investigation into a potential pimping operation: while surfing the Internet, police had happened upon a twenty-five-year-old Estonian woman named Lia offering sexual services from the building. A fifty-two-year-old man was videotaped arriving in his Volvo at 5:47 p.m. Twenty-three minutes later he emerged with a satisfied grin. Several months later, a white envelope arrived at his home with *Polismyndigheten i Stockholms län* (Stockholm County Police) embossed on the top left-hand corner. For the married father of two, it was the beginning of a nightmare. In court he vehemently denied buying sex from Lia, claiming he only went to see her "to talk." The judge didn't buy it. The *torsk* was found guilty of procurement and fined twenty-five hundred dollars.

With the police finally on board, the Swedish government shifted its focus to persuading women to get out of the trade. A key element of the legislation provides an avenue of escape by offering social support to help these women reshape their lives. The Stockholm social-service agency Prostitutionsenheten reported that, of the 130 women it had been in contact with from 2000 to 2003, 78 had left prostitution, many of whom pointed to the legislation as "an important incentive" to their seeking help.

"Women tell me that the law was the first time somebody cared about them . . . [they] actually saw this was a form of violence against women and not something that they wanted to be in and that it made them contact social workers to leave," Ekberg says.

But not everyone in Sweden is a supporter. There are a handful of vocal detractors. Petra Östergren, a Swedish writer and social commentator, points out that most prostituted women she has interviewed "reject the idea that there is something intrinsically wrong with their profession, or that they should be subjected to therapy or retrained."

Östergren maintains that women in prostitution find the law "paradoxical, illogical, and discriminatory" and that it "further obstructs their work and exposes them to danger." She says that women working on the streets in some bigger cities claim there is now "a greater percentage of perverted customers" and that "the nice and kind customers have disappeared." A perverted john, she explains, is someone who demands "more violent forms of sex," like "sex with feces and urine," and who is "more prone to humiliate, degrade, and violate" the woman and refuses to use condoms.

According to Östergren, "the sex workers say it is now harder for them to assess the clients," and the johns are "more stressed and scared." Negotiations take place quickly and outdoors, which, she maintains, increases the likelihood of a woman ending up with a dangerous client. "Since there are fewer customers on the streets, many women who sell sex in order to finance a drug habit can no longer refuse these customers, as they were previously able to."

Other critics argue that the law has pushed the sex trade underground, making life far more difficult and dangerous for prostituted women. Ekberg disagrees. "The prostitution industry never operates completely underground. At the most, it is out of sight of the general population. So if you get rid of street prostitution, it's not that it's gone underground. It's just that regular people don't see it."

Despite the odd voice or two coming out against it, public support for the *Sexköpslagen* is overwhelming. Three polls conducted between 1999 and 2002 found that approximately 80 percent of the population supports the law and the principles behind it. Of the small number that wants it repealed, the majority are men.

To get its message out, the Swedish government has spearheaded major public-awareness campaigns against sexual exploitation. Sex education programs aimed at changing attitudes are held in high schools, local community centers, and sports clubs. The military is also targeted, and soldiers are warned that the law applies to Swedish peacekeepers stationed anywhere around the world. Should a peacekeeper buy a local or trafficked woman where he is stationed, he will be arrested, sent home, and brought to trial.

As part of one program, more than sixty thousand high

school students have been shown *Lilja 4-Ever*, a brutal and disturbing film about a sixteen-year-old who is a victim of sex trafficking from Estonia to Sweden. The one-day seminar also permits the students to discuss gender equality, rape, pornography, sexual violence, attitudes toward girls, and the exploitation of girls on the Internet. And the students are responding.

In one embarrassing incident in April 2004, a group of high-school students on a "friendship mission" to Mombassa, Kenya, got worked up when informed by locals that their teachers were acting inappropriately. So the teenagers grabbed a video camera and followed their chaperones into the red-light district, where they taped them chatting briefly with some women and then disappearing into a brothel. "We went to Kenya to help these people and then our teachers exploited them. It was disgusting," one of the students said. On returning to Sweden, the students went to their headmaster demanding action against the wayward teachers. When he refused, they made the videotape public.

The Swedish government has also launched a poster campaign. Ekberg says she wanted a campaign that "wasn't like the usual poster campaigns," the kind featuring "a woman in high heels, short skirt with a décolletage, standing in the twilight at night, leaning over a car." In her posters, there's something inside the car, but "we never see the something," she explains. "We wanted to take the guy out of the car and show, for once, that it is a fact: the root cause of prostitution is that men buy.

"These posters were gigantic," she says. "We had them all over Sweden, in bus shelters, on subways, on trams, wherever you can think of. One says 'Time to flush the johns out of the Baltic' because . . . we wanted to stop men from traveling to the Baltic countries."

Another poster shows the faces of everyday johns. The government had a difficult time recruiting male models, because "nobody really wanted to hang around Sweden and be pointed out as a possible buyer." In the end, Ekberg managed to persuade some colleagues — a "political adviser and some state secretaries" — to pose.

The message is sinking in. Jenny Sonesson, secretary-general of the Liberal Party's women's movement, says that the key objective was to reinforce social stigmas about buying sex so that men who might otherwise frequent a brothel or the street would think twice before visiting prostitutes in Sweden or abroad. "Swedish men are now ashamed about buying sex. It's just not socially accepted," she says.

But tell that to some of the judges. Among convicted johns are four of them, including Supreme Court Justice Leif Thorsson, who paid a fine of more than $6,700 in 2005. Police discovered Thorsson's phone number in a young male prostitute's cell phone, along with text messages from the judge. The incident caused a furor in Sweden when the judiciary ruled that Thorsson could keep his job and when Bo Svenson, the head of the Supreme Court, joked that Thorsson's tryst could be an advantage on the bench: "One could say that he has a deeper knowledge of the subject." Svenson later apologized for his comment.

The Swedish Association of Judges also weighed in, remarking that Thorsson's actions were not only criminal but demonstrated a severe lack of judgment from one of the more senior guardians of the law. Opinion polls showed the majority of Swedes were not taking the matter lightly. They wanted Thorsson to do the honorable thing and step down.

He continues to sit on the bench.

Following the example of its Scandinavian neighbor, Norway's government introduced a new law in April 2008 to stamp out prostitution by criminalizing johns. In proposing the bill, Norwegian justice minister Knut Storberget said, "We want to send a clear message to men that buying sex is unacceptable. Men who do it are taking part in an international crime involving human beings who are trafficked for sex.

"People are not merchandise," he added. "By criminalizing the purchase of sexual favors, Norway will become less attractive in the eye of human traffickers." The minister also noted that the government "has launched several initiatives to help as many people as possible to get out of prostitution."

In November 2008, Norway's parliament passed the law by a vote of forty-four in favor and twenty-eight against. It went into effect on January 1, 2009.

Also in November 2008, British Home Secretary Jacqui Smith announced legislation to target johns who buy sex from trafficked women. In explaining the government's rationale, Smith said: "We need to send out a message to men and to society in general that most women do not choose to be in prostitution, whereas the buyers have a free choice."

Under the proposed law, it will be a criminal offense to pay for sex with someone who is controlled for another person's gain, and johns will not be able to use the defense that they didn't know that the woman was trafficked, controlled by a pimp, or in debt to her drug dealer. Convicted johns would face a fine equaling up to $1,500 and receive a criminal record. Moreover, anyone who pays for sex knowing that the woman has been forcibly trafficked could also face rape charges, which carries a potential life sentence.

While critics argued that Britain should follow Sweden's lead, the government claimed that such a move would be "a step too far," arguing that the sex trade in Sweden was tiny compared with the scale of the problem in Britain, which has an estimated 80,000 women involved in prostitution — the majority having been trafficked from Eastern Europe, Africa, and the Far East.

Minister for Women Harriet Harman, who has spent years campaigning against prostitution, has described the flow of women brought into Britain by human traffickers as a modern slave trade and said that it only exists because men are prepared to buy sex: "So, to protect women, we must stop men buying sex from the victims of human trafficking."

16

BACK TO
SCHOOL

*Part of the problem is that these guys are jerks. They're
knuckle-dragging, bone-headed bad guys and they really
don't care if their actions hurt the women or the community.*
—MICHAEL SHIVELY, CRIMINOLOGIST

NEAR MIDNIGHT ON A FRIDAY, the deserted stroll suddenly jolts to life
with the pounding beat of rap. The music pulsates from two over-
sized speakers inside a black Honda Civic. The driver, wearing
rhinestone-studded knock-off Versace sunglasses, is bopping up
and down, trying to exude the essence of cool. It's the third time
he has circled the block, his sights set on a slinky blond in mesh
stockings, a micromini, and a red tank top. This time, the dude
pulls over to the curb.

"Hey, pretty mama! What ya doin'?" he shouts through the
rolled-down passenger-side window.

The woman looks over at him and smiles.

"Wanna go for a ride?" he asks.

"I'm working."

"Come on over here!" he insists with what he hopes is an enticing grin.

She walks over and sticks her head into the open window.

"Let's say we go for a little ride," the driver suggests.

"What do you want?"

"A little oral persuasion, if you get my meaning."

"Yeah, I get it. Fifty."

"Hey, I'm not askin' for the whole enchilada. How's about twenty?"

The woman pauses. "Forty."

"You drive a hard bargain. Get in," he says, the sexual tension palpable as he flips open his wallet.

But just as he is about to pull away, a police cruiser, roof lights flashing, races around the corner and comes to a screeching stop in front of his car.

Busted!

The hooker is a vice cop, and the john has just been stung.

THEY ARRIVE ONE AFTER THE OTHER, baseball caps pulled low over their foreheads. Many are wearing sunglasses and glance furtively up and down the street before darting into the building. They are all men, and every single one is a john. But the hour is early — a little after eight on a Saturday morning. It's not the early bird special at an Asian massage parlor. These guys, all forty-two of them, are going to school, a special kind of school named in their honor: john school.

Aside from paying for sex, this motley crew has one embarrassing experience in common: they've all been busted in nighttime street sweeps, "reverse stings" by female undercover cops posing as hookers. Today these wayward johns are in for a hefty dose of R & R, but not the usual kind. At john school in San Francisco, R & R means "reeducation and rehabilitation," as well as a whole lot of enlightenment.

Not one of them wants to be here. Their disdain is etched on their hangdog faces. But they were ordered by the court to attend or suffer a far worse consequence: a criminal record. There are no knowing nods or glances, no high fives or smirks as the men shuffle into the meeting room. Most look annoyed, not only because they've had to pay a thousand-dollar fine — a hell of a lot more than a cheap fifty-dollar blow job — but because everyone in the room knows their shame.

The six-hour course offered here is the original john school that is now being emulated in more than two dozen cities across North America. Known officially as the San Francisco First Offender Prostitution Program (FOPP), it is designed to impress upon these men that cruising the city streets for hookers is a very dumb and unmanly thing to do. If what drives them is an erection, today they are in for an ice-cold shower.

"This is stupid," one man mutters as he flops into a chair.

I try to strike up a conversation. "How did you get caught?" I ask.

"I'm watching a little porn at home, so I get a little horny and decide I want a blow job," he tells me. "I head to the Tenderloin [district] . . . and *bang*! The bitch is a cop. Now I'm out a grand. I can't believe my luck."

I scan the room, and I am somewhat surprised. Most of the men are in their thirties and forties. A couple of guys are in their twenties, and a few in their fifties. They are a microcosm of San Francisco's population: whites, Asians, Latinos, blacks. About one-third are wearing wedding bands. Most are definitely blue-collar, but there are at least a half dozen who are likely professionals. A few are actually not bad looking. Sitting toward the back and off to the sides are a half dozen particularly angry men with attitude.

Sergeant Paul Yep of the San Francisco Police Department's vice squad opens the proceedings with what's meant to be a wake-up call. "I know that it's Saturday morning and it's nice outside, but you are all fortunate to be here. If you were arrested in [nearby] Oakland, your car would have been towed and you'd have to go to court," he says. "So there will be no sleeping . . . Stay awake and finish the class."

Yep informs the men that they will be hearing from a series of speakers over the next six hours. "Some of them are going to share their personal experiences with you. You don't have to agree with anything they say, but be respectful."

First up is Assistant District Attorney Marsanne Weese from the vice-crimes division of the attorney general's office. Her talk is a forty-five minute crash course on solicitation and the law: all the things that can go awry when soliciting on the streets, through an escort service, or on the Web.

Her audience sits up and takes notice.

Weese points out that, while in most American cities first-time offenders would have to go to court, in San Francisco the aim is not to convict. "This is something we want to educate you on. What we're trying to do is inform you that this is something the state takes very seriously, and the reason it takes it seriously is because there is a lot of crime in areas where solicitation takes place."

The prosecutor goes on to describe the misdemeanor of solicitation. "My job as a district attorney is to prove the elements of a crime to a jury, and in solicitation there are only two elements I have to prove — that there was an agreement and there's the act," she explains. "In a sting operation, online or over the phone, all the police have to do is get you to agree. It's not entrapment. So when an undercover vice officer says, 'Sex for forty dollars,' and someone says yes, that's an agreement. But that's not a crime. However, when you walk with her and show her the money, that's the act. And that's all I have to prove in solicitation."

Weese also discusses how the crime of solicitation can escalate into more serious criminal charges. Most johns, she notes, tend to be under the influence when prowling the streets, which can lead to a DUI charge. Then there is the actual sex, which can result in a charge of lewd conduct in public.

But the real crimes, the ones that end up with serious prison time, happen when a john picks up a woman and something goes awry. Weese recounts a case in which a woman was badly beaten in the face. "She had gone into a laneway with a client in the Tenderloin. A few minutes pass, and the police get a call of a rape. The police catch the two in a sex act, and the prostitute tells them, 'He raped me.' So the officers arrest the solicitor, and now he's looking at rape and assault, both felony charges, and he's looking at a minimum of sixteen months in state prison. The man tells the police he didn't rape her, but the woman has injuries consistent with rape."

The john spent three months in county jail awaiting trial, and just before his court date the district attorney's office learned of an undercover drug operation that had been going on in the same area on the night of the alleged assault and rape. The street scene had been videotaped. The tape captured the john and the woman walking together and disappearing around the corner just minutes before the police were called. It also confirmed that the woman already had the injuries in question, so the charges were quickly dropped.

Weese describes another case in which police stopped a car and the woman, who "knows the deal," claimed she was dragged inside. "Now he's looking at kidnapping."

The men take all this in.

She warns them about their own safety, citing violent pimps and women who assault and rob johns. "They know you're soliciting, and they know you've got cash," she says. "In the last nine months, we've had a lot more assaults and robberies [of johns by pimps]."

She has her audience's attention, but the biggest wake-up call is still to come. The assistant district attorney notes that, in her jurisdiction, if a john gets caught with a minor, " 'I didn't know' will not be taken as an excuse. You will be charged and prosecuted for statutory rape. We don't even charge for solicitation. If the minor is between the ages of sixteen and eighteen, that's sixteen months minimum in state prison. If she's younger, it's a minimum of three years state prison."

Weese recounts a case in which a twenty-four-year-old from

Delaware, who was in the city working on a contract, picked up a streetwalker. The police noticed the two in a parked car and rapped on the windshield as the man was being orally pleasured. The woman carried no identification, but it turned out she was sixteen. "He told the officers he had no idea. 'She told me she was eighteen. I asked her age.' But whether or not he knew how old she was, he was charged with statutory rape."

Several of the men glance at each other in chastened silence. Most never bother to ask the age of the women they pick up, but from the expression on several of their faces, it appears they knew that some were likely minors.

Next up is a public-health nurse who gives a frank talk on the heat of the moment, "getting laid," and STDs. "Having a lot of sex partners is not a bad thing," he begins, "but without protection, it is definitely not a good thing." He runs a graphic, stomach-churning, libido-killing slide presentation showing photographs of swollen, dripping, oozing, disease-infected penises and vaginas.

After a short break, the most intense part of the day begins. Norma Hotaling, the executive director and founder of SAGE (Standing Against Global Exploitation) enters the room. She surveys the latest cast of johns.

"Good morning," she begins.

Only three men half-heartedly respond.

"You're right, it's probably not a good morning to you right now, but hopefully by the end of the day you'll feel a little different," she says.

Norma pauses. She knows her audience well. She can read these men like a cheap novel. She has spoken to more than five thousand johns in the past dozen years. She knows how their minds operate, and she isn't the least bit intimidated.

She asks them to remove their baseball caps. The men hesitate, so she bellows: "Take off those hats!"

She continues. "The one thing I know about men involved in prostitution is you get used to having a lot of power and control over a woman. It won't work with me."

The hats come off, and most of the johns go straight into protection mode, arms folded tightly across their chests, legs crossed.

Norma begins by telling the johns about SAGE.

Its main focus is to help women in prostitution escape the streets. Many of the women who walk through our door have a lot of issues. Many have been raped thirty, forty, fifty times. They've been molested in their childhoods. Some of them have children that were conceived when they worked in the sex industry. Men like you deposited sperm in them because you didn't want to use a condom, and they have these children who are in the child welfare system or somewhere else.

Many of the women and girls we work with have been gang-raped. They've experienced gang rape at thirteen and fourteen years of age. They've been arrested over and over again for prostitution . . . They've been recruited by pimps and traffickers and trafficked all over the United States and sometimes outside the U.S. And . . . and these are children!

A lot of the men are staring down at their sneakers. The tension is palpable.

"The people we see have serious diseases. Their souls and

their spirits have been raped and beaten. But somehow they found the courage and strength to walk through our door. They walk through the door almost dead. They have no shine or sparkle in their eyes."

She stops for a moment. Her eyes narrow. "I sense a lot of attitude in the room, and I sense it when I talk about women being raped and molested and betrayed. They end up on the street, in your car, with a smile on their face telling you they like you because that's what you want to hear.

"I hope that for a moment you could put the attitudes aside and hear that I'm talking about real people in clearly desperate situations who have been hurt throughout their lives. If they don't make it through the doors of SAGE, they end up in Dumpsters, ditches, in shallow graves and pine boxes with no one to bury them."

The johns shift uneasily in their seats.

"Some of them do make it to SAGE and they do get their lives together and they do change. Their cheeks start to glow, and their eyes start to sparkle again and they stop shaking," Norma explains.

She takes a deep breath and then assumes her other role, that of cofounder of the john school these men are attending. "We've had over five thousand men go through this program. This program is designed for you. It is not designed to shame or blame you. It is designed to give you information that many of you have probably never thought of, because what we know about the men that are involved in the sex trade is that you don't take any time to sit down and think about your involvement.

"You men crossed the line, thinking your life was going to be nirvana. How many of you thought after you spent your fifty or one hundred dollars that your life was nirvana?"

Only one john raises his hand.

"Was it good for you?" Norma asks.

"No," he mumbles.

"This program is also designed so that you get the latest information on STDs and HIV. . . . If you're picking up somebody you just met and you're not using a condom, I bet you they're not using condoms with everybody else. So if you think they're safe, I'm here to tell you they're not!

"Crack users [involved in prostitution] have a lot of sex with people without condoms, and you don't know that ten minutes ago they were in a room with five guys and they were having sex with all of them without condoms," she explained.

"How many of you have had sex with a prostituted woman without a condom?" she asks. None of the men dares to raise a hand.

"What are you going to say to your wife or your girlfriend when you pass on an STD or HIV?"

The men shift nervously in their chairs.

Norma tells the students that when she first started doing "this kind of work," people asked her all the time, "Why do you work with those people, those immoral, bad people?" They weren't talking about the johns, she says. "They were talking about the women . . . these 'hos' . . . And I tell them the other reason: because I used to be one of them. I am an ex-prostitute. I could have ended up in a pine box." Several of the johns look up at this grandmotherly woman, stunned.

Norma's story is not uncommon among women who become prostitutes. After being sexually abused as a child, she tried to numb her pain with drugs. Soon she was selling her body to sustain a drug habit that cost her three hundred dollars a day.

"I was a heroin addict when I was on the streets. I carried knives. I was suicidal. I was trafficked as a kid, bought and sold and bought and sold and bought and sold over again. I worked the Tenderloin and lived in the park for eight years. When I was involved in prostitution, I didn't get to go home. Today, I get to go home."

After twenty-one years of selling her body on the streets of San Francisco, Norma committed herself to a detox program and turned her life around. She went back to school and found her calling—to help other women escape the shackles of prostitution. "I see the beauty of the women on the street, and I really know who they could be. I see myself in them. I see those times when I was out there and desperate. That's what drives me to do the work I do. I say to the women, 'I am just like you and there's hope. There's a place for you to come where there's love. It's safe and we'll help you heal.'"

The fifty-six-year-old crusader faces the classroom filled with johns. "I'm standing here on a day when I really don't want to be here, because on Tuesday I'm going in for surgery because I have cancer," she says. "I'm here today one more time because of you, because of the women, and because some of you are going to get something out of this program and it's going to change your lives for the better."

Norma is now in tears. One of the johns gets up from his chair, walks up to the podium, and hands her a Kleenex.

"I'm here to tell you there's a life out there where you don't have to live a lie," she continues. "There's a life out there where you can be honest with yourself and not in denial."

When she's done, the johns give Norma a warm and honest round of applause. Several approach her to thank her. One man, looking extremely chastened, tells her that he is ashamed of himself.

"I never knew these things you spoke of today. I am very sorry for what I have done, and I will never do this again," he says. This was the last appearance Norma would make at the john school. She died on December 16, 2008.

When the men return after lunch, the attitude is wiped clean from most faces. The afternoon sessions deal with the impact on neighborhoods where johns cruise. There is a talk on child exploitation, a presentation by Sex and Love Addicts Anonymous, and a discussion about the trafficking of women and children into prostitution.

At the end of the day, the men head home, many to wives or girlfriends. Some have been enlightened, but the expressions of a few suggest that they just don't get it and don't want to.

"I feel like such a jerk," one of the men tells me as he is leaving the building. "I could have really fucked up my life and ruined my marriage. I'm just glad I got this chance."

A twenty-something john, his baseball cap firmly back on his head, winces when I ask what affected him most from the program. "The slides on those diseases. That shot my lunch. It made me feel like puking. It's enough to turn you off of sex," he says. "I'm really going to be careful from now on."

"When you go to see a hooker?" I ask.

"No, that's a thing of the past. I don't need this shit in my life," he says. "I'm going to work on a real relationship. I don't want to be contributing to any more of this suffering stuff."

A third man with a hard-bitten face and a faded tattoo of Jesus on his left arm shrugs his shoulders when I ask what he thought of the day. "It's all propaganda. It's not all that bad out there. The women are making easy money. I just make sure I don't go for the ones who look like they're being abused by a pimp."

"Like the woman who arrested you?" I interject.

"Yeah, nothing like entrapment!" he grumbles as he trudges out to wave down a cab.

THE FIRST OFFENDER PROSTITUTION PROGRAM began in San Francisco in 1996. Since then, 5,800 men have gone through the program. The school has been replicated in twelve American cities as well as in Canada, the United Kingdom, and Korea. Yet for years it has been the target of criticism by the supporters of legalization.

One outspoken critic is pro-prostitution advocate Carol Leigh, director of the Bay Area Sex Workers Network in San Francisco. She has accused FOPP of using scare tactics and presenting a lopsided view of the sex trade.

"We shouldn't be increasing guilt around sexuality," she says. "At the school, they're not presenting prostitution in its entirety. There's quite a diversity of attitudes toward sex work in the city, and the [john] schools only present one view — that women are angry toward their clients. It's very problematic that the city is calling this education." Leigh insists that, though she thinks johns should be educated about women and children trafficked into the sex trade and exploited, it should not be done "in a punitive context."

Critics have also questioned how a one-day course could achieve even the slightest deterrence. They refused to believe that a course so simple and so short could dissuade johns from returning to their clandestine meanderings. One die-hard skeptic was Michael Shively, a criminologist at Abt Associates, a Massachusetts-based research firm. Right from the get-go, he had serious reservations about what he described as a program "put together on the back of a napkin."

Shively, who has a reputation as a tough, solid, and objective researcher, is the primary author of an exhaustive two-year study on FOPP, commissioned by the National Institute of Justice. He sat in on john school classes in San Francisco and admits he was impressed by what he saw, but he still harbored strong doubts as to its efficacy. He was convinced that once the evaluation was done, he would be telling Norma Hotaling that it was not effective.

When we talked, Shively noted that, as a rule, offender-treatment programs designed to change behavior need to be sustained over several months. "One-day programs generally do nothing for people. It needs to be intense . . . a lot of intervention over a period of time, usually a minimum of four to six months. When I looked at the First Offender Prostitution Program, it violated every principle of effective intervention."

To evaluate the program, the research team pored over two decades of data for San Francisco and the rest of California — ten years before the program and ten years since its inception.

"We looked at the arrest rates year after year [before implementation] . . . and then *boom!* john school, and it drops by half and stays at that level over the subsequent years. We literally spent six months trying to make the effects go away, not because we wished it to be so, but because it was such a dramatic impact considering how nonintensive and unsustained the intervention is. It's a day talking to men."

In trying to reconcile the results, Shively became a believer. "Connecting the dots between each piece of the john school class, whether it's the testimony of survivors or the police, the DA on legal ramifications, the nurse talking about health . . . we don't know which piece did it, but we do know it's had a big effect."

Shively believes the success boils down to two appeals being made by the people who talk to the johns. "The first is to self-interest. They're telling the guys, If you continue to do this, here's what will happen to you. You will take health problems back to people — like your wife or girlfriend — that don't deserve them. You will have serious legal consequences. You can be the victim of a crime. . . . You're not asking them to be nice guys, you're just saying it's bad for you and here's why." The second appeal is to altruism. "It's trying to get the guys to realize the harm they're causing, develop empathy for the women," he says. This, he believes, can be a motivation for change.

"Part of the problem is that these guys are jerks. They're knuckle-dragging, bone-headed bad guys, and they really don't care if their actions hurt the women or the community," he says. "It's just that they have stupid ideas about what sex is, what intimacy is. They truly believe prostitution is a victimless crime. When you grow up as a male in this culture, it isn't hard to end up with a screwed-up belief system about women and intimacy, and the john school covers that."

Because the San Francisco evaluation yielded such a stunning surprise, the research team shifted its attention to San Diego, where the program had been implemented in the year 2000. "One of the reasons we have confidence in the results is because San Diego started a john school in a different year," Shively explains. "And when you look at the arrest rates from 1995 to 2000, there is a sudden drop in 2000 by half and it stays that way.

"The punch line is the program works. The data are very strong, and we're confident that this program does what it intends to do," he says. "The collective evidence strongly supports the conclusion that the john school significantly discourages johns from reoffending.

"I'm in a strange position as a researcher," Shively adds, "because we usually tend to be skeptical and objective. But when you get results that are extremely positive, you end up sounding like an advocate. I've been doing research for twenty years, and I've never seen a program that works as well as this."

17

GET THE
PREDATOR JOHNS

*The jury's verdict is a reminder that pedophiles who attempt to
evade detection and prosecution by committing sex crimes
overseas face serious consequences.*

—ROBERT SCHOCH, SPECIAL AGENT IN CHARGE OF THE
IMMIGRATION AND CUSTOMS ENFORCEMENT (ICE)
OFFICE OF INVESTIGATIONS, LOS ANGELES

AT THE FIRST WORLD CONGRESS Against Commercial Sexual Exploitation of Children, held in Stockholm, Sweden, in 1996, alarm bells were sounded about the escalation and horror of buying, selling, trafficking, and use of children in prostitution and pornography. Two years later, the International Labor Organization warned that the "commercial sexual exploitation of children has . . . become an issue of global concern, and the indicators are that it is on the rise."

Five years later, at the second World Congress, held in Yoko-
hama, Japan, in 2001, one report after another warned that the
situation had gotten far worse; the age of child victims of prostitution was getting younger and younger. More than three thousand delegates from one hundred thirty countries sat in stunned
silence, listening to the harrowing stories of children who have
had their innocence brutally ripped away by predator johns —
Romanian children trafficked to Western Europe; teenagers from
the ghettos of Brazil offering sex to tourists in exchange for pocket
money; Russian street kids forced into "survival sex"; and young
Vietnamese or Nepalese girls sold to brothels in Cambodia and
India.

Today, throughout the world, predator johns are on the prowl
for younger and younger victims to abuse sexually. Child advo-
cacy organizations like ECPAT (End Child Prostitution, Child
Pornography and Trafficking of Children for Sexual Purposes)
and UNICEF (the United Nations International Children's
Educational Fund) estimate that hundreds of thousands of children — mainly girls but a significant number of boys — fall
victim to commercial sexual exploitation every year. In the desperate shantytowns of Third World nations — Costa Rica, Brazil,
Mexico, and Honduras; Thailand, the Philippines, and Cambodia; Gambia, Kenya, and South Africa; and Sri Lanka — and
in countries reeling from staggering social upheaval, like Russia,
Ukraine, and Romania, the millions of dollars spent by foreign
sex tourists pay for the rape of defenseless children.

The lives of these innocent victims are almost too horrific to
recount — children as young as five forced to service between two

and thirty men per week. That's anywhere from more than one hundred to fifteen hundred men a year.

Over the past two decades, a lot of words of concern have poured from the mouths of world leaders, and a lot of promises for action have been made. Yet for child victims, precious little seems to change. The promised end is nowhere in sight.

Packs of predator johns continue to head out from the United States, Canada, and the European Union, and from Japan, South Korea, and Australia, flush with cash and bereft of morals. They travel to impoverished countries to hunt down children because they know that laws are weak, economies are in shambles, national resolve is shaky, and corruption is rampant. They know that if they happen to stumble into a legal quagmire, they can probably bribe their way out.

While many predator johns are pedophiles who *preferentially* seek out children for sexual relationships, a disturbing and growing number are what are called *situational abusers*. These are men who don't consistently seek out children for sex but will take advantage of "why-not sex" with children if the opportunity arises. These men, oftentimes stirred by the titillation of child porn or the desire for something totally different, have no qualms about engaging in paid sex with girls who could be their daughters or granddaughters.

The distorted rationalizations and justifications offered by these opportunistic johns are truly mind-boggling. Often they convince themselves that they are doing nothing wrong, that it is culturally acceptable to have sex with children in the countries they visit. They pretend to believe that Third World nations do not have the same social taboos against sex with children as the West, and that the children are less sexually inhibited. These traveling perpetrators feel free to experiment with child sex while abroad because of the anonymity that comes with being in a foreign land — anonymity that provides them with freedom from the legal and perhaps personal restraints forbidding this kind of behavior in their homeland. Even more disturbing is that so many of these men sidestep any pangs of guilt by convincing themselves that they are helping the child's family escape economic hardship by exchanging money for sex. This is the ultimate conscience pacifier.

More and more tourists are targeting children and adolescents for another reason: because they believe them to be free of HIV/AIDS. In fact, these young victims are less likely to practice safe sex because they know nothing about it, and they are unable to oppose the will of the men who abuse them.

Trouble is, the situational abusers rarely get caught. They pass through the child brothels so quickly, it is virtually impossible for authorities to nail them. The men who do get arrested are the hardcore pedophiles who stick around long enough to capture the attention of locals. They also have an almost compulsive desire to document their encounters with children by taking photographs and making videos, trophies of their exploitation.

Child Sex Tourism Laws

To combat this shameful scourge, most Western nations — including the United States, Canada, Australia, the United Kingdom, and Sweden — have passed laws making it illegal for their citizens to travel abroad to engage in sexual acts with a minor. If perpetrators are caught, they can be prosecuted in their home country. However, with the exception of the United States, these laws ring hollow, because they have not been backed up by effective enforcement measures.

Benjamin Perrin, a Canadian who helped found the Future Group, an organization fighting the trafficking of children for sex, noted that only one Canadian, Donald Bakker, has been convicted under Canada's child-sex-tourism law, enacted in 1997. And even his arrest and conviction was not a result of a targeted child-sex-tourism investigation; it came about by sheer happenstance.

"Canada has one of the worst records in the world on enforcing this [kind of] law. This is becoming an international sore spot for Canada," Perrin said. "Are we going to back up our tough talk on child sexual exploitation with action?"

Unfortunately, Canada, like virtually every other country that has passed laws against child-sex-tourism, has not posted any investigators to foreign destinations favored by child predators. Only the United States has, and its action has sent out a chilling message to American child-sex tourists.

It has been illegal for Americans to travel abroad with the intent to have sex with someone under the age of eighteen since September 13, 1994, when President Bill Clinton signed into law an extension of the Mann Act. It gave authorities a new tool for fighting the sexual abuse of children overseas by U.S. citizens. Persons convicted under this law could face a maximum of ten years in prison plus fines of up to $250,000. The law appeared to be a step in the right direction, but it soon proved extremely difficult to enforce. The problem inhered in just one word: intent. It was nearly impossible for prosecutors to prove that an offender had the requisite intent when he left home. For example, a man heading out on a business trip who ends up having sex with a child overseas could escape prosecution in the United States by claiming that he did not leave home thinking this would happen.

For almost a decade, U.S. prosecutors managed to snag and reel in only one offender. In 1998, Florida Atlantic University mathematics professor Marvin Hersh, aka Mario, was arrested in Boca Raton and charged with traveling for the purpose of illegal sexual contact with a minor and aggravated sexual abuse of a child in Honduras. The fifty-eight-year-old was also charged with trafficking a fourteen-year-old Honduran boy back to Florida as his sex toy.

At his trial a year later, evidence was introduced describing at length the professor's elaborate efforts over several years to engage in multiple sexual encounters with young, poverty-stricken boys, mainly from Honduras and Thailand, going back to 1990. In Honduras, on the streets of La Ceiba, Hersh hooked a seventeen-year-old who was "very hungry." The teenager agreed to accompany the American to a restaurant and then to a hotel, where he allowed him to perform oral sex on him. The boy later introduced Hersh to each of his three younger brothers, the youngest being ten. Over time, the professor had repeated sexual encounters will all the brothers.

During the trial, Juan — the boy smuggled into the United States — testified that he thought the professor "was one of God's marvels. Since he was so nice, I did it from the bottom of my heart." Juan testified that he had engaged in sexual relations with Hersh because he was poor. "I had the need and I wanted [Hersh] to help my family out," adding that the American had befriended the family, given the boys Nintendo Gameboys, and paid the rent.

In total, Hersh traveled to Honduras eight times in 1994 and 1995. During one visit, he told the boys' parents that their children would have many educational advantages if they moved with him to the United States. In August 1995, the parents allowed Juan to travel to the States with the professor. In preparation, Hersh went to California, where he obtained a false birth certificate for the boy in the name of John Anthony Hersh, born in Los Angeles in 1985. He also applied for a U.S. passport and a social security card in the same name, listing the boy as his son. While living in Florida, Juan went to school during the day and at night slept in Hersh's bed.

In 1996, the professor's ex-wife tipped the FBI. Hersh told investigators that Juan was his son — the product of an illicit affair — and he denied all allegations of sexual abuse. But in a search of his home, investigators discovered a suitcase containing hand-drawn maps of where to find young boys for sex in several Third World countries. They also found computer images of boys engaged in sexual activities and photos of Hersh sexually abusing boys as young as eight.

Throughout the trial, the professor maintained his innocence, claiming he was nothing more than a generous benefactor. The jury didn't buy it. In March 1999, Hersh was convicted of ten charges stemming from his sexual exploitation of Honduran boys while traveling abroad. Three months later, he was sentenced to 105 years in prison. Hersh was the first — and only — American prosecuted and convicted under the amended provision of the Mann Act.

While offering a sobering glimpse into the world of traveling pedophiles, the trial of Marvin Hersh dramatically illustrated for lawmakers that the Mann Act desperately had to be strengthened. The intent loophole needed to be plugged.

On April 30, 2003, President George Bush signed into law the Prosecutorial Remedies and Other Tools to End the Exploitation of Children Today Act, better known as the PROTECT Act. The new law made it an offense to travel abroad to engage in sex with a minor, whether intended or not. It also toughened penalties for child-sex tourism, increasing the maximum prison term from fifteen to thirty years, and established Operation Predator — a joint initiative between U.S. Immigration and Customs Enforcement (ICE) and the Department of Homeland Security — with sweeping powers to investigate these crimes. Since Operation Predator began, more than a dozen men have been successfully prosecuted.

Seventy-year-old Michael Lewis Clark was the first American to be convicted under the PROTECT Act. He was arrested in Cambodia by local authorities in June 2003 for engaging in illegal sexual activity with two boys, ages ten and thirteen. A joint investigation by ICE and Cambodian authorities determined that Clark may have molested as many as fifty children in Cambodia. He was extradited to Seattle in March 2004, where he pleaded guilty to engaging in illicit sexual conduct with minors in foreign places. On June 25, 2004, Clark was sentenced to ninety-seven months in prison.

More than 50 percent of the sex tourists arrested abroad for having sex with children have been previously convicted of child sex crimes back in their home countries. It is a sobering statistic. One such person is sixty-one-year-old Richard Arthur Schmidt. In February 2004, Schmidt was extradited from Cambodia and brought home to Baltimore, Maryland, handcuffed to an ICE agent. He was charged with multiple violations of the PRO-TECT Act involving the molestation of boys in the Philippines and Cambodia. Schmidt had previously been convicted of child sex crimes in Maryland three times. In 2000, he was released on parole after serving thirteen years of an eighteen-year sentence. Three years later, ICE agents in Bangkok learned that the man had been molesting boys in the region. Schmidt pleaded guilty, and on May 25, 2005, he was sentenced to fifteen years in prison.

ICE agents don't just sit back waiting for American johns to sexually assault a foreign child abroad. The act gives them the tools to track down predator johns before they strike. Eighty-five-year-old John W. Seljan found that out the hard way. He was arrested at Los Angeles International Airport as he attempted to board a flight to the Philippines in October 2003. Intercepts of correspondence indicated he was on his way to have sex with Filipino girls age nine and twelve. At the time of his arrest, the elderly man was in possession of pornographic materials and sexual aids, and he had nearly one hundred pounds of chocolates in his luggage. On March 28, 2005, Seljan was sentenced to twenty years in prison on six counts related to child-sex tourism.

While the act zeros in on U.S. citizens or residents, it also targets "any person who travels into the United States" en route to a foreign destination to engage in child-sex tourism. Two foreigners — one from France, the other from Germany — learned about this section of the law within moments of deplaning. Thirty-year-old Frenchman Sebastien Sarraute and Manfred Knittel, a fifty-three-year-old German, landed in Tucson, Arizona, a month apart in 2004 on international flights. The men were heading to Mexico to have sex with girls ranging in age from six to fourteen. Knittel and Sarraute pleaded guilty and were each sentenced in August 2005 to fifty-one months in prison, after which time they will be deported.

The United States is the only real sheriff on the world stage actively pursuing child-sex tourists and prosecuting American offenders at home. The task is extremely challenging for ICE. Evidence gathered in foreign jurisdictions is often difficult to use in American courts. The difficulty of bringing very young children from abroad to testify is another complication. More often than not, however, evidence seized from the predators themselves will lead to a successful prosecution. These men hang themselves with their own rope by writing extensively about their sexual exploits in diaries, photographing themselves with their victims, and videotaping their sexual debauchery. For these predator johns, their trophies prove to be their downfall.

Edilberto Datan thought no one would find his trophies. On November 4, 2004, when he returned from a two-month vacation in the Philippines, U.S. Customs and Border Protection officers at Los Angeles International Airport searched his luggage and found computer memory sticks taped inside the San Diego resident's jeans pocket. ICE was immediately contacted. On the sticks were approximately one hundred sexually explicit images of

Filipino boys. A search of Datan's home revealed an extensive child pornography collection. The sixty-one-year-old pleaded guilty in March 2005, admitting he had sex with four Filipino boys. On June 17, 2005, he was sentenced to seventeen years in federal prison and ordered to pay $16,475 in restitution to eight of his young victims.

ICE agents have even caught American predators heading to Third World nations to work as teachers and aid workers, jobs that put them in close and continuous contact with children. On June 19, 2006, acting on a tip from workers with the International Justice Mission, Cambodian police and ICE agents raided a house in Phnom Penh. It was occupied by Michael Joseph Pepe, a burly fifty-three-year-old retired U.S. Marine Corps captain who worked in the city as a teacher. Police rescued three young girls, aged nine to eleven, whom the American had been raping and torturing. Pepe was arrested along with the mother of one of girls found in the home. She was charged with selling her daughter to the suspect for three hundred dollars. The mother of the other two children was arrested for renting her daughters to Pepe for thirty dollars a month. A Vietnamese pimp was also arrested. She had been paid a finder's fee of ten dollars for each victim she brought to the American. She had also instructed the girls on how to perform sex.

In the raid, police seized a trove of evidence, including rope and cloth strips used to restrain the girls, child pornography, a computer hard drive, children's clothes, Viagra pills, mood-altering drugs, children's games, and newspaper articles about pedophiles. A subsequent analysis of the man's computer revealed a virtual library of hundreds of images of nude and semiclothed children, some bound at the wrists and ankles, performing various sexual acts with Pepe.

After being expelled from Cambodia on February 2, 2007, Pepe arrived in handcuffs, under police escort, in Los Angeles to face a raft of charges under the PROTECT Act. According to the court affidavit, ICE agents interviewed four of Pepe's victims, ranging in age from nine to twelve, who stated that he had sexually abused them. One eleven-year-old girl, who had been drugged by Pepe, told authorities that she woke up in a pool of blood. Medical examinations found that she had injuries consistent with forced intercourse.

During the trial, six of the seven girls testified that Pepe drugged, bound, beat, and raped them. Several victims testified that they were required to give him sexual massages and perform oral sex on him on a daily basis.

Pepe was found guilty and faces up to 210 years in prison.

Robert Schoch, special agent in charge of the ICE office of investigations in Los Angeles, described the verdict as "particularly gratifying and not surprising given the horrendous evidence introduced during this trial about the defendant's sexual exploitation of these vulnerable youths.

"This case represented one of the most egregious examples of international sex tourism we have ever investigated, and the jury's verdict is a reminder that pedophiles who attempt to evade detection and prosecution by committing sex crimes overseas face serious consequences," Schoch said.

In December 2008 an overseas ICE investigation led to the arrest of a Russian-born millionaire businessman in Philadelphia for his alleged involvement in child prostitution in his former homeland. Andrew Mogilyansky, thirty-eight, was charged with organizing a child prostitution ring in Moscow that involved orphaned girls trafficked from St. Petersburg. Mogilyansky, who is married, is a dual citizen of Russia and the United States and resides in Richboro, Pennsylvania. He came to the United States in 1989.

According to the indictment, from 2002 to 2004 Mogilyansky conspired with a Russian man, Andrei Borisovich Tarasov, and three others to create an online prostitution ring in Russia involving women and girls. The ring advertised the business on the Web site Berenika, named for a mythical Russian princess. "These adult and minor females were housed at an apartment in Moscow, Russia, and routinely transported to another Moscow apartment to engage in commercial sexual acts with 'clients' of the business, who arranged encounters initially through the 'Berenika' Web site," the indictment alleges. It goes on to state that Mogilyansky invested money into the Berenika business and that he "recruited young minor females from an orphanage in St. Petersburg, Russia, to work as prostitutes in Moscow," adding that he engaged in sexual activity with the girls in an apartment he owned in that city before sending them to Moscow to work in prostitution. The indictment identified the three orphan girls, all fourteen and younger, as M.S., E.K., and J.N.

At a press conference in Philadelphia, acting U.S. Attorney Laurie Magid said she's dealt with child pornographers and predators in her time but this case is different. "The defendant went out of his way, in fact halfway around the world, to find perhaps the weakest population," Magid asserted. "He believed that if he went far enough away, he would avoid the interest of law enforcement. He was wrong. Very, very wrong."

She noted that, "All of the victims in this case were young girls who were orphans. The defendant took what little they had — their innocence and their dignity. As the indictment alleges, not only did he molest them for his own pleasure but he treated these children as a commodity — useful, marketable, and ultimately disposable.

"He took those girls to his apartment in St. Petersburg, where he molested them. He molested them as a way of introducing them to his child prostitution business. After he molested these girls, he sent them to Moscow to work as prostitutes for him," Magid added. "Mogilyansky is now facing criminal charges and a potentially lengthy sentence in an American prison for the horrible acts that he committed on Russian soil."

Mogilyansky has been charged with one count of traveling for the purpose of engaging in illicit sexual conduct and three counts of engaging in illicit sexual conduct. If convicted of all charges, he faces a maximum sentence of thirty years in prison on each count and a million-dollar fine. Tarasov and the other accomplices in the prostitution ring were arrested, tried, and convicted in Russia in 2004. Tarasov is currently serving a ten-year sentence. At some point in 2004, Russian authorities sought Mogilyansky for the alleged sex crimes, but he evaded capture and flew back to the United States, with which Russia has no extradition treaty.

Mogilyansky's lawyer, George Newman, declined to comment on details of the case. "We deny the allegations and look forward to contesting them in court," he said.

According to court documents, Mogilyansky is owner of IFEX Global Inc., a company that distributes fire-extinguishing equipment and also has a car-export business. The indictment said that IFEX was valued at more than $10 million in 2004, while Mogilyansky's personal wealth was valued at $5.3 million in 2006. He is also founder and chairman of the International Foundation for Terror Act Victims, which aids victims, particularly orphaned and injured children, of terrorism in Ossetia, Russia, following the school massacre there in 2004. The organization has raised more than $1.2 million so far.

Problems at Home

While Western leaders decry the contemptible activities of traveling johns who target children abroad, the problem of prostituted youth back in their home countries has reached alarming proportions. The United States, Canada, Australia, United Kingdom, and every nation in the European Union are in crisis over the growing numbers of teenagers — the vast majority of them girls — being pressed into the flesh trade.

The best data available suggest that between one hundred thousand and three hundred thousand kids a year are exploited through the commercial sex industry in North America every year. The average age of coercion and recruitment into prostitution is twelve to fourteen, and the vast majority is controlled by pimps who dragoon these young victims to service upwards of a dozen johns each night. These children are rotated from city to city every three to four weeks by their pimps.

In a single month, May 2007, more than four hundred

children from twenty-eight different U.S. states were found working in prostitution in Las Vegas, according to Linda Smith, president and founder of Shared Hope International (SHI). In March
2008, the nonprofit organization, based in Vancouver, Washington, released a blistering report dubbing the gambling mecca as
the hub for child trafficking in the United States. It pointed out
that the "high-risk conditions of Las Vegas," including easy access
to alcohol and drugs, twenty-four-hour gambling, and a "hyper-
sexualized entertainment industry," fuel the problem of "domestic minor sex trafficking."

SHI investigators who went undercover to determine the extent of domestic child-sex trafficking learned that, for the fired-
up john, child sex is easy to find. "If you pay the price you can
get what you want, and I can get it for you. Now if you want
something really young, that's two hundred dollars, it's just going
to cost you a little bit more than that," a pimp told an undercover investigator.

Smith, a longtime crusader against the trafficking of children
into the global sex trade, said she thought she had seen the absolute worst after visiting sex-tourism outposts on several continents. But she got the shock of her life when she began looking
into the issue in her own backyard. "I was so naive," Smith said.
"I was going all over the world, when twelve-year-old girls are
being trafficked at truck stops here. I said, 'If I don't know, others don't know.' The reality is our children are being trafficked."
And the unconscionable reality is that throughout North America minors arrested in prostitution raids are labeled "child prostitutes." They are treated by the justice system as criminals,
instead of being diverted to social programs within child welfare

systems that can give them the kind of counseling and rehabilitation services they need to break free of their pimps.

Meanwhile, the vast majority of johns who use and abuse these girls are still able to disappear into the night. When they get caught with a youth in prostitution, they plead ignorance. "Oh, I thought she was eighteen. She told me she was eighteen," they swear, as if they really asked her age when she climbed into their vehicle. It takes only a few minutes of conversation to figure out if someone is just a child. But an aroused john rarely uses the head on his shoulders.

What is truly disconcerting is that over and over the authorities — mostly male cops — buy this pathetic excuse. Yet sex with a minor is statutory rape. It's a crime, and "I didn't know" is not a defense. By law, these johns should be arrested, charged, and prosecuted. One would expect that a fifty-year-old man caught having sex in his van with a fourteen-year-old would automatically be arrested and charged with statutory rape. More than likely, however, the cops will instruct the man to go home, telling him that it's his lucky night. Then they will drive off with the fourteen-year-old — the victim — handcuffed in the backseat of the police cruiser. She will be charged and locked up in a youth detention center, along with young offenders arrested for assault, armed robbery, or murder. "Right now, there's no cost. There has to be a cost to the purchaser, the customer who buys sex from a child," says Linda Smith.

Western society is incredibly two-faced when it comes to prostituted children. It professes to be caring and protective of its youth. It charges teachers if they fail to report suspected cases of child abuse. It fines parents who don't strap their kids into car seats. It passes laws requiring children to wear bicycle helmets. It fines corner-store owners if they are caught selling cigarettes or liquor to minors. It does this to protect children from harm, to keep them safe. It does this because society believes children and adolescents are too young to make informed decisions and need to be protected.

Yet when it comes to youth involved in prostitution, a completely different and hypocritical dynamic comes into play. In most cities throughout North America and the Western world, a fourteen-year-old girl caught in prostitution is viewed through a sinister lens. Because she is on a street corner wearing spike heels, spandex, and gaudy makeup; because she is a runaway, maybe the product of an abusive family; because she has accepted cash for sex, she is seen as a perversion of childhood. She is a bad kid, somehow deemed to have the capacity to consent to her rape. As a result, she is not treated by child protective services and the courts as a child in need of protection but as a young offender, punished for a crime that has been committed against her.

Not surprisingly, when johns are asked about having had sex with a prostituted minor, to a man they vociferously deny ever having been with anyone under the age of eighteen. On Internet chat lines and discussion boards, they express revulsion at men who do this. Yet throughout the Western world numerous studies show that as many as 80 percent of women in prostitution entered the trade well before they turned eighteen. In the United States and Canada, the average age of entry is fourteen and getting younger. When these girls reach legal age, they suddenly appear in escort ads, offered up as "barely legal." It is safe to assume that most of these young women didn't suddenly wake up on their eighteenth birthdays to the epiphany that prostitution was precisely the exciting career opportunity they had been looking for. It's also a sure bet that virtually every one of them was forced to service packs of johns long before she turned eighteen.

And the johns know that.

The message to all johns — whether traveling abroad or cruising the back streets of their hometowns — should be the same. Children are off limits. They are never prostitutes. They are victims of the worst kind of sexual exploitation, and when men rent their bodies it is rape.

On September 26, 2008, New York State governor David Paterson signed into law a bill shielding sexually exploited girls and boys from being charged with prostitution. Known as the Safe Harbor for Exploited Youth Act, it will divert children under the age of eighteen who have been arrested for prostitution into counseling and treatment programs, provided they agree to aid in the prosecution of their pimps. Safe harbor, however, will not be offered to repeat offenders or to those who have failed to comply with previous court orders.

Governor Paterson noted that the law will ensure "that sexually exploited youth receive counseling and emergency services as well as long term housing solutions. . . . As a society we must do everything in our power to prevent sexual exploitation, but when it does occur we must be prepared to assist our youth with appropriate outreach services. For too long we have been disciplining young children who are the victims of brutal sexual exploitation instead of providing them with the necessary services to reintegrate them into society and ensure they receive adequate crisis intervention." Safe harbor will not go into effect until the

spring of 2010, in order to allow the state time to set up necessary services.

IN A VIRGINIA HOTEL that normally caters to business travelers and va-
cationers, undercover FBI agents and local police officers were
meeting with a different kind of clientele. Throughout a Friday
evening, several prostituted women arrived at Room 403 thinking they'd made an appointment with a john. Instead, it was a
sting, and the entire event was captured on hidden cameras.

The arrests that followed were similar to those played out
across the United States in October 2008, during a three-day
sweep dubbed Operation Cross Country II. The objective: to
rescue child prostitutes and get them into protective services, and
to disrupt the pimps and criminal organizations that victimize
children.

The FBI, along with the Department of Justice, the National
Center for Missing and Exploited Children (NCMEC), and
ninety-two local, state, and federal agencies in twenty-nine U.S.
cities, conducted a series of stings as part of the FBI's Innocence
Lost initiative.

In total, forty-seven children, some as young as thirteen, were
rescued. All but one were girls. Ten of those children had been
listed as missing in the NCMEC database. The operation, which
targeted call centers, truck stops, casinos, and Web sites, dis-
mantled a dozen large-scale prostitution rings and resulted in the
arrests of 73 pimps and 518 prostituted women.

At a press conference at FBI headquarters in Washington,
Deputy Director John Pistole said, "Sex trafficking of children
remains one of the most violent and unconscionable crimes com-

mitted in this country. There are few law enforcement missions more important than protecting our nation's children."

Ernie Allen, chief executive of NCMEC, pointed out that in June 2008, at the announcement of Operation Cross Country I, "I made the comment that millions of Americans think this is the kind of problem that only happens somewhere else — Southeast Asia, Central America, Eastern Europe. Operation Cross Country Two is the latest evidence that this is a problem that's happening on Main Street, USA.

"In the past, this is a problem that has been attacked solely at the local level," Allen continued. "And one of our underlying premises in Innocence Lost is that this is organized crime — not Mafia, not La Cosa Nostra, but organized nonetheless. These people are moving kids from city to city. There is a network. These kids have become commodities for sale or trade. They are involved in twenty-first century slavery."

"Make no mistake, the minors who were interdicted as part of this operation are victims of the most extreme form of sex trafficking," said Matthew Friedrich, acting assistant attorney general in the Justice Department's criminal division. "It sadly remains the case, even now in 2008, that there remain instances of children in the United States manipulated into prostitution by pimps willing to make a fast buck based on the most vulnerable among us.

"The best protection for victims is the incarceration of the offender. This is so because children manipulated into becoming prostitutes are often forced to remain there through violence and through intimidation," Friedrich pointed out.

Since the FBI launched the Innocence Lost initiative in 2003,

575 child victims have been rescued, and 365 individuals have been convicted on a combination of state and federal charges. The following are some of the cases investigated during the first five years of Innocence Lost.

Kansas City – Don L. Elbert III forced three underage sisters, two of whom were fourteen-year-old twins, into prostitution. Elbert pleaded guilty to child sex trafficking in May 2007, and on January 10, 2008, he was sentenced to eight years in prison and fifteen years of supervised release and was ordered to pay $524,571 in restitution.

Los Angeles – Juan Rico Doss was indicted in June 2005 on one count of conspiracy, two counts of sex trafficking of children, and three counts of transportation of minors for prostitution. Doss transported two teenage girls between Los Angeles, Sacramento, Oakland, and Reno. His wife, Jacquay Ford, was also involved in the girls' exploitation. She was indicted and testified against Doss. Ford was sentenced to fifteen months. Doss received a life sentence.

Detroit – Robert Lewis Young, aka Blue Diamond, transported juveniles from Hawaii to Chicago and Detroit. Electronic surveillance of Young's phone was initiated in June 2005. On March 17, 2007, Young was sentenced to twenty-five years supervised release and ordered to pay $67,000 in child support for his own twelve children. On October 30, 2007, one of Young's pimp partners, Jody Spears, was sentenced to eight years. On May 29, 2008, Gary Kimmel, an associate of Young's in Chicago, pled guilty to one count of money laundering and agreed to forfeit $405,000.

Atlantic City – Matthew Thompkins, aka Knowledge, was a U.S. Postal Service employee who operated a prostitution ring involving as many as forty women whom he forced into prostitution. His youngest victim was fourteen years old. In August 2005, electronic monitoring on two of his telephones began, and four months later he was indicted. Investigators estimated his assets totaled in excess of three million dollars. On March 27, 2008, Thompkins was sentenced to 23.3 years and lifetime supervised release. On the same date, his associate Demetrius Lemus was sentenced to eight years — the reduced sentence due to his cooperation with prosecutors.

Toledo – Kevin Murphy trafficked women and children to Washington, D.C., and other cities for the purpose of prostitution. Agents in Washington, D.C., assisted in recovering a juvenile victim. Five victims testified to the grand jury, which resulted in a multiple-count indictment against Murphy. On October 26, 2007, he was sentenced to ten years.

Washington, D.C. – Sunni Ham forced two underage girls into prostitution in Washington, D.C. He made them wear revealing clothing while they performed sex acts for money. On June 12, 2007, Ham was sentenced to more than eight years.

Sacramento – On June 21, 2006, Will Moss Jr., aka Slim, was found guilty of twelve counts relating to sex trafficking of children and various firearms offenses. Moss employed minors for the purpose of prostitution, transported them across state lines, and controlled them through force and intimidation. They were assaulted and raped by Moss on numerous occasions. On February 9, 2007, Moss was sentenced to forty years in federal prison and ten years of supervision. Upon release from prison, he must register as a sex offender.

Pittsburgh – Michael Simmons, Stephanie Gease, and Deshonqua Strait were all convicted in relation to a case of child prostitution. Simmons was found guilty of transporting a child from Pennsylvania to California and sentenced to seventeen and a half years. Gease, Simmons' aunt and former foster mother, was sentenced to eight months for purchasing a bus ticket and escorting the child to the bus station. Strait was sentenced to one year for training and supervising the child.

Washington, D.C. – Gary Gates and Tamisha Hayward operated an online escort/prostitution business known as Red Light Special and Pandora's Box. Clients contacted a telephone number posted on the Web site to set up dates. Hayward reserved hotel rooms for the girls using Priceline.com. On April 23, 2004, Gates and Hayward were indicted on thirteen counts of sex trafficking of children, eleven counts of coercion and enticement, five counts of transportation of minors, and two counts of transportation for illegal sexual activity. On September 8, 2004, through plea agreements, Gates was sentenced to more than fourteen years and Hayward to more than eight.

Oklahoma City – Stormy Nights was a large-scale child prostitution investigation focused on the interstate prostitution of children at truck stops and call services. Stormy Nights used a number of sophisticated investigative techniques, including wiretaps, GPS, and pen registers. On May 10, 2004, nine federal arrest warrants and three federal search warrants were executed in and around the Oklahoma City area. These individuals were charged with a variety of federal offenses that included transportation of an individual with intent to engage in criminal sexual activity; aiding and abetting; transportation of a person under the age of eighteen with intent to engage in criminal sexual activity; promotion, management, establishment, or carrying on of any unlawful activity; sex trafficking of children; coercion of a person under the age of eighteen to engage in a sexual act; felon in possession of a firearm; interstate and foreign travel or transportation in aid of racketeering; and money laundering. Sentences for these individuals ranged in length up to seventeen and a half years.

San Francisco – On September 20, 2002, Theodore Love, aka Ace Love, was arrested on state charges for promoting prostitution. In his residence were six females, two of whom were juveniles, age thirteen and seventeen. Love transported the women and children to Las Vegas, Washington, D.C., and Los Angeles and forced them to work as prostitutes. Love advertised his escort company, The Love Zone, in *Spectator* magazine and on the Internet at Eros Guide. On September 25, 2003, Love was indicted federally, charged with sex trafficking of children and transportation of minors with intent to engage in criminal sexual activity. Love pled guilty and was sentenced to more than seven years in prison.

Atlanta – Mariece Chevalia Sims, aka Maurice C. Sims, and Dwayne B. Thigpen abducted a sixteen-year-old from Arkansas and forced her into prostitution in Texarkana, Arkansas; Gulfport, Mississippi; and Atlanta, Georgia. Sims and Thigpen sexually assaulted and continually threatened the victim. On August 12, 2003, Sims and Thigpen were charged with kidnapping and transportation of minors with intent to engage in criminal sexual activity. A year later, Thigpen pled guilty to one count of transportation with intent to engage in criminal sexual activity, and in September 2004, Sims was found guilty at trial of kidnapping, forced labor, sex trafficking of children, and transportation with intent to engage in criminal sexual activity. On December 16, 2004, Thigpen was sentenced to five years in prison and five years of supervised release. Sims was sentenced to life and was ordered to pay $500 in fines.

EPILOGUE

THE TRUTH IS SIMPLE: if there were no demand, prostitution would not exist. Prostitution is not about women's sexuality. It's about men. If men the world over did not demand paid sex, there would be no need to corral, break, and submit millions of women and children to this dehumanizing existence.

What have these women and children endured to be with these men? The violation of their bodies and the denial of their essence as human beings. What has it cost the "clients," the johns? Nothing more than a few dollars.

Now multiply that by tens of millions of johns the world over. With billions of dollars streaming in, the profits are enormous. To ensure future profits, there must always be enough women willing to enter this so-called profession to satisfy the bottomless demand. Trouble is there never are . . . and never will be. Young girls don't dream of becoming call girls, and the vast majority of women don't relish selling their bodies to survive. Those who resort to prostitution do so because there are few if any other options.

Enter the traffickers, who through brute force ensure that
there is an endless supply ready to satisfy the burgeoning demand — women of all ages, ethnicities, shapes, and sizes, women
trained to submit to the full range of what johns demand. There's
no question about it: the skyrocketing demand has contributed
to global sex trafficking, yet we continue to look at prostitution
as a women's problem, to consider the victims as somehow to
blame. We continue to think of women who sell their bodies as
opportunistic, dirty, pitiful. When we do speak of them, we use
the language of the streets — we talk of "hookers," and "whores."
We do this while somehow ignoring the other half of the equation, as though these women are acting alone. We let ourselves
forget that the women are pawns.

At the very crux of the debate over prostitution is the entrenched notion that the sex trade is inevitable; that it has been
around since man first stood erect, and that it is here to stay. And
there too is the problem. When we ask ourselves what we can do
about prostitution, we inevitably think of the women standing
out on the streets. We wonder what we can do to clean up our
cities, to banish this scourge — these women — from our communities, but we turn a blind eye to the caravans of men who
circle city blocks in search of paid sex.

If we really want to do something about prostitution, we need
to acknowledge the role of johns, and johns have to take responsibility for their actions. If prostitution is about choice, it's about
the man's choice to pay women for sex. Johns *choose* to go to a
"working girl" rather than invest in a relationship. They choose
to go on sex junkets to impoverished nations because they are
disillusioned with or afraid of Western women. They choose to

turn a blind eye to the grim reality of the women and girls whose bodies they rent. They choose to impose their will on extremely vulnerable women. The johns are the ones who have a choice, and they are the ones who win when prostitution goes legal.

So what do we do?

Target the johns. Learn from the example of Sweden and criminalize the buying of sex. Teach them what's at stake, whether through education, tough sentencing, or otherwise. Hold them accountable for their actions. Men soliciting sex from women in prostitution need to face consequences for their behavior, and a good first step is john school. Police enforcement is important but it is at best a Band-Aid. The focus should not be on publicly naming and shaming but on exploring their motivation and trying to make them understand the full ramifications of their behavior — for themselves and the women.

Abandon the fantasy of legalization. The last thing prostitution needs is a government-sanctioned air of respectability. It doesn't matter what governments or pro-prostitution lobbies say or do. Legalization will never sanitize the selling and buying of sex. It will never put an end to the violence, and it will never stop the degradation that the women endure night after night. The stigma of prostitution is part and parcel of the trade and no amount of whitewashing or sugarcoating will ever change that.

Change societal attitudes: What is desperately needed is an all-out campaign aimed at changing social attitudes about prostitution. Society must confront just how damaged masculinity is today and how destructive male behavior has become, both inward and outward. Prostitution seriously undercuts the possibility of creating relationships of equality, respect, and honesty between men and women in all aspects of life. It instills in boys and men the idea that women and girls are objects for sexual use rather than equal human beings. It endangers any possibility of equality in *all* relationships between men and women. Particularly worrisome is that the ranks of johns are being bolstered by new generations of younger and younger men ever more strongly conditioned by society's mass-produced illusions of sexuality. Music videos, TV commercials, magazine ads, Hollywood movies, and pornography teach young men to view women, girls, and sex as a commodity that can be bought and sold. For real change to occur, we have to turn the tables and point the finger of blame at the real perpetrators — the johns, the pimps, the princes of porn. Society has to radically rethink men's responsibility in prostitution, and prostitution must be seen and defined as a male issue. To put the brakes on the flourishing demand for paid sex, we need to do away with patriarchal attitudes and half-baked excuses. No, it is not in a man's nature to always need sex, and no, it's not cool or manly to go out and pay for it.

We urgently need intervention programs that work on changing the attitudes of men, and no doubt the easiest target for enlightenment are first-time buyers and teenage boys.

Start young: Parents and educators need to pull their heads out of the sand and deal with the fact that very young children are being assaulted by unsettling pornography, much of it hardcore. Once these children enter the netherworld of pornography, their innocence is lost. Their fragile minds are distorted, their views of relationships and women tainted or skewed.

Educate boys: Boys need frank, open discussions about sex, sexuality, and what it means to be a man, because what they are seeing can have a devastating effect on them. We need to teach boys about loving and lasting relationships built on respect for girls and women.

Enforce the laws: Every country has in place laws regarding trafficking, abduction, coercion, assault, and rape. Unwavering prosecution and heavy prison time for pimps and traffickers will help put the brakes on this sexual calamity.

Help the women: For the women and girls who are forced into this tragic existence, the only avenue of escape is a real job—a serious chance at a better life. That is all they ask for, and the well-heeled nations of the West have to contribute meaningfully to the solution. They need to address the economic and social inequities that force women into prostitution. They must find ways of helping these women, not only with skills training, but with genuine offers of employment that don't require them to take off their clothes. For the vast majority of women and girls in the trade, prostitution is not a chance at life—never was, never will be. It is enslavement and much worse—it is modern-day sexual terrorism.

Governments should also make it a priority to ensure that every penny made off the backs of these women and children is taken from the bank accounts of those profiting from the trade. The money should be distributed to the victims and to aid agencies that are trying to rescue women and children and help them put their shattered lives back together.

Many people throw their hands up in complete surrender, arguing that it is unrealistic to think that prostitution can ever be abolished. "Why even bother?" That's a dangerous question to ask. By conceding defeat and surrendering to the pro-prostitution forces, we are basically accepting that these women and girls deserve to be fodder for the flesh trade.

We need to act now. It may seem too intimidating, ugly, entrenched, and pervasive a problem, but we have to try because of what is at stake — the lives of millions of women and girls the world over.

This entire social tragedy boils down to one word: *dignity* — the dignity of women and girls worldwide. In prostitution there is no dignity, no empowerment, no equality in any form. True equality between men and women will always be beyond reach as long as men feel they have the right to rent a woman's body. It is not a right, and it never should be. We need to do everything we can to abolish prostitution.

ACKNOWLEDGMENTS

A LOT OF PEOPLE PLAYED A ROLE in the writing of this book, and they deserve a ton of credit. First and foremost, I want to thank Lesia Stangret. She was my guiding light throughout this arduous and trying project, assisting me with her insights, direction, research, support, and above all, a critical editorial eye.

I particularly want to thank Natasha Daneman, my agent at Westwood Creative Artists, who immediately recognized the importance of this book and fought hard to bring it to reality.

At Arcade publishing in New York, I want to thank Calvert Barksdale for his editorial insights and for keeping me on track; Sarah R. Doerries for her fine copyediting; and Richard and Jeannette Seaver for their vision and commitment to the book.

In my research on this grim topic, I have had conversations and interviews with scores of dedicated people – men and women who see prostitution for what it truly is, a devastating worldwide human rights abuse. I want to thank Norma Ramos, Melissa Farley, Laura Lederer, John R. Miller, Mark P. Lagon, Eleanor Kennelly Gaetan, Norma Hotaling, Michael Shively, Irene Soltys, Peggy Sakow, Liliane Kohl, Joy Smith, Sheila Jeffreys, Dorchen A.

Leidholdt, Janice Redmond, Julie Bindel, Gunilla Ekberg, Daisy Kler, Andrea Mozarowski, Brett Mitchell, Jeff Silverstein, Marleen Trotter, Hannah James, Gary Haugen, Pat A. Reilly at ICE, RCMP Sergeant Lori Lowe, and Vancouver detectives Benedikte (Ben) Wilkinson and Ron Bieg.

INDEX

Made in the USA
Monee, IL
07 May 2022

96067110R00194